Football Officials

GuidebooK

Mechanics For Crews of Four and Five Officials

by Jeffrey Stern, George Demetriou & Jerry Grunska

From the Publishers of *Referee* Magazine
and the National Association of Sports Officials

FOOTBALL OFFICIALS GUIDEBOOK
Mechanics for Crews of Four and Five Officials

by Jeffrey Stern, Associate Editor, *Referee* magazine, George Demetriou & Jerry Grunska

Graphics and layout by Matt Bowen

Copyright © 1999 by Referee Enterprises, Inc., P.O. Box 161, Franksville, Wis. 53126.

Printed in the United States of America

ISBN 1-58208-008-9

Table of Contents

CREW OF FIVE p. 105

CREW OF FOUR p. 201

Table of contents continued on following page

Table of contents continued from previous page

Acknowledgements

Like a well-officiated game, this book was the product of great teamwork. I'd like to especially thank my co-authors, Jerry Grunska and George Demetriou, who graciously shared their vast technical knowledge and writing skills. Grunska was a football official for more than 40 years and has been *Referee's* football "Doing It" columnist since 1986. A retired educator, he lives in Evergreen, Colo. Demetriou has been *Referee's* football "By the Rules" columnist since 1993. An official since 1968, he works for MCI Worldcom and lives in Colorado Springs, Colo.

I'm also grateful for the editorial and technical advice offered by *Referee* editor Bill Topp. The many diagrams and other visual effects in the book are the work of *Referee* publication design manager Matt Bowen. Don Dalton, athletic director and retired head football coach at Burlington (Wis.) High School, was instrumental in providing information on offensive formations and tendencies. Thanks also to Tom Brandon, retired head football coach at Racine (Wis.) Case High School, whose players served as models for many of the illustrations throughout the book, and to Jeff McDorman of the Racine Parks and Recreation Department, who provided equipment used in illustrations.

Jeffrey Stern
Associate Editor
Referee magazine

Introduction

Until I began work on *Football Officials Guidebook*, I never really knew what was meant by the phrase "labor of love." The farther the book progressed, the more I realized how deep my passion for football officiating really is.

Producing this book also reinforced the importance of doing things the right way on the football field. If you don't already subscribe to the methods and philosophies included here, I hope you will at least try them. The book is designed to help the first-year official as well as the seasoned veteran.

Of course, *Football Officials Guidebook* is just that: a guide. Some of the concepts within these pages will not agree with the National Federation or Collegiate Commissioners Association (CCA) manuals, or coincide with state or local association practices. This book includes mechanics differences — and there are many! We've also included what we think is the best way to do things, based on years of discussions with referees all over the world.

The variations and deviations from the Federation and CCA manuals will, at worst, show you some things you don't want to (or aren't allowed to) try. At best, it will open a new way of thinking for you and quickly change for the better the way you referee your games. Like any guidebook, you won't embrace it all; but what you do like will make you better.

I hope you like what we've done and that you learn as much reading it as I did writing it. Drop me a note and let me know what you think.

Jeffrey Stern
Associate Editor
Referee magazine

Chapter 1

Definition of Terms

Balanced formation — An offensive formation in which three linemen are on either side of the snapper.

Ballcarrier — The player in possession of the ball. Also known as the runner.

Belly play — A running play in which the ballcarrier (or a player pretending to be a runner) hides the ball by carrying it in front of his belly and bending slightly at the waist.

Blitz — A defensive strategy in which several players commit to rushing the passer. See "Showing blitz."

Box — Apparatus (also known as the down marker) used by the chain crew to show ball position and the current down.

Brush blocks — Tactic in which an offensive player makes minimal contact with an opponent. The purpose of a brush block is not to move or direct the opponent, but to momentarily impede the opponent, then move downfield. Brush blocks are common on punts and screen passes.

CCA — Acronym for the Collegiate Commissioners' Association. The CCA produces the official football manual for the NCAA. The CCA manual is used throughout college football and is referred to often in this book.

Chain crew (or chain gang) — Non-officials in charge of the line-to-gain equipment and box.

Chuck — Signal used to indicate which team has called a timeout. See Signal Chart, page 45. Also, a term used to describe contact by a defender on a pass receiver.

Cleaning up after the play — Mechanic in which the official not responsible for the ballcarrier observes action behind and around the ballcarrier.

Dead-ball officiating — Activity during the time immediately after the ball becomes dead. Good dead-ball officials don't stop officiating when the ball is dead. They continue to watch the players and prevent problems.

Digger — Official who removes players from a pile and determines which team has recovered a fumble. See pages 30-32 .

Downfield — Refers to the direction the offensive team is moving with the ball. On a scrimmage down, it is the area beyond the neutral zone. Opposite of "Upfield."

Echoing a signal — Giving the same signal as a crewmate (i.e. stop the clock, touchdown).

Federation — Short for the National Federation of State High School Associations. The Federation is the governing body for high school athletics and produces the official football manual for the Federation. The Federation manual is used throughout high school football and is referred to often in this book.

Flat — The area behind the offensive linemen where backs go to receive short passes. A pass to a back in the flat is thrown shortly after the snap, thus making it different from a screen pass.

Free kick — A kick from a tee that starts either half or follows a score. A kickoff is a free kick.

Give up — Turning attention from a specific player (usually the runner) because the player has entered another official's coverage area.

Halo concept — Technique involving imaginary circles around players that help define coverage areas for officials. See Visual Definition, page 17, and Coverage Philosophy, page 20.

Hashmarks (or hashes) — Also known as the inbounds marks, the lines on the field from which the ball is snapped if it becomes dead in a side zone or out of bounds.

Inbounds marks — See "Hashmarks."

Inside-out look — Pivot that turns an official's back toward the middle of the field, allowing him an angle to action in a side zone or on the sideline.

Key — An action or reaction by a player that gives the official a tip as to what type of play the offense will run; a player an official observes for all or part of a down.

Line-to-gain equipment — Ten-yard chain connected at each end to poles used to indicate the line team A has to reach in order to achieve a first down. The box is also considered to be part of the line-to-gain equipment. See "Box," "Chain gang" and "Stakes."

Look through — Use of depth-of-field vision to observe a player lined up inside the nearest player. See Visual Definition, page 15.

Makeup call — The practice of consciously making a call that favors one team in an effort to "even up" a previous call that hurt that team. Although circumstances sometimes give the impression an official's decision is a makeup call, good officials do not purposely make makeup calls.

Mirror a spot — Mechanic, usually used by wing officials, in which one official marks the spot of forward progress and another indicates the same spot from across the field. See Basic Mechanics, Chapter 35, and Visual Definition, page 15.

NCAA — Acronym for the National Collegiate Athletic Association. The NCAA is the governing body for collegiate athletics. The NCAA uses the official football manual produced by the CCA. Both groups will be referenced throughout this book.

Nine-yard marks (or numbers) — The yardline identification numbers painted on the field. The distance from the sideline to the top of the numbers is nine yards.

No-call — A conscious decision by the official that an action was not worthy of a penalty.

Officiate back to the ball — Mechanic in which a wing official who has moved toward team B's goalline moves back toward the play in order to determine the spot of forward progress.

Onside kick — A free kick intentionally kicked a short distance in the hope of recovering the ball. Not to be confused with a squib kick.

Pick play — Pass play on which one receiver runs a short route, drawing a defender, and another receiver runs a slightly deeper route. The receiver on the short route blocks an opponent, freeing his teammate from coverage. The act is illegal if a pass crosses the neutral zone.

Pinch ends — Mechanic used in goalline and short-yardage situations in which the wing officials' initial position is closer to the widest offensive end than normal.

Pitchout — A backward pass, usually thrown by the quarterback to a running back.

Placekick — A kick when the ball is placed on a tee or when the ball is held by a teammate.

Player designations — For ease of reference throughout this book, team A is the team that was in possession of the ball when the ball was snapped; team B is the team that was on defense when the ball was snapped; team K is the team that free-kicked the ball or kicked a scrimmage kick (including field goals and kick trys); and team R is the team that was to receive the free kick or scrimmage kick or was defending on the field goal or kick try attempt. Similarly, A1 is player for team A, B2 a player for team B, etc.

Point of attack — On a running play, the area in advance of the runner through which he runs; on a passing play, anywhere in the vicinity of the passer or any player attempting to reach the passer; on a kick play, anywhere in the vicinity of the kicker or any player attempting to reach the kicker or block the kick.

Preventive officiating — Refers to actions by officials who prevent problems from occurring by talking to players and coaches. Preventive officiating is often related to dead-ball officiating.

Pulling — Tactic by offensive linemen used especially on sweeps. After the snap, a pulling lineman moves quickly from his normal position to the end of the line or the opposite side of the formation in order to block an opponent.

Punch — Supplementary signal used to indicate a pass was backward and not forward. See Signal Chart, page 58, and Supplementary Signals, page 57.

Runner — See "Ballcarrier."

Screen pass — Short pass play on which the receiver (usually a back) catches the ball behind a wall of blockers.

Scrimmage kick — A kick made from scrimmage that precedes a change of team possession. A punt, field goal and kick try are scrimmage kicks.

Scrimmage kick formation — An offensive formation in which the punter or holder and placekicker are at least seven yards behind the snapper. Not to be confused with a "Shotgun," which is a formation generally used for scrimmage plays and not for kicking plays.

Selling the call — Placing emphasis on a call with louder voice and whistle, and slightly more demonstrative signals. Selling only occurs on close calls and should be used sparingly. It is designed to help the call gain acceptance and show the official's decisiveness.

Short side (of the field) — The side of the field from the hashmark to the nearer sideline when the ball is snapped from the hashmark; opposite of the "Wide side." See Visual Definition, page 15.

Shotgun — An offensive formation in which the quarterback is several yards behind the snapper (see "Scrimmage kick formation").

Showing blitz — The defense places eight or more players within four yards of the snap, making no secret of the fact it intends to place pressure on the quarterback or kicker. See "Blitz."

Shuffle step — Movement used mainly by wing officials on pass plays. The torso remains perpendicular to the line of scrimmage and the feet are alternately scraped along the ground (not a crossover step) in order to move downfield.

Side zone — The area of the field between the sidelines and the hashmarks. See Visual Definition, page 15.

Slotback — An offensive player who lines up in the offensive backfield and in the open area (the "slot") between the offensive tackle and a wideout.

Square off — Ninety-degree turn made by an official when marking the spot of forward progress. See Visual Definition, page 17.

Squib kick — A free kick, usually low and short, kicked in an effort to prevent a fast runner from returning the kick.

Stacked — One player lined up directly behind a teammate (e.g. a linebacker positioned immediately behind a defensive tackle).

Stakes (or sticks) — Poles at either end of the chain used to indicate the line team A has to reach in order to

achieve a first down. See "Line to gain equipment" and "Chain crew."

Straightlining — See Visual Definition, page 16.

Strong side — For the purposes of this book, the side of the offensive line on which there are more eligible receivers outside of the tackles; opposite of "Weak side." See Visual Definition, page 17.

Trap block — Tactic in which offensive linemen permit a defensive lineman to penetrate the line, then block the defender from the side.

Trips — Three eligible receivers on one side of an offensive formation.

Upfield — The direction the defense or receiving team is moving. Opposite of "Downfield."

V — Triangular alignment used by officials to relay the ball from a side zone to the hashmark. See Basic Mechanics, page 29, and Visual Definition, page 17.

Weak side — For the purposes of this book, it is the side of the offensive line on which there are fewer eligible receivers outside of the tackles; opposite of the "Strong side." See Visual Definition, page 17.

Wide side (of the field) — The area from the opposite hashmark through the middle of the field and side zone to the sideline when the ball is snapped from the opposite hashmark. Opposite of the "Short side." See Visual Definition, page 15.

Wideout — An eligible receiver who lines up outside the last player on the offensive line, on the line of scrimmage.

Wing official (or wingman) — The linesman or line judge.

Downfield ➝

Look through — Wing officials don't always key on the player directly in front of them. In those cases, the official uses depth-of-field vision to observe a player lined up inside the nearest player. In the PlayPic, the wing official is looking through the split end and is keying on the tackle (the gray-shaded player).

Mirror a spot — When an official in charge of determining forward progress marks the spot, another official should mark the same spot from across the field. Mirroring lends credibility to the determination of forward progress and allows for better ball retrieval in certain situations.

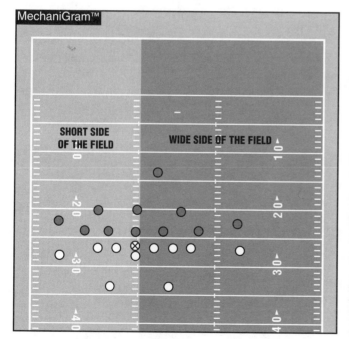

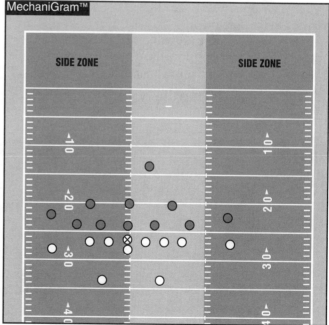

Short side (of the field) — The side of the field from the hashmark to the nearer sideline when the ball is snapped from the hashmark is called the short side. The opposite of the short side is the wide side.

Side zone — The area of the field between the sidelines and the hashmarks is known as the side zone.

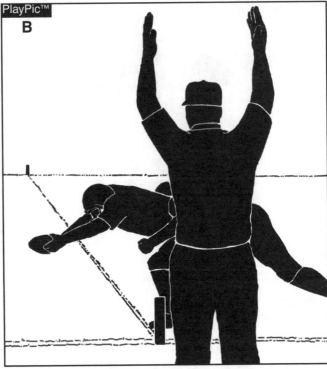

Straightlining — Straightlining occurs when your view of a play is obstructed by the players themselves. In effect, you are in a straight line with the players and have no angle to see between them.

Moving quickly to obtain an angle perpendicular rather than parallel to the players eliminates straightlining. Keep your head up and continually watch the play when moving.

The most common straightlining concerns are trailing a runner and pursuing tackler and ruling on passes at the sideline.

PlayPic A illustrates straightlining involving a runner. From that position, the official cannot see if the defender has grasped the runner's facemask, if the ball is coming loose from the runner's grasp and where the spot of forward progress will be when the runner is

downed (particularly if the runner is approaching the goalline).

PlayPic B shows the official in good position to observe the ball, the runner, the tackler and the goalline.

The straightlined official in PlayPic C cannot see if the receiver has the ball in his grasp before he crosses the sideline. The official in PlayPic D has the proper angle to observe the receiver, his feet and the ball.

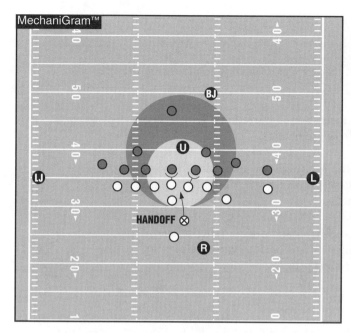

Halo concept — Technique involving imaginary circles around players that help define coverage areas for officials. On a running play up the middle for example, the umpire observes the main halo (light gray shading), around the runner. The wing officials and back judge (five-man crew) observe the secondary halo (darker gray shading), looking for holding, illegal blocks and other fouls. The halos shift in depth, width and location as the runner advances and varies his direction left or right.

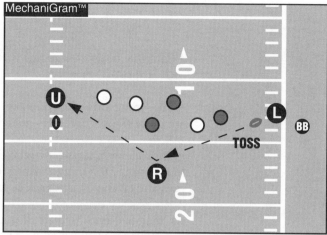

V — The method used by officials to relay the ball from a side zone to the hashmark is called the V because of its triangular shape. The covering official marks the spot, which is mirrored by the umpire, who is standing at the hashmark. The referee catches the toss from a position between the hashmark and the covering official and two to three yards behind the dead-ball spot. The referee then pivots and flips the ball to the umpire. In a five-man crew, if the back judge is the covering official, he can leave the ball on the ground at the spot while the appropriate wingman can retrieve a ball from the ballboy and flip the ball to the umpire. Once the ball has been set by the umpire, the wingman picks up the ball at his feet and gives it to the ballboy.

The back judge may also be the middle man in the V on plays that end downfield.

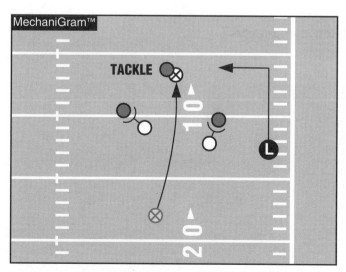

Square off —The covering official should make a 90-degree turn when marking the spot of forward progress. Squaring off lends credibility to the determination of forward progress.

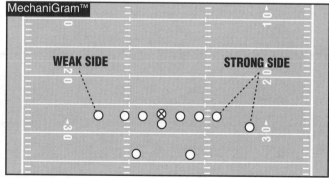

Strong side — For the purposes of this book, the side of the offensive line on which there are more eligible receivers outside of the tackles is known as the strong side. The opposite of the strong side is the weak side. Recognizing the strong side is important in determining keys in a five-man crew.

• Squaring off is a 90-degree turn made by an official when marking the spot of forward progress.

• The strong side of an offensive formation is the side on which there are more eligible receivers outside of the tackles.

• The defense shows blitz when it places eight or more players within four yards of the snap, making no secret of the fact it intends to place pressure on the quarterback or kicker

• Officiating back to the ball is a mechanic in which a wing official who has moved toward team B's goalline moves back toward the play in order to determine the spot of forward progress.

Quiz

Without referring back, you should be able to answer the following true-false questions.

1. The wing officials can pinch the ends on any scrimmage down.

2. Preventive officiating is heading off problems by talking to players and coaches.

3. Selling every call lends credibility to the call.

4. A pick play is a defensive maneuver.

5. The wide side is the side of the field from the hashmark to the nearer sideline when the ball is snapped from the hashmark.

1. False 2. True 3. False 4. False 5. False

Chapter 2

Philosophy

COVERAGE PHILOSOPHY

Movement and compromise are the characteristics of football officiating. Twenty-two players are moving around, competing for space and position; the officials must utilize hustle, angles, distance and planned compromises to observe and control the action.

Hustle

Hustle is an overused word today. Everyone knows it's needed to succeed, but what does it really mean when relating it to football officiating? Think of it this way: NCAA Division I and NFL games are officiated by seven-man crews. Why? Because of the speed, size, quickness and the physical nature of games at those levels, seven officials can better control a game than four, five or six officials. The extra sets of eyes and ears prevent many problems. Plus, athletic budgets allow it at those levels, something that would be difficult at NCAA Division III, high school and youth levels.

The game control expectations are no different with four or five officials, yet there are fewer people to help control the game. Significant movement by all officials is critical for proper field coverage. Hustle gives you a chance. In essence, four or five officials must work hard enough to cover a field that is the same size but better covered by seven officials at higher levels. That equates to more running and a well-placed concern for angles.

Movements

All officials must work hard at understanding then obtaining proper angles. Your line of sight must provide you with an opportunity to view a developing play or part of a play. You must be able to see completely through the play, which means your vision must be unobstructed by the players directly involved in the play and others near the play.

When the ball is snapped, all 22 players are in motion. An official's angle and distance adjustments are constant as play is in motion. A step or two in the right direction may open up a whole new viewing experience, free from obstruction; a step in the wrong direction will screen you from the critical game action.

Far too often officials who can't (or won't) run well don't move with the flow of the play. They're afraid of getting in the way and aren't confident they can move quickly enough to avoid players and get good angles. The game suffers because coverage suffers. A good wing official, for instance, flows downfield with the play when a runner is in his coverage area and moves toward the center of the field to watch the players behind the play when the run is on the opposite sideline.

Why such an emphasis on movement? Movement allows the non-covering officials to watch players away from the ball, the critical component to combating physical play. Rough play is a point of emphasis nearly every year. When a wing official moves off the sideline, he can watch the areas behind the run, where rough play often occurs.

The covering wing official also moves along the sideline to improve angles. There's usually at least three and sometimes six or seven players around the ball, either trying to throw blocks or attempting to make the tackle. Movement is critical to watching action around the ball. It's also paramount to game control.

Proper movements when the play is over are also important. Because the ball is live for only a few seconds every play, there's a tendency to think about spotting the ball for the next play and forgetting about the players. If officials ignore post-play action, players get physical with each other and game control suffers. All officials must observe player action after the ball has been whistled dead.

A complete understanding of field coverage

Proper coverage is enhanced by good eye contact and a "feel" for where your crewmates are looking. You must learn about all aspects of football officiating to know who is covering what. Once you've mastered that, practical onfield application develops through communication, including eye contact and understanding. At the risk of being obvious, you've got to know exactly what both you and your crewmates are expected to do in specific situations — then effectively communicate with your crewmates — to truly master football officiating. When you understand why angles and distance are important and how and when to obtain them, you'll find yourself in great position throughout each game.

Halo coverage

Both manuals define officials' areas of jurisdiction, but many officials may have misconceptions about them. The halo principle is designed to not only provide coverage when the ball is in those areas, but to ensure that all 22 players are observed on every play.

When a player is in possession of the ball (or the ball is loose on the ground, such as a rolling punt or a fumble), the halo surrounding the ball and all players in around it is called the main halo. There is no hard-and-fast definition for the size of halos; use two to five yards as an average. The official nearest the main halo is responsible for the actions of players within the halo.

The remaining officials are responsible for the secondary halos, which surround the players in their area.

Take for example a normal scrimmage down. When the quarterback takes the snap and spins to hand the ball to the halfback, the quarterback, the halfback and any other team A players in the vicinity (possibly the fullback, a pulling lineman or a receiver who was in motion) are inside the main halo, which is observed by the referee. But once the play moves into and beyond the line of scrimmage, the referee should no longer be watching the ballcarrier; he should instead be observing what happens to the quarterback, those other team A players mentioned above and perhaps any team B players who have broken through the line. The main halo becomes the responsibility of the appropriate wing official (or the umpire if the run is right up the middle).

Punt and interception returns are somewhat problematic, because the back judge (or either wing official in a four-man crew) may be the only official with a clearly defined responsibility, while other officials' assignments are somewhat nebulous.

Let's put a two- to four-yard imaginary halo around a punt receiver and say that the back judge (line judge in a four-man crew) is responsible for it. Who else should be looking at that small halo? Maybe the line judge, after he has observed players converging on the spot where the punt will come down. But the rest of the officials on the field should program themselves to watch players in the secondary halo, a semicircular area 10 to 20 yards ahead of the receiver.

The linesman, for example, should concentrate on the flow of players downfield and watch for someone signaling for a fair catch ahead of the receiver (because such a player would be outside the main halo). The runback, however, may take the ball into the linesman's own side zone, in which case he will shift his focus from the secondary halo and observe the runner coming toward him. His job includes spotting a clip or a facemask foul within a limited area near the runner, as well as action on the runner himself. The halo can narrow to four yards in radius while the runner is advancing, and it'll compact even more as the runner approaches the official.

When the runner has moved upfield, all halos shift. That's the turning point, the pivotal factor in coverage. The line judge in this example should take the secondary halo in front of the runner, 15 or 20 yards ahead of the runner. The scope of the line judge's observation can be extremely wide, because all the action is directly in front of him.

As the runner advances, the main halo moves with

him and other members of the crew have to make a sudden shift of focus. The back judge should trail the play actively on runbacks, and he must be prepared to sweep past the sidelines to assist in direct coverage if the runner should wind up out of bounds. When the runner goes beyond the sideline, the back judge must follow him.

When the punt flies overhead, the umpire will be in the midst of players streaming downfield and will actually be inside the secondary halo described earlier (the secondary circle in front of the receiver's immediate perimeter). The umpire should watch the players who are trying to get into position to make the tackle and the opponents who are blocking them.

Some punters choose not to try to become involved in the pursuit and simply admire their punt as it flies downfield. If the referee is also looking at the ball far downfield, he could fail to see an unnecessary and illegal block on the punter. Even if the punter is no longer covered by roughing the kicker rules, an opponent should not get a free shot at punishing a player who is not moving to participate in the play.

OFFICIATING PHILOSOPHY

"Three of the most important elements of football officiating are reading keys, developing trust (in yourself and your crewmates) and communicating."

While no single sentence can really summarize football officiating, that one gives you the framework for success. To do it effectively, you've got some homework to do.

The greatest single thing you can do to help improve your officiating is gain a better understanding of the game itself. Anticipation is critical in officiating. You give yourself a much better chance of getting in proper position and making the correct call if you anticipate what is going to happen. That doesn't mean anticipate the call; that is a major error. It means knowing what's likely to happen and adjusting accordingly. The only way you can get better at anticipating is by becoming a student of the game.

To elevate your officiating, you must learn about offensive and defensive strategies. If you know what each team is trying to do (well beyond "scoring more points than the other team"), your game awareness, communication, field coverage and judgment will improve.

This book places a great deal of emphasis on recognizing plays and adjusting accordingly. In order to do that, you must first understand each element of the sentence.

Reading keys

When officiating a game you must recognize, understand and react to each play situation. The down, distance, score and time remaining in a game often dictate offensive plays; they also greatly affect your field coverage. When the offense breaks the huddle, what formation are they in? Are there three wide receivers on one side of the formation? Two tight ends? Is the quarterback under center or in a shotgun formation? By recognizing the formation, you can anticipate what's coming next.

Reading keys also means primarily watching the players' movements. Depending on the position you're working, the players who provide your keys will vary. Let's say you're the umpire. As the ball is snapped, you see the offensive linemen fire forward. That tells you the play is likely a run. Say a guard pulls and joins the tackle on the opposite side of the line in a double-team block. That should indicate the point of attack; a team rarely goes to the trouble of using a pulling guard to deceive the defense. Now that the point of attack is established, you can focus on the blocking in that area and determine how that contact affected the play.

Obviously, the defense is providing keys of its own. You must watch how defensive players line up, if the safety is close to the line and indicating a blitz, and so on.

The more you know about the game, the less chance you have of getting surprised. It takes more than studying the rules and mechanics. A complete official knows what's going on from the players', coaches' and officials' perspectives.

This book emphasizes offensive plays that combat defensive strategies. It will help you understand what players are trying to do so you can be prepared on the field to make the proper coverage adjustments.

Developing trust

When it comes down to it, trust is a vital element in officiating. You must trust yourself and the knowledge you've obtained to see you through game situations. You must also trust your crewmates not only to handle situations properly, but to implement proper field coverage.

You must develop trust with your crewmates so that only penalties that merit enforcement are called. If you throw a flag and a crewmate asks, "Are you sure that's what you saw? I had a better look and I didn't see it," you must trust that the crewmate's motives are pure. You must also set aside personal pride and pick up the flag if you truly believe the crewmate is correct.

You must also trust that if you go to a crewmate with the same question, he will have the proper reaction.

Trust also comes into play regarding field coverage. In almost no instance should every official be watching the player with the ball. The non-covering officials must watch the players who are not involved in running with the ball or tackling the runner, especially when the play is over. Think about it: Usually there are only a couple of players around the ball. That leaves the majority of the players in other areas. If all of the officials had their eyes glued to the ball, the majority of the players would be unattended. That's when problems occur, like rough play or trash-talking. If the non-covering officials watch the players in their vicinity during and after the play, the game stays under control.

You must trust your crewmates to handle things correctly when you're the covering official and vice versa. We have a tendency to want to watch the ball even when we're not supposed to. Maybe that stems from watching games on TV, because the cameras always focus on the ball. Maybe it comes from the belief that more exciting things happen around the ball. Whatever the reason, you must trust your crewmates to handle it. If you don't, dead-ball coverage is non-existent and the game suffers.

Officials who trust each other in handling situations and field coverage responsibilities form the building blocks to successful officiating. Fight the urge to watch the ball all the time. Your game will stay under control, your judgment will improve and you will become a better crewmate and a better official.

Communicating

Effective communication rounds out the successful official. It makes sense: If you've got a lot of knowledge and make good decisions but can't effectively communicate with others, no one can tell that you've got a lot of knowledge and make good decisions. Good communicators make good officials.

Communication goes well beyond words. It includes body language and signals. There is a great deal of emphasis on proper, clear signals throughout this book. Why? Signals are our language. They're our way of telling others what's going on. Bad signals mean poor communication. Good signals show decisiveness, clearly indicate what's going on and even help calls become accepted.

Learn how to read keys, trust yourself and your crewmates and communicate effectively. You'll find yourself improving every time you step onto the field.

Chapter 3

Football
Officiating
Basics

Good officials project professionalism on and off the field. Among the areas where you can stand out:

Accepting games

Before even getting on the field, you obviously need to be hired. Assigning methods vary from state to state, level to level and association to association.

Learn what the process is from other local officials and association leaders. Then, follow the system. Do not compromise your principles to get games. In some areas, it's improper to contact coaches directly for games. If that's the case, don't do it. You'd be sacrificing your integrity just for an assignment. It's not worth it.

In other areas, officials must get games from coaches or athletic directors. While that practice often gives the appearance of favoritism and impropriety, follow the procedures that are accepted and don't deviate. Be careful.

Once you've figured out the procedure and accepted an assignment, keep it. Few things upset assignors more than turned-back games. Obviously emergencies do happen, but they should be few in number. Officials who continually have problems making assignments eventually don't get called.

It's tempting to turn back a game when a better one comes along. Some assignors allow turn-backs if the official has a chance to move up a level, for example from a JV game to varsity. Others frown upon it no matter what. If you know you can't turn a game back without upsetting someone, don't do it.

If you've got an opportunity to take a game that moves you up a level and your assignor is open-minded, be honest about it. Don't commit to the new game until you've talked to the assignor for the game you've already got.

If you get caught being dishonest about assignments, you're going to burn the bridge on both ends. The assignor you lied to won't call. The assignor you lied for won't call because that assignor is smart enough to know that if you did it to someone else to move up, you'll do it again! You gain more credibility by keeping the assignment you've got. After all, if you're worthy of a chance to move up, other assignments will come your way.

When you receive a contract in the mail, return it in a timely fashion. Think of your officiating as a business. As the business owner, realize how important contracts are to your business. If they are returned late or incomplete your business will suffer because you're less likely to get other contracts. Get the contract back in the mail as soon as you get it.

Conditioning

Football officiating requires you to be in good physical condition. Consider taking a physical examination before each season. Stay in shape rather than get in shape. Being physically fit is a lifestyle. If you never get out of shape it won't be such a chore getting ready for the season.

Arriving at game site

The proper amount of time varies by level and by local practice. General rule: Arrive at least 45 minutes before kickoff. For varsity and college games, 90 minutes is more acceptable. Allow enough time to stretch out, get dressed, have a pregame with the crew and conduct pregame duties without rushing.

Whenever possible, a crew should travel to and from the game site together. Among the benefits to sharing a ride are:

• **Cost reduction** — Crew members can save gas money by car pooling. If the same official does all of the driving in a season, the rest of the crew can contribute to a gasoline fund or buy the driver's postgame meal.

• **Building togetherness** — If you want to get to know someone, there's nothing like a dozen or so long motor trips to break the ice. As the years go on and you become more comfortable with the officials on the crew, you'll find you can discuss almost any personal, professional or officiating problem and receive sound advice, heartfelt consolation or hearty congratulations.

• **Relaxation and preparation** — Passengers can skim the rulebook, discuss unusual situations and otherwise prepare mentally for the game or catch a nap on the way home.

Arrive at the game site well in advance of the scheduled start time. Allow enough time to get stuck in traffic and still make it in plenty of time.

When arriving at the game site, park in a well-lit area and, if possible, near an exit not used by most fans. If possible, park with open space in front of and behind your car to ensure no one can box you in after the game. Put all valuables (like a briefcase, clothes, etc.) in your trunk so thieves have less of a reason to break into your car.

Dress

At most levels, officials have private lockerrooms. When that's the case, do not go to the game dressed in any part of your uniform. It just looks unprofessional. Make a good first impression on game management by wearing clean, pressed clothes to and from the game. Jeans, shorts, T-shirts, baseball caps, sneakers, shorts, sandals, sweatsuits and jogging attire are inappropriate. Wedding rings may be worn on the field, but other rings, necklaces, bracelets and earrings may not. As a backup in case a watch malfunctions during the game, at least one official (preferably the line judge) who doesn't have timing responsibilites should wear a watch.

Carry your uniform in a garment bag or gym bag. The bag should be neat (no frayed edges, etc.) and entirely black. Some associations have their group's logo or the official's name embroidered on the bag. That's acceptable if that's what officials in the area are doing. If no one else in the area is doing it, don't do it just to stand out.

Many officials at the high school and college levels use all black, wheeled, airline-type luggage. They keep your clothes clean and pressed and, because of the wheels, are easy to transport.

Your uniform should be clean and well kept and should include:

• **Shirt:** Standard black and white vertical stripes are worn. Officials should have shirts with short and long sleeves. All crew members should wear the same length sleeves. Do not wear a long-sleeved garment underneath a short-sleeved shirt. T-shirts and turtlenecks (for cold weather) should be black. The undershirt should not have any letters or pictures that could be seen through your striped shirt. Shirts should always be tucked in. Association patches are allowed if it's accepted in the area.

• **Pants:** White knickers with a black belt. The overlap at the bottom of the knickers should not be more than four inches below the knee. The belt must be black, one and one-quarter to two inches wide, with a nondescript buckle. When state associations allow, white shorts may be worn. Knickers are standard attire for college games and scrimmages. White compression shorts should be worn underneath the knickers. Shirts should be tucked inside the compression shorts to prevent stripes from showing through the knickers.

• **Shoes:** Entirely black shoes are most acceptable; however, some state associations and college conferences allow black with minimal white markings (like shoe logos). Black laces are always worn.

• **Socks:** The one-piece football stocking is almost universally worn. The Federation requires socks with northwestern stripes (one-half inch white, one-half inch black, one inch white, one-half inch black, one-half inch white). The width of the black showing below the knickers should be the same as the wide black band below the striping pattern. The CCA specifies that the white portion of the sock above the top of the shoe heel should be between three and four inches wide. A black portion above the white should be between two and two and one-quarter inches wide. The alternating black and white stripes should be one-half to five-eighths of an inch wide. The black between the top of the top white stripes and the bottom of the knickers should be between two and two and one-quarter inches wide.

• **Cap:** A black cap with white piping should be worn by all but the referee. The referee's white hat must be clean. All caps should be fitted; adjustable caps appear unprofessional.

• **Whistle:** If a whistle on a lanyard is used, both must be black. The whistle should be plastic. Metal whistles (even with rubber caps) are outdated and appear unprofessional. Carry a spare in your pants pocket. If a finger whistle is used, it should also be black plastic.

• **Jacket:** The CCA does not allow jackets to be worn during games. When high school associations allow jackets to be worn during the game, the jacket should be black and white striped. Jackets may be worn before the game during warmups. All officials should either wear jackets or go without.

• **Accessories:** Each official must have:

✔ At least one penalty flag (two are recommended). Each flag should be 15 by 15 inches and have a center weight. Most officials put rubber bands around the weight to form a ball which aids the flight and direction of the flag when it is thrown. Do not use a flag with a metal clip. The flags may be carried in the belt or in pockets; your association may have a policy. Wherever it is carried, as little of the flag as possible should be visible so the official doesn't appear flag-happy.

✔ At least one beanbag to mark non-penalty spots. Beanbags should be white and worn in the belt.

✔ An information card (to record timeouts, captains, etc.) and a writing utensil.

✔ A wristband, rubber band or other device to keep track of downs. The umpire should wear a second device to keep track of the area of the field from which the ball was last snapped.

• **Other accessories:** Gloves, when worn, should be black. The referee should have a coin. The linesman should have a dial that is clipped to the chain as an aid for measurements, etc., and an extra snap clip to aid setting the box after the first and third quarters.

Meeting with game management

Upon arrival at the game site, inform someone from game management that you have arrived. At the youth level, the game manager is likely a league supervisor. In high school and small college, it's probably the host athletic director or representative. Letting them know you're there immediately means they don't have to wonder if the officials arrived.

The game manager likely will show you to your lockerroom. With the game manager:

• Confirm kickoff time.

• Ask if there's going to be an extended halftime for parent's night, homecoming, etc. If there is, make sure the game manager informs both teams before the game.

• Ask where the teams and officials should go if weather (e.g. lightning, torrential rain) or emergency (e.g. bomb threat) forces suspension of the game.

• Find out where the game manager will be located during the game. You may need to find the game manager quickly during the game to take care of crowd control or other administrative duties.

• Find out how many athletic trainers will be on the sidelines and if an ambulance and crew will be on site in case of injury.

• Find out if anyone is going to escort the crew to your lockerroom at halftime and immediately after the game. Make sure your lockerroom is locked after you leave and someone is there to open it when needed. It's very upsetting when you want to get into your lockerroom at halftime or after the game and no one is there to open the door. Also, find out if game management has arranged for someone to inform the teams and officials when it is time to return to the field for the second half. If not, let the game manager know the officials will take care of that duty.

By taking care of duties with game management before the game, you won't have to worry about those details during the game.

After the game

If facilities are available, shower and change back into the same clothes you arrived in. Don't leave with your uniform on. You want to leave with a professional appearance, just as the one you had when you arrived.

Leave the game site with your crew. There's safety in numbers. If you and your crew are going to stop for a bite to eat, consider stopping out of the town you just officiated in. You don't want to be a local celebrity or a target.

Communicating with the governing body

If conduct or game reports are necessary, they should be sent promptly to the proper authorities. Send all reports within 24 hours of the game.

If there was a problem during the game that warrants a report to your supervisor, consider calling the supervisor as soon as possible before mailing the report. Supervisors usually like to hear about problems first from the officials so they don't get surprised when the angry coach or administrator calls.

Report all items that are supposed to be reported. Most governing bodies require all ejections to be reported. If you don't report yours, the governing body can't discipline the offender. You may think the altercation was minor and doesn't warrant suspension, etc. That's not your call! Report all ejections (if required) and let the governing bodies make their decisions. Sometimes, officials don't report because they think they're doing the offender a favor. What if the offender has been ejected four or five times throughout the season but only one has been reported? The authorities won't be aware of the continuing problem and can't take care of business. You are hurting yourself and other officials by not reporting properly.

Frequent study

Learning is an ongoing process. A complete knowledge of the rules and mechanics is essential. Study the rules throughout the year, with special emphasis on new rules at the beginning of the season. Test-taking and small group discussion are effective educational tools.

Chapter 4

Basic Mechanics

DUTIES BETWEEN DOWNS

The seemingly mundane task of counting players must be done on every play. There is no excuse for allowing one team a manpower advantage for even one play.

In certain situations (kickoffs, for example) *Referee* recommends telling a team it has too few players on the field. That is preventive officiating. At the youth or non-varsity high school level, the appropriate official should tell the kicker, "I'm not going to give you the ball until you have 11 players out here." At the high school varsity level and above, the appropriate official should tell the kicker, "You don't have 11 players out here."

On scrimmage downs, however, no such warning should be given because in most cases the ready for play has sounded and it's likely a play (or penalty) is imminent. The section on supplementary signals (pages 57-60) provides details on the signals that officials should use to communicate the number of players on the field.

The counting assignments:

FEDERATION

Five-man crew
- Free kick. The referee, line judge, back judge and the umpire count team R; the linesman counts team K.
- Scoring kick. The referee and umpire count team K; the back judge counts team R.
- Scrimmage kick. The referee and umpire count team K; the linesman, line judge and back judge count team R.
- Plays from scrimmage. The referee and umpire count team A; the linesman, line judge and back judge count team B.

Four-man crew
- Free kick. The referee and linesman count team K; the umpire and line judge count team R.
- Scoring kick. The referee and umpire count team K; the line judge counts team R.
- Scrimmage kick. The referee and umpire count team K; the linesman and line judge count team R.
- Plays from scrimmage. The referee and umpire count team A; the linesman and line judge count team B.

NCAA

Five-man crew
- Free kick. The back judge counts team R; the umpire counts team K.
- Scoring kick. The referee and umpire count team K; the linesman and line judge count the players on the side of the field whose team is on their respective sidelines; the back judge counts team R.
- Scrimmage kick. The referee and umpire count team K; the linesman and line judge count the players on the

side of the field whose team is on their respective sidelines; the back judge counts team R.
- Plays from scrimmage. The referee and umpire count team A; the linesman and line judge count the players on the side of the field whose team is on their respective sidelines; the back judge counts team B.

Four-man crew
- Free kick. The referee counts team K; the line judge counts team R; the linesman and umpire count the players on the side of the field whose team is on their respective sidelines.
- Scoring kick. The referee and umpire count team K; the linesman and line judge count the players on the side of the field whose team is on their respective sidelines.
- Scrimmage kick. The referee and umpire count team K; the linesman and line judge count the players on the side of the field whose team is on their respective sidelines.
- Plays from scrimmage. The referee and umpire count team A; the linesman and line judge count the players on the side of the field whose team is on their respective sidelines.

Down and distance
Using signals to indicate the next down are often presented to the audience and to one another in an offhand way, indicating a kind of mindless ritual, when in reality they should be employed as succinct and forceful reminders of the exact goings on in the game.

The indicating of the downs in a highly visual way promotes crew concentration. The referee should pause after the ball is placed for the down (or before it is placed if he chooses), and while signaling the down with upraised arm and fingers, he should call out the number of the down in a loud voice.

The Federation manual says referees should announce the down before every play, but few referees follow that directive. It is useful, however, to relay information about the distance on every down. The concentration of officials can waver if they just operate in a casual way regarding the game situation and the line-to-gain. *Referee* recommends that the umpire turn to each wing official with a strong verbal signal and a direct look, while relaying information about the down with hand gestures. The back judge (five-man crew) should also lift an arm signaling the down, but only after seeing both wing officials reflect the umpire's signal.

The appropriate number of fingers are raised to indicate the down (one finger for first down, two for second, three for third); a fist indicates fourth down.

Before the snap
The referee and the umpire are the officials who can best

control the pace and flow of a game. Their actions and mechanics can be the difference between a crew that looks sharp and one that appears slipshod or harried.

When a play ends in a side zone, a good umpire hustles to the nearest hashmark in order to take the spot from the covering official. That frees up the wingman to retrieve the ball. The covering official must not abandon the spot until the umpire arrives and verbally releases him, nor should he drop a beanbag and get the ball. Another mistake for the wingman to avoid is holding the spot and making the umpire come into the side zone to get the ball.

When it is obvious a first down has been achieved in the linesman's side zone, a hustling crew can use the same techniques to speed the process of setting the chains. The linesman holds the spot until the umpire arrives to mirror the spot. The umpire, seeing that the ball is well beyond the lead stake, takes the spot from the linesman so the linesman can get to the sideline and move the chain crew.

Hustle and communication are vital. The umpire cannot take his time getting to the spot. It is also important for both officials to be good dead-ball officials. They must not stare down at the spot; it is vital they keep their heads up and watch players in the vicinity.

The referee should hustle to the ball once the spot has been determined. A glance toward the chains tells the referee if a first down has been achieved. A good line judge will tell the referee the status of the play — "They got it" if it's obvious team A has achieved a first down; "Second (or third or fourth) down" if team A is obviously short. "Take a look" tells the referee the ball is close to the lead stake. The line judge isn't ordering a measurement; he's merely cautioning the referee not to make a hasty decision. The clock should not be stopped unless it is obvious a first down has been made. If the referee decides to measure, the referee alone should stop the clock.

Once the ball is set, the umpire straddles it and waits for the referee to blow the ready for play before moving to his position. The referee should not blow the ready for play until checking that the linesman and chains are in place and until all officials have verbally and visually confirmed the down.

The umpire remains over the ball for two reasons. First, to ensure the ball is not snapped before the ready for play. Secondly, the umpire and referee can confirm the status of the clock. If the crew has just enforced a penalty, the umpire can remind the referee whether the clock should start on the ready or on the snap. The umpire can also advise the referee to withhold the whistle if the chain crew is not in position or there is some other delay. Good umpires tell the referee if the latter's between-downs pace is lagging or rushed.

Perhaps the most important communication between umpire and referee comes on penalty enforcement. The officials must be certain they agree on the yardage, enforcement spot and added penalty (automatic first down, loss of down, etc.) before the umpire steps off the penalty.

Ball relay

Nothing makes a crew look unprofessional and sloppy like a slipshod ball relay system. Unless you have seen a crew that has to chase the football because it was thrown too high or too low for the intended receiver to catch, you can't believe how comical it appears. Since you're not on the field to entertain the spectators between plays, here are some tips to remember when getting the ball from the dead-ball spot to the spot from which it will next be snapped.

Foremost, remember that your playing days are over. No one — least of all the crewmate on the receiving end — cares if you can throw a hard overhand pass with a tight spiral from 35 yards away. Never throw the ball more than 20 yards. Use an underhanded motion to deliver a chest-high pass. If you have to take a couple of steps to shorten the distance between yourself and a crewmate, do it. That is especially important in inclement weather. If you've gone to the trouble of getting a dry ball from the sideline, walk the ball in to the umpire to eliminate the possibility that it will get dropped onto the wet turf. If you wanted to use a wet, muddy ball, you wouldn't have exchanged it for a dry one, right?

Unless field conditions dictate, there is no need to exchange balls when the play ends in the middle of the field.

Good ballboys will help facilitate the ball relay (see Chapter 11, Instructing the Chain Crew, Timer and Ballboys). Whether you have ballboys or not, the key to getting the ball to the umpire is the "V." (See Visual Definition, page 17.) The covering official marks the spot, which is mirrored by the umpire, who is standing at the hashmark. The referee (or back judge when the play ends farther downfield) catches the toss from a position between the hashmark and the covering official and two to three yards behind the dead-ball spot. The referee then pivots and flips the ball to the umpire.

In a five-man crew, if the back judge is the covering official, he can leave the ball on the ground at the spot while the linesman or line judge (depending on which side zone the ball is in) can retrieve a new ball from the ballboy and flip the ball to the umpire. Once the ball has been set by the umpire, the back judge picks up the ball at his feet and gives it to the ballboy.

FUMBLES

Officials have specific duties when a pile forms on top of a fumble. The ball will be spotted and the process will be much simpler if each crew member does his job.

When an official sees a fumble, he must drop a beanbag at the yardline at which the ball was fumbled (the spot may be used for penalty enforcement if a foul occurs while the ball is loose). He must also continue officiating.

If the covering official sees a player recover the fumble from a prone position, he should blow the play dead. If the defense recovers, the stop-the-clock signal is given, followed by a point in the direction of the recovering team. If the offense recovers, the covering official should only signal the next down (unless a first down was achieved; in that case, the stop-the-clock signal is given, followed by a point in the direction of the recovering team).

If a fumble results in players from both team forming a pile that prevents the covering official from determining possession, the ball must be "dug out" of the pile. The official closest to the pile becomes the "digger," the official responsible for unpiling the players and determining who has recovered the fumble. The official nearest the digger signals the clock to stop and looks at the clock to be sure it is stopped. The remaining nearby officials echo the signal.

Assuming the pile consists of four or more players, the digger begins by getting the players on top of the pile to get up. One method is to tap those players and say, "You're out," or "You don't have it; get up." Pay attention when you get close to the pile; you don't want a mouthful of helmet. The digger can't be shy about getting dirty. The ball is somewhere on the ground; the digger should be, too.

If the players are slow to unpile, another official can approach the pile and assist the digger; the remaining officials should practice dead-ball officiating and observe the players not on the pile.

Another digger's trick is to grasp the arm of the player who is clearly in possession of the ball at the bottom of the pile. By saying, "I've got the ball; everyone off the pile," the digger can ensure the proper team is awarded possession while getting the players to disperse.

If the digger can clearly see the ball or is certain he knows which player has covered it, he verbally relays that information to the referee. If team A has recovered, the referee announces the next down and restarts the clock (or signals the first down if team A

has achieved a first down). If team B has recovered, the referee alone signals the change of possession.

The digger can help statisticians and spectators by pointing to or otherwise identifying the player who recovered the fumble once the pile has dispersed.

When a fumble is recovered betweentwo officials and the pile consists of four or fewer players, there is usually no need for a digger. The officials should make eye contact and confirm what they've seen (e.g. "I've got red ball." "So do I."). If they agree, both give the proper signals. If they don't agree, one must serve as the digger.

Anytime the referee is in the area of the pile, the recovery information should be verbally relayed to the referee. The referee alone then signals.

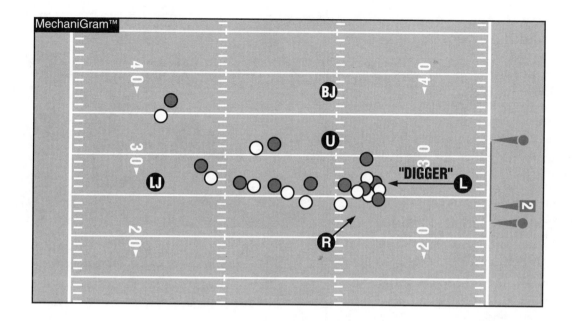

CHALK TALK: FUMBLE IN LINESMAN'S SIDE ZONE

Because the fumble has occurred in the linesman's side zone, he becomes the "digger," the official responsible for unpiling the players and determining who has recovered the fumble. The referee slowly approaches the pile while signaling the clock to stop. The referee should look at the clock to be sure it is stopped. The remaining officials echo the signal.

Assuming the pile consists of four or more players, the digger begins by getting the players on top of the pile to get up. One method is to tap those players and say, "You're out," or "You don't have it; get up." If the players are slow to unpile, the umpire can approach the pile and assist the digger; the remaining officials should practice dead-ball officiating and observe the players not on the pile.

Once the digger can see the ball or determine the player who has covered it, he verbally relays that information to the referee. If team A has recovered, the referee announces the next down and restarts the clock (or signals the first down if team A has achieved a first down). If team B has recovered, the referee alone signals the change of possession.

MECHANICS ILLUSTRATED: 'DIGGING OUT' FUMBLES

In PlayPic A, a running play has ended with a fumble in the side zone on the linesman's side of the field and it is unclear which team recovered. Because he is closest to the pile, the linesman becomes the "digger," the official responsible for unpiling the players and determining who has recovered the fumble. The official nearest the digger (the referee in this instance) signals the clock to stop and looks at the clock to be sure it is stopped. The remaining officials echo the signal.

Assuming the pile consists of four or more players, the digger begins by getting the players on top of the pile to get up. One method is to tap those players and say, "You're out," or "You don't have it; get up." Pay attention when you get close to the pile; you don't want a mouthful of helmet. If the players are slow to unpile, the umpire can approach the pile and assist the linesman. That's a natural movement since the ball will next be snapped from the hashmark.

In PlayPic B, an official (the line judge or back judge, depending on the size of the crew) is using dead-ball officiating techniques to ensure an altercation doesn't erupt. He is close enough to the players so they know he is there but not so far away he has to shout to be heard.

Once the digger can see the ball or determine the player who has covered it, he will verbally relay information to the referee (PlayPic C). If team A has recovered, the referee announces the next down and restarts the clock. If team B has recovered (as in PlayPic C), he alone signals the change of possession.

The digger can help statisticians and spectators by pointing to or otherwise identifying the player who recovered the fumble once the pile has dispersed.

PlayPic™ A

PlayPic™ B

PlayPic™ C

FORWARD PROGRESS AND SPOTTING THE BALL

Perhaps the most important job for any football official is determining the runner's forward progress and spotting the ball for the next down. Each is a highly visible task that will be performed dozens of times during a game. They are the bread and butter of football officiating. Doing those jobs improperly, due to poor judgment or mechanics, will result in loud protests from players, coaches and spectators and will severely damage an official's career.

Forward progress should be handled by the wing official moving up and down the field with the runner, parallel to the sideline, and then moving to the selected place at right angles to the sidelines ("squaring off"). Not only does squaring off look sharper than arriving at a spot in an arc, it adds credibility to the call.

Some wing officials indicate forward progress by sticking one foot far ahead of the other and either patting a knee repeatedly or pointing at the ground in staccato jabs. Such gestures are not desirable behaviors because on occasion the umpire or referee may take a spot from the opposite official, making the gesturing official look foolish. Unless a first down or a touchdown is at issue, a wingman's spot should be decidedly undemonstrative. Simply placing the downfield foot (the one closest to team B's goalline) is sufficient for marking a spot.

Wing officials, primarily responsible for identifying forward progress on scrimmage downs, must remember that the progress point is the spot under the ball in player possession when that player is downed by rule. Where a knee or hip touches the ground is only an indicator that kills the play. Wing officials should also be firm about awarding any runner his furthest advance if a swarm of defenders roll the runner backward.

Wing officials should not penetrate the hashmarks for a spot unless the spot needs to be sold (such as on a fourth down play when team A only needs to advance the ball a short distance in order to achieve a first down). When the play ends between the hashes, the wings can give the spot from approximately midway between the hashmark and the sideline. When the play ends in his side zone, the covering wing can mark the spot with the downfield foot, retrieve the ball and flip it to the middle man of the "V" so it can be relayed to the umpire at the hashmark.

Several situations arise in which it is difficult to obtain an accurate spot or where officials sometimes make mistakes. One of those occurs when a runner is downed near a sideline but momentum carries the runner beyond where he contacted the ground. Often he may have been tripped up and either stumbled or flew through the air after being knocked off-balance. In such cases the runner may land inbounds and then either skid or roll past the sideline.

First of all, the clock should not be killed on such a play; the covering official must give the wind-the-clock signal to keep the clock running. The covering official must make an instant decision whether or not to fix the spot by remaining on it. If a runner (together with tacklers) slides into a team bench area, and if the play gained less than five yards, the wing official may choose to mark the progress spot with a beanbag and then move outside to protect the players himself, realizing that another official (most of the time the back judge in a five-man crew or the referee in a four-man crew) is likely to be tardy, having to run a considerable distance. The referee should be prepared to serve as a backup on such a play.

If the gain is substantial, however, the back judge (five-man crew) or referee (four-man crew) should swing outside (saying "I'm here") and retrieve both the players and the ball. The wing official may then retain his progress spot while watching post-play action out of bounds.

If the covering wing needs to go out of bounds to help his crewmate break up a confrontation, he should drop a beanbag and make sure the progress spot is secured.

Another progress problem occurs on buttonhook passes, particularly those caught near a sideline, where those patterns are usually run. The basic problem in obtaining an accurate spot is that the sideline official is either in front of or behind the receiver, and often a reception is followed instantly by contact, with the receiver being shoved toward the line of scrimmage.

The receiver should be given the full benefit of progress, the point where contact and ball possession occurred. Pro and college officials operate in partnership on such plays, with the opposite wing official deciding on the progress spot, and the covering official picking up that spot after the play by glancing across the field. That is excellent cooperative officiating.

Again, the covering official should be sure to use an arm wind to keep the clock running if the play is dead near the sideline.

One difficulty in determining forward progress is that the wing official may not see the ball when a runner is downed. That is particularly true when a runner hits the center of the line and falls under a pile of players. In such instances the wing official who makes the call can stop at an approximate spot and then adjust slightly as players unpile and the ball comes into view. Any adjustment should be made carefully, with a slight shuffle or sidestep. The official should stand erect, hands at the sides, feet together, toes pointing at the ball, with the downfield foot (the foot closest to team B's goalline) ahead of the other and in line with the foremost point of the football. A word to the umpire that you have the spot can be helpful.

Another difficulty for the wingman in obtaining a good spot is that a runner may not fall to the ground at all but instead may be stopped and held in an upright position. The wing official must first of all be sure that the runner has indeed been halted and secured. The official should kill the play with a whistle and stand motionless to indicate where the ball was when the whistle sounded. The covering official should remain in the side zone unless either the lead stake on the chain or the goalline are threatened.

A third problem in obtaining a true progress spot is a play on which the runner bounces off defenders. Sometimes a runner hits the line and is turned back but not secured by defenders, whereupon the runner tries for another hole. At times the runner may actually advance by darting into an alternate opening, but just as often he may be bent backward at a spot behind where he initially tried to penetrate the line. The official must be sure to award the runner only the advance made on his own, when he ran freely, ignoring the first or second smash into the mass of defenders.

But the official must also avoid setting up a progress point where the runner landed if he was driven back from his furthest downfield penetration.

A runner may also be driven backward on a sweep on which a defender hoists the runner in an aggressive tackle and propels him in the opposite direction. At times a runner is a side zone may be dumped five yards from where contact was initiated, being vulnerable because defenders have had an opportunity to develop considerable velocity in tackling. In such instances the official must quickly decide whether to cover the downed runner or remain at the progress spot.

Such a decision depends upon the position of the backup official (the referee in a four-man crew or the referee or back judge in a five-man crew). If the backup official started from the runner's side zone, he may easily get to the pile and defuse player animosities (runners often get angry when they are driven backward and flung to the ground). If the backup official was stationed on the far side at the snap, he may not be of much help in policing the grounded players, in which case the wing official should mark the progress spot with a beanbag and move quickly to extract players from the runner.

An alert umpire will hustle to the spot and align himself with the progress spot so he can retain that spot if the covering wing official has to step between players.

Another important mechanic is called "officiating back to the ball." When the ball is snapped close to team B's goalline (see Chapters 18 and 26, Goalline Plays), the wing officials must move quickly to team B's goalline in order to rule on a potential touchdown. If the runner is downed short of the goalline, the wing official moves back toward the play in order to determine the spot of forward progress.

MECHANICS ILLUSTRATED:
MIRRORING THE SPOT

Good crews establish and maintain a rhythm in spotting, retrieving and setting the ball. The covering official and the umpire can work together to establish a good tempo.

In PlayPic A, ball has become dead in a side zone. The wing official has marked the spot of forward progress and the umpire is hustling to the hashmark to mirror the spot.

PlayPic B shows the umpire holding the spot, freeing up the wingman to retrieve the ball. The covering official must not abandon the spot until the umpire arrives and verbally releases him, nor should he drop a beanbag and get the ball. Another mistake for the wingman to avoid is holding the spot and making the umpire come into the side zone to get the ball.

When it is obvious a first down has been achieved in the linesman's side zone, a hustling crew can use the same techniques to speed the process of setting the chains. In PlayPic C, the linesman holds the spot until the umpire arrives to mirror the spot. The umpire, seeing that the ball is well beyond the lead stake and mirroring the spot, frees the linesman to get to the sideline and move the chain crew.

Hustle and communication are vital. The umpire cannot take his time getting to the spot. It is also important for both officials to be good dead-ball officials. They must not stare down at the spot; it is vital they keep their heads up and watch players in the vicinity.

MECHANICS ILLUSTRATED: SETTING THE BALL

The umpire can set the ball one of three ways — facing the offense, facing the defense and directly facing the wing official providing the spot. There is no right or wrong method; the choice belongs to the umpire.

PlayPic A illustrates the umpire facing the defense. That method allows the umpire to speak to the defensive players unobtrusively. Facing the offense, as shown in PlayPic B, makes it easier for the umpire to communicate with the referee and see him give the ready-for-play signal. In PlayPic C, the umpire is straddling the ball, which allows communication with the defense and referee.

Whichever way you choose, keep the following information in mind:

• Once the ball is set, remain over the ball until the ready signal has been given. Facing the referee allows the referee and umpire to remain in visual contact with each other. Remind the offense to wait for the whistle before getting into their stances or calling signals.

• The wingman who can see the ball will mark forward progress, particularly when the play ends between the hashmarks. Take forward progress from the wingman. The umpire should rarely (if ever) be responsible for the spot, even if the play ends at his feet. Things happen that the umpire simply cannot see from the middle of the field; trust your wings to give you the proper spot.

• When the play has ended out of bounds, use the sideline yardage stripes (assuming the field has them) as a guide in placing the ball. For instance, if the spot is between the 31 and 32 yardlines say to yourself, "The back end of the ball is closer to the 31 than the 32." If the ball becomes dead in a side zone, the wing official will be closer than the yard marks and it should be easier to find the proper spot.

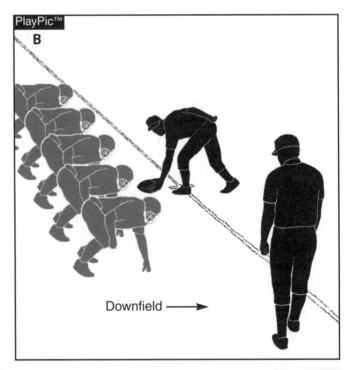

Downfield ⟶

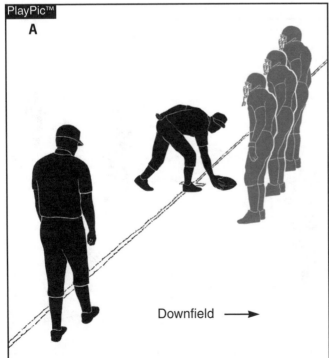

Downfield ⟶

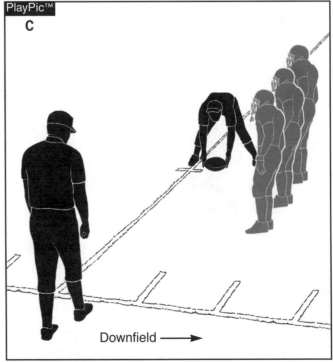

Downfield ⟶

• Officials must count players on every down, especially on downs following timeouts or injuries, when substitutions are common.

• Every official should acknowledge the down, verbally and by signaling.

• The "digger" on a fumble can't be shy about getting dirty. The ball is somewhere on the ground; the covering official should be, too.

• Squaring off to mark a spot adds credibility to the officials' decision.

Quiz

Without referring back, you should be able to answer the following true-false questions.

1. The umpire has no player-counting responsibilities.

2. When a pile forms on top of a fumble, the official closest to the pile becomes the "digger."

3. The downfield foot is the one closest to team B's goalline.

4. Mirroring the spot allows the referee to quickly determine whether team A has achieved a first down or if the current series will continue.

5. Before the ready for play signal is blown, the umpire remains over the ball to ensure the ball is not snapped and so that the umpire and referee can confirm the status of the clock.

1. False 2. True 3. True 4. True 5. True

Chapter 5

The Pregame

PREGAME CONFERENCE

The great importance placed on the pregame conference with officiating partners has made the concept almost cliché. Nearly everyone in officiating — camp directors, clinicians, book authors, columnists, veteran officials — all say a pregame conference is a significant ingredient of success. They're all right: If you can talk about it before it happens on the field, you're better prepared to deal with it.

There are as many different pregame conferences as there are officials. There is no magic formula for a "successful" pregame conference. There are a number of topics, however, that should be included:

Rule changes/major differences
Cover recent rule changes, especially in the beginning of the season when the rules and interpretations may still be a bit unclear. Cover major rule differences when you work different levels of play — for example, going from high school to small college games or high school to youth ball.

Special coverage
Discuss what to do in the event of hurry-up offense, obvious onside kick situation, etc. If the weather is threatening, discuss how the crew will handle a suspension of play due to lightning. The crew should also decide how it will handle fights or similar altercations.

Making the call
Go over signals between officials (receivers on or off the line, "two sticks" for a first down, etc.). Discuss which crew members are responsible for counting players and what signals will be used to indicate a team has enough, too many or too few players. Remind officials who are sharing coverage to make eye contact and to practice good dead-ball officiating.

Reporting fouls to the referee
The referee should tell crew members how he wants fouls reported to him. Does he want the official to identify the offending team by uniform color or by referring to them as offense and defense? Remind officials to indicate the status of the ball at the time of the foul (loose ball, dead ball, etc.) and the result of the play (incomplete pass, scoring kick was good, etc.). Remind wing officials they are to tell the coach who committed the foul, the nature of the infraction and any special enforcement (loss of down, quarter extended for an untimed down, etc.).

Timeout responsibilities
Who's timing the timeout? Where are the officials positioned during the timeout? How are you going to inform the teams that the timeout is over? Who will tell the coach how many timeouts each team has remaining? *Referee* recommends the coach be told how many timeouts each team has left after every charged team timeout.

Bench decorum
This is a key element, often overlooked in pregame conferences. It is especially important if the crew does not work together often. Make sure that the officials involved have roughly the same idea about what conduct is out of line and what isn't. Remind wing officials to find the "get back" coach, the assistant who will help keep players and team personnel out of the coaching belt.

Injured officials
Discuss how the crew will adjust assignments if an official is injured or becomes too ill to work. Which officials will move where is up to the crew, but generally a four-man crew works without a line judge and a five-man crew works without a back judge when a crewmate is ill or injured. When a crew is reduced to two officials, *Referee* recommends that one official work as the referee and the other as a linesman.

Halftime
Are you going to let the coaches and teams leave the field before heading off yourselves? *Referee* recommends that the officials meet at a designated place on the field, allow the teams to leave and have the referee signal the timer to start the clock. Also, someone needs to make sure the officials and teams are properly notified of the time on the clock so they can return in time. The game manager should let the officials know if someone has been designated or if the officials will be responsible.

Leaving the field
Will the crew leave the field together or is each official to leave on his own?

Game expectations
If you know of some team history that may affect the game, discuss it. For example, if the two teams were involved in a fight the last time they met, you may want to talk about those ramifications on the game and the players' and coaches' attitudes.

PREGAME DUTIES

Meeting with coaches
Whenever possible, the pregame meeting with the coaches should be conducted off the field. In that instance, the referee and the umpire should visit each lockerroom, then report back to the rest of the crew in the officials' lockerroom. If the meeting with the coaches occurs on the field, meet with the visiting coach first if possible. Either way, the meeting should begin with the referee introducing himself and giving the coach a card listing names of crew members.

With the umpire within earshot, ask the coach if all players are properly equipped (NCAA rules allow a team representative other than the coach to make the verification). Have the umpire inspect any suspect equipment or tapings. Ask if the team plans on using any unique formations or trick plays. Foreknowledge helps the crew be prepared for such instances and increases the chances the play will be officiated correctly.

Get the captains' numbers. Some crews also obtain the captains' names. If an official wishes to speak to a captain during the game, perhaps to seek his help in calming an angry teammate, the captain will respond better if he is called by name rather than number. Some crews also ask the coach what his choice would be if his team wins the coin toss. In the excitement that is felt before the game, captains sometimes blurt out something other than their coach's wishes. If you've asked the coach and the captain gives a different answer, a preventive officiating technique is to ask the captain, "Are you sure that's what you want?"

Inform the coach when the coin flip is to take place (conference or association rules may dictate; "normal" is three minutes before game). Tell him that his team will be notified by an official when there is three minutes left on the halftime clock. With that notice, the team is expected to be on the field for the three-minute warmup. Also, if there is a planned extended halftime, make sure the coach is aware of it.

The crew should take the field together. College rules mandate that at least one official must be on the field in uniform 60 minutes before kickoff; unless conference or state association rules state otherwise, 30 minutes is "normal" for other levels.

Once on the field, the officials' duties are as follows:

Referee

• **Inspect the field.** The referee should walk down both sidelines and along each endline at a brisk but unhurried pace. You don't need to inspect every blade of grass, but if you discover potholes, broken glass or other hazards, ask game management to have the problem taken care of immediately. If the field is marked for another sport (many football fields are also used for soccer), make sure the crew knows which lines are being used for football. Make sure the goalposts are straight and free of decoration and that the goalpost pads are securely fastened. Check the pylons to ensure they are properly placed.

• **Spot-check players.** Make a casual visual inspection of players as they warm up. Look for tinted eyeshields, knotted jerseys, towels with decorations and other uniform-related violations. Before the game, ask the head coach to have the players make the necessary corrections.

• **Check with the crew.** Verify that the umpire has inspected any tapings or protective equipment, that the linesman has met with the chain crew and that the line judge has met with the timer and the ballboys. Discuss unusual plays or formations either team may have.

Umpire

• **Spot-check players.** Make a casual visual inspection of players as they warm up. Look for tinted eyeshields, knotted jerseys, towels with decorations and other uniform-related violations. Before the game, ask the head coach to have the players make the necessary corrections.

Linesman

• **Inspect the box and chains.** Make sure the chain is securely attached to the poles and is free of kinks. If there is no tape at the midway point of the chain (to facilitate the determination of whether a five-yard defensive penalty will result in a first down), ask a trainer for tape and mark the chain. The ends of the box and chain poles must be properly covered. If they are not, ask game management to remedy the situation.

• **Meet with the chain crew.** See chapter 11.

Line judge

• **Inspect the field.** The line judge should walk down both sidelines and along each endline at a brisk but unhurried pace. You don't need to inspect every blade of grass, but if you discover potholes, broken glass or other hazards, ask game management to have the problem taken care of immediately. If the field is marked for another sport (many football fields are also used for soccer), make sure the crew knows which lines are being used for football. Make sure the goalposts are straight and free of decoration and that the goalpost pads are securely fastened. Check the pylons to ensure they are properly placed.

• **Keep track of the game balls (four-man crew).** Ensure that game balls are kept separate from practice balls; players are not allowed to warm up with the game balls. If the game balls are delivered to the officials' lockerroom before the game, the air pressure can be checked with a gauge. Air can be removed from balls that are over-inflated; balls that are under-inflated should be returned to game management and corrected or not used. If the game balls are given to the officials on the field, a visual and touch inspection should be used. Once approved, game balls should be marked (e.g. official's initials) so only approved balls are used in the game.

• **Meet with the ballboys and timer (four-man crew).** See chapter 11.

• **Meet with the auxiliary down box operator (when applicable).** See chapter 11.

Back judge (five-man crew)

• **Keep track of the game balls.** Ensure that game balls are kept separate from practice balls; players are not allowed to warm up with the game balls. If the game balls are delivered to the officials' lockerroom before the game, the air pressure can be checked with a gauge. Air can be removed from balls that are over-inflated; balls that are under-inflated should be returned to game management and corrected or not used. If the game balls are given to the officials on the field, a visual and touch inspection should be used. Once approved, game balls should be marked (e.g. official's initials) so only approved balls are used in the game.

• **Meet with the ballboys and timer.** See chapter 11.

When duties are completed

After onfield pregame duties have been completed, the referee, linesman and back judge (five-man crew) move to midfield on the linesman's side of the field while the umpire and line judge move to midfield on the opposite side.

That is an ideal time to casually observe both teams for information that will be helpful during the game: Is the quarterback right-handed or left-handed? How strong are the punter's and kicker's legs? How is the wind affecting kicks? Watch both teams without giving the appearance they are being inspected. Before the kickoff, exchange information with other crew members.

Avoid using pregame time for non-essential chat with players, coaches, spectators or others, especially if it could give the appearance of favoritism.

OUTLINE

Pregame duties
Coaches' certification
Spot check players' equipment
Check and mark balls
Identify medical staff
Instruction of chain crew and alternates
Instruction of ballboys and timer
Inspection of field

Coin toss procedure
First half procedure
Second half options

Free kicks
Positions
Instructions to teams
Restraining lines
Count players
Starting clock
Momentum into end zone
Touchback
Untouched kick out of bounds
Blocking below waist
Kick-catch interference
Fair catch
Onside kicks
Free kick after safety

Scrimmage plays — general
Positions
Crew communication
Count players
Substitutions
Legality of offensive line — wing officials' signals
Eligibility of receivers
Man in motion
Dead-ball fouls

Scrimmage plays — runs
Coverage of runner — in backfield, between tackles, sweeps, pitchouts
Action in front of runner
Dead ball coverage
Forward progress — out of bounds
Goalline/short-yardage situations
Coverage of fumbles, ensuing advances and returns

Scrimmage plays — passes
Coverage of passer — roughing
Passer/pass behind/beyond line of scrimmage — clarify jurisdiction Forward/backward pass
Intentional grounding — clarify jurisdiction
Ineligibles downfield

Keys and zones
Coverage of receivers
Complete/incomplete
Pass interference — offensive, defensive
Coverage on interception — momentum into end zone, blocking below waist

Punts
Positions
Contact on kicker
Blocked/touched on line of scrimmage — ball beyond/behind neutral zone
Kick-catch interference
Fair catch
Untouched in end zone
Out of bounds — marking spot
Illegal touching
Coverage of runback — runner, other action, blocking below waist
Fakes

Field goals and try attempts
Positions — coverage of posts
Contact on kicker/holder
Blocked/touched on line of scrimmage — ball beyond/behind neutral zone
Fakes
Coverage when defense gain possession

General duties
Fumble pileups
Ball relay

End of quarter
Changing end after first and third quarters
Halftime
End of game

Timeouts
Records
Positions and duties

Measurements

Fouls and enforcement
Reporting — who, what, where, when
Recording fouls
Options
Signals
Enforcement

Reserve positions in case of injury
If one official is hurt
If two officials are hurt

Chapter 6

Philosophy of
Signals

Clear and concise communication is a necessary ingredient for any successful person, regardless of the profession. The same is true for officials. When people hear the word "communication," most think of how a person speaks to an individual or group. A sometimes overlooked yet critically important communication method is body language.

In many ways, an official's body language is just as important as any verbal communication. Just as an official can get into trouble for using profanity when speaking to a player or coach, poor body language can escalate a negative situation. Conversely, positive body language can help ease and control a potential conflict.

Think about this: Why do we bother to give signals? It's because we need to tell others (players, coaches, fans, etc.) what happened on the field and it's impossible to yell loud enough for everyone to hear. Sounds condescendingly simple, but keeping that basic principle in mind will make you more aware of what signals you use and how you give them.

Throwing the flag
When you call a foul, your body language sends a message to everyone watching. Slamming your flag to the ground shows you are too emotional. Avoid the practice of throwing the flag at the offender. Indicating the yardline at which the foul occurred is crucial, but it can be accomplished by dropping the flag in front of you and on the proper yardline. When a violation occurs at the snap, throw the flag as high as possible and in front of you. No official wants to be hit with his own flag and wing officials don't want the flag to land in the bench area.

Selling a call
Selling a call is like raising your voice: Sometimes it is necessary and effective. Do it too often and people get angry or turned off. Sell a call only when necessary. Obvious calls need good signals too, but close calls need a little extra emphasis to communicate to everyone clearly. Don't over-sell; you don't want to appear that you're caught up in the emotion of the game.

Using approved signals
Follow the prescribed signals in the manuals. It's important because people have come to accept and understand them. Again, think about signals as words. If two English-speaking people were talking and one briefly switched to a foreign language, confusion would set in. The same is true for signals. By using unauthorized signals, you're speaking a foreign language and confusion reigns.

There are, however, some commonly accepted signals that are not included in the Federation or CCA manuals. Listed as "additional signals" in the "signals chart," consider using them if your governing bodies allow.

Signaling to the pressbox
As a referee, your presentation to the pressbox is equally important. That's one of the few times where all eyes are focused on you.

Come to a complete stop. Keep your head up. Pick out a spot about halfway up the stands and focus your eyes on that spot. You should have no facial expression; you're neither happy nor unhappy to be performing this duty. Slowly give the signal and point to the offending team. The referee must avoid jabbing his arm when signaling; it is another sign the official is angry or feels a sense of "gotcha" toward the offending team.

Whether or not you are allowed to use a microphone to report fouls, the number of the offending player should not be announced. Take a short pause between facets of the announcement and coordinate your signals with what you are saying. Avoid using the phrase "We have" when announcing a penalty.

An example of proper wording when reporting the penalty: "Holding (pause), on the offense (pause), repeat the down (pause), third down." Some referees add the distance of the penalty and the enforcement spot: "Clipping (pause), on the receiving team (pause), 15 yards from the spot of the foul (pause), first down."

In subvarsity games, youth games or games at which there is no public address announcer, *Referee* recommends giving the signal to both sidelines. Consider giving the announcer a copy of the signal chart. Although most fans and coaches know the signals for common fouls such as holding or encroachment, other signals are less common. Giving the announcer a copy of the chart improves the chances the announcer will properly convey your signal to the crowd.

Slow down and think about your signals as a language. If you "speak" slowly and clearly and use the right "words," the correct message and tone will get across.

Referee-only signals
The referee is the only official who signals penalties. Under some circumstances, other officials may give other signals illustrated in the signals chart that follows. For instance, any official may give the stop-the-clock signal when the ball becomes dead out of bounds or a request for a charged timeout has been granted.

Unless preceded by an asterisk (*), the illustrated signals are for the referee only.

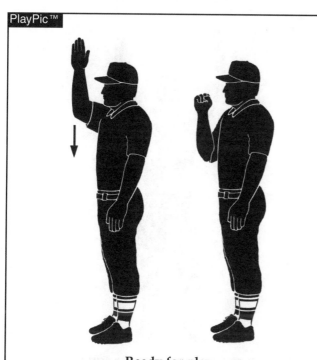

Ready for play

Extend one arm fully upward and "pull a light chain" while simultaneously blowing the whistle.

*Start the clock

Three easy swings of one arm at full extension while facing the clock operator; rotate the arm in front of the body, not to the side.

Untimed down

Twirl the index finger overhead to indicate the clock will not run for the play (e.g. a try).

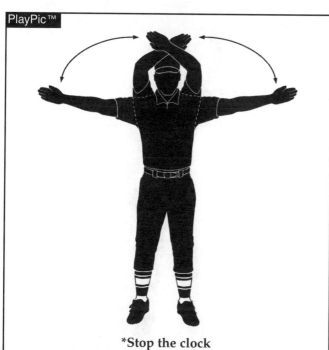

*Stop the clock

After two strokes, glance at the clock; if it hasn't stopped, the signal can be continued until no longer necessary.

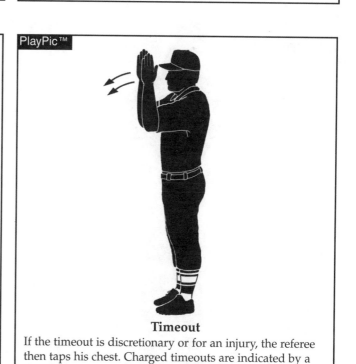

Timeout

If the timeout is discretionary or for an injury, the referee then taps his chest. Charged timeouts are indicated by a chucking motion three times in the direction of the requesting team. If the timeout is a team's third and final charged timeout for a half, NCAA wants it to be indicated by three pulls on an imaginary steam whistle.

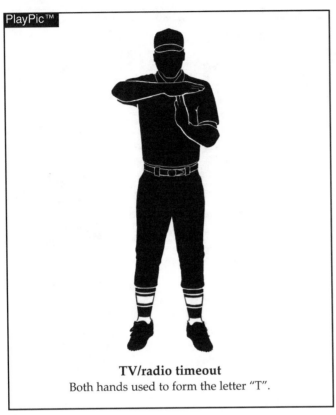

TV/radio timeout
Both hands used to form the letter "T".

*Touchdown/successful try/successful field goal
Arms should be fully extended in a straight line toward the sky.

*Safety
Hands together in front of your body above head height.

Dead-ball foul
For dead-ball fouls only; not to be used to indicate the runner is down.

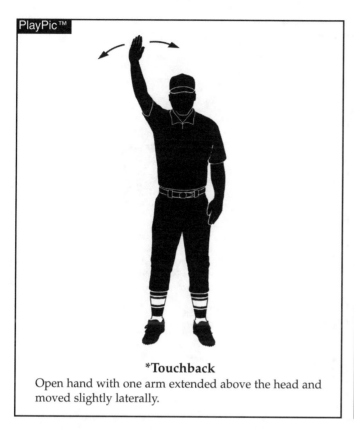

*Touchback
Open hand with one arm extended above the head and moved slightly laterally.

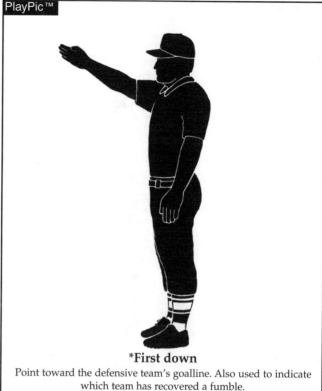

*First down
Point toward the defensive team's goalline. Also used to indicate which team has recovered a fumble.

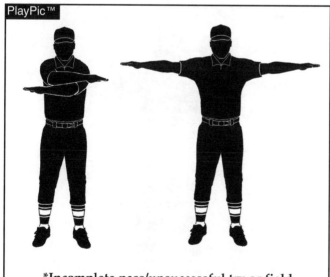

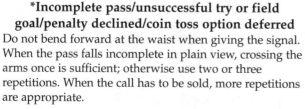

*Incomplete pass/unsuccessful try or field goal/penalty declined/coin toss option deferred
Do not bend forward at the waist when giving the signal. When the pass falls incomplete in plain view, crossing the arms once is sufficient; otherwise use two or three repetitions. When the call has to be sold, more repetitions are appropriate.

*Legal touching
One hand slid across the palm of the other.

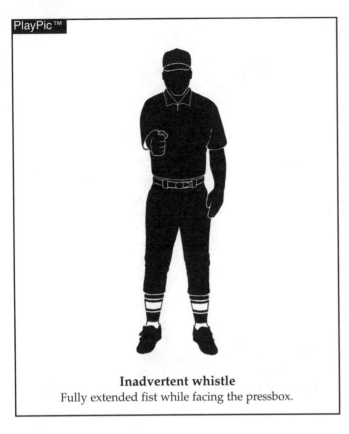

Inadvertent whistle
Fully extended fist while facing the pressbox.

Disregard flag
Flag waved two or three times above the head.

End of period
Full extension of one arm overhead with the ball in hand.

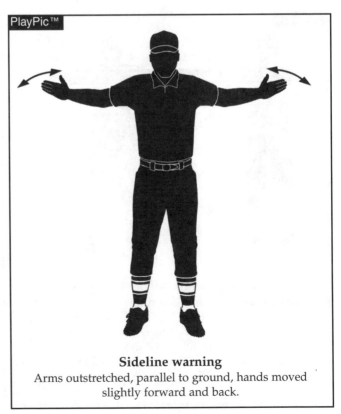

Sideline warning
Arms outstretched, parallel to ground, hands moved
slightly forward and back.

Illegal touching (NCAA only)
first touching (Federation only)
Elbows out, upper arms parallel to the ground with the hands motionless on the shoulders.

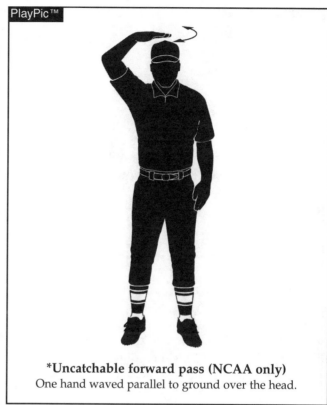

*Uncatchable forward pass (NCAA only)
One hand waved parallel to ground over the head.

Defense offside (NCAA only)
encroachment (Federation only)
Hands motionless on hips for a couple of seconds.

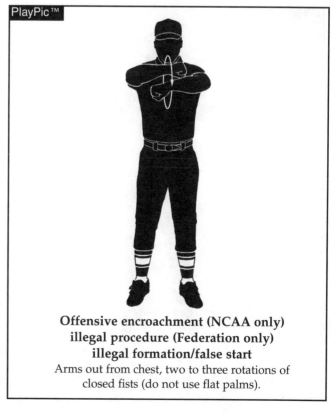

Offensive encroachment (NCAA only)
illegal procedure (Federation only)
illegal formation/false start
Arms out from chest, two to three rotations of closed fists (do not use flat palms).

Illegal motion
Two chops out from the chest parallel to ground with the right palm down.

Illegal shift
Two chops out from the chest parallel to ground with both palms down.

Delay of game
Fold the arms at chest height and hold for a few seconds.

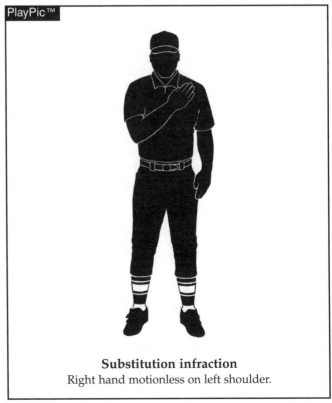

Substitution infraction
Right hand motionless on left shoulder.

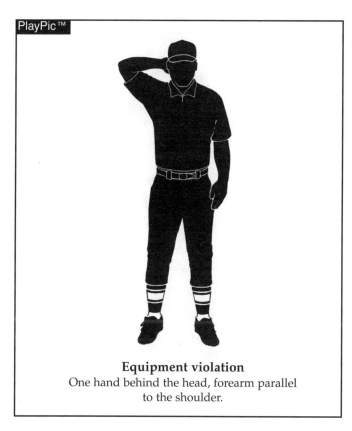

Equipment violation
One hand behind the head, forearm parallel
to the shoulder.

Illegal helmet contact
One fist held to the side of the head.

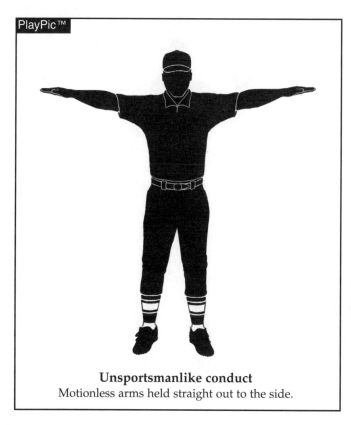

Unsportsmanlike conduct
Motionless arms held straight out to the side.

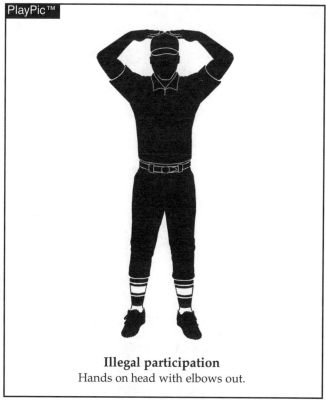

Illegal participation
Hands on head with elbows out.

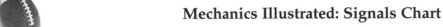

Sideline interference

Face away from the pressbox; arms crossed behind the back.

**Running into (NCAA only)
roughing the kicker or holder**

Short leg kick. (NCAA, precede with the personal foul signal, to distinguish from running into the kicker. In Federation, only the kicking signal is called for, but most referees use both signals.)

Illegal batting/kicking (for illegal kicking, follow with point toward foot)

Elbow out with upper arm parallel to ground, left hand motionless on left shoulder. (For illegal kicking, follow this signal by pointing to a toe.)

**Invalid fair-catch signal (Federation only)
illegal fair-catch signal**

One arm at a 90-degree arm angle.

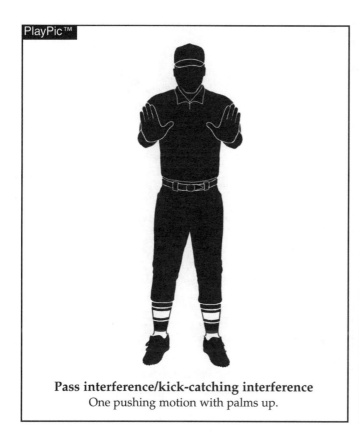

Pass interference/kick-catching interference
One pushing motion with palms up.

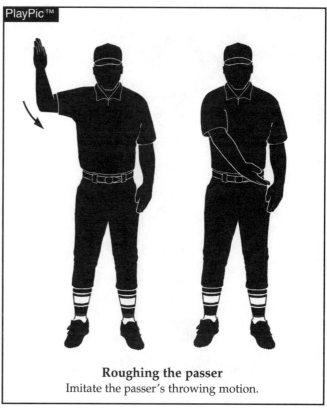

Roughing the passer
Imitate the passer's throwing motion.

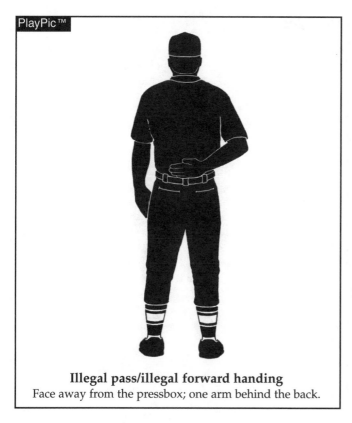

Illegal pass/illegal forward handing
Face away from the pressbox; one arm behind the back.

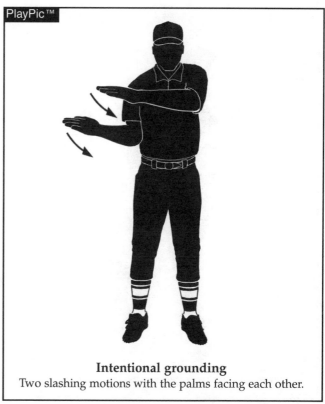

Intentional grounding
Two slashing motions with the palms facing each other.

Ineligible downfield on pass
The palm of one hand on top of the head.

Personal foul
The wrist of one hand struck one with the
side of the other fist.

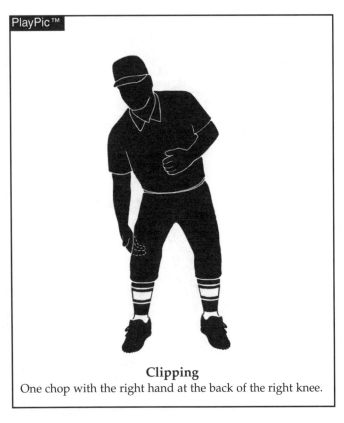

Clipping
One chop with the right hand at the back of the right knee.

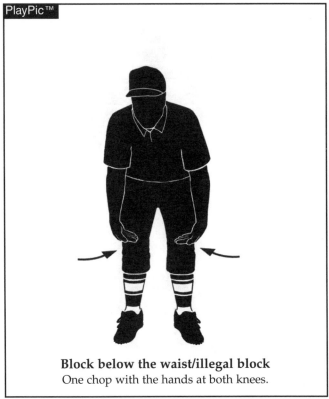

Block below the waist/illegal block
One chop with the hands at both knees.

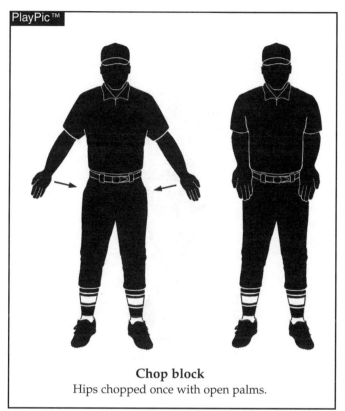

Chop block

Hips chopped once with open palms.

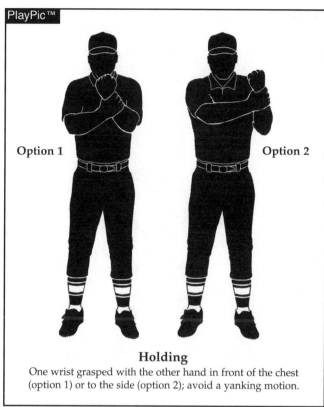

Option 1   Option 2

Holding

One wrist grasped with the other hand in front of the chest
(option 1) or to the side (option 2); avoid a yanking motion.

**Illegal block in the back (NCAA only)
illegal use of hands**

The right wrist, palm open, grasped with the left hand
and pushed away slightly.

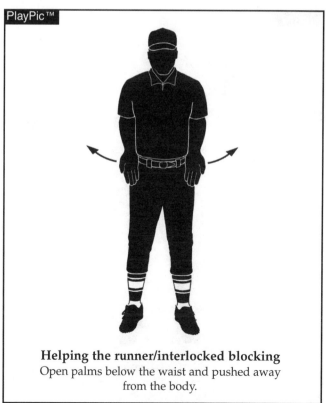

Helping the runner/interlocked blocking

Open palms below the waist and pushed away
from the body.

Grasping facemask or helmet opening
Fist in front of the face pulled down (NCAA only: The major foul is preceded with the personal foul signal).

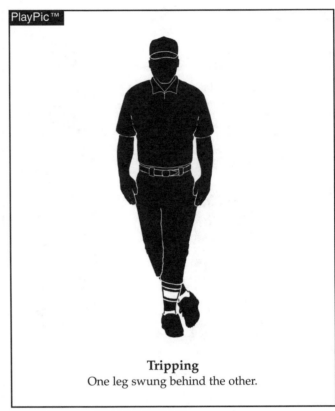

Tripping
One leg swung behind the other.

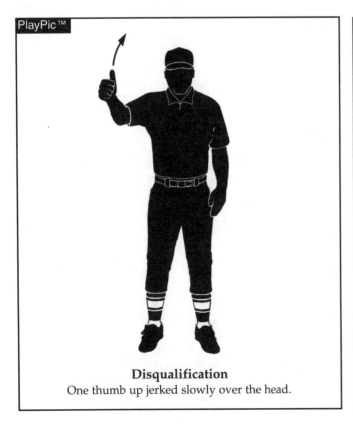

Disqualification
One thumb up jerked slowly over the head.

Loss of down
Hands behind the head, forearms parallel to the shoulders.

CREW AND SUPPLEMENTARY SIGNALS

Officials should not be reserved about talking to each other when the situation and distance between officials allow. The verbal communication should not be idle chit-chat but the passing along of game-related information.

Referee recommends having all officials verbally relay the down between every play. Another situation in which officials should verbalize: When the ball is to be snapped inside the 10 yardline, officials should point out the goalline to each other. Some crews say something like, "Know how it got there," reminding each other to think about the force or impetus that put a loose ball into the end zone before signaling touchdown, safety or touchback.

Officials may even talk to each other during a play; for example, when one official gives up coverage of the runner to another on a kick return, the official taking the runner should say something to his crewmate to let him know the coverage has shifted.

However, communication between officials should be sparse from the time the offense has broken the huddle until after the ball is snapped. In that interim, crews should use approved crew communication signals to relay vital information.

Crew communication signals, as well as signals to help amplify or explain officials' decisions (supplementary signals), are illustrated and explained in this section.

Crew communication signals

The "punch" signal (a fist held at shoulder level with the arm fully extended toward the offensive backfield) has two uses. Before the snap, it alerts the wing official on the opposite side of the field that the receiver nearest the signaling official is off the line of scrimmage.

Why is that important? In a five-man crew, it helps the back judge and the opposite wing figure out which receivers are being keyed by which officials. For instance, if the receivers in team A's formation are a split end and flanker on the linesman's side and a tight end on the line judge's side, the strength is to the linesman's side; the back judge keys on the split end and the linesman on the flanker. But if the flanker goes in motion and reaches the line judge's side before the snap, the back judge's key becomes the tight end on the line judge's side and the line judge's key changes from the tight end to the motion man.

In a four-man crew, the signal is a reminder to the non-signaling wing that a flanker may go in motion and that the signaling wing has more than one eligibles on his side of the field.

The punch is also used between a referee and wing official to indicate a pass was thrown backward rather than forward. The referee and wing must make eye contact to prevent a situation in which one official is signaling the pass was backward and another blows it dead as an incomplete forward pass.

If a backward pass is muffed, the punch signal alerts the rest of the crew that the loose ball may be recovered and advanced by either team. The signal also lets the other officials know that pass interference rules are not applicable (unless, of course, the receiver throws a forward pass after catching the backward pass).

If there are only 10 players on the field, the counting officials should indicate it by placing the palms flat against the chest, fingers spread wide. It's important to indicate there are only 10 players in case the 11th player enters the field just before the snap. If the player is an eligible receiver, the officials must be sure the receiver met rule requirements regarding distance from the snap and to be certain there are seven players on the line of scrimmage.

Eleven players on the field should be acknowledged with a thumb's up at shoulder height. If there are 12 players on the field, the counting officials should indicate it by placing the palm of one hand in front of the face, fingertips touching the bill of the cap. If the count occurs at a time when illegal substitution rules apply, the counting officials should blow their whistles, give the stop-the-clock signal and throw their flags.

When snapper protection rules apply (Federation) or fourth-down fumble rules apply (NCAA), officials should use the rolling fists signal (the same motion used to signal false start). The signal also reminds officials to stop the clock at the end of the play if they are the covering official.

Federation recommends three other signals: Crossed fists in front of the chest indicating "two sticks" (team A has more than 10 yards to go — thus both poles on the chains — for a first down); arms at waist level with palms facing the sideline and moved in a pushing motion to indicate to the referee the previous play ended out of bounds; and one hand pressed to a cheek to indicate an unbalanced line (another factor in determining keys).

Supplementary signals

Only one supplementary signal is allowed and only in NCAA. The signal — both hands in front of the chest and pushed toward the side — is used when a scoring kick is wide or a receiver caught the pass out of bounds. *Referee* recommends that signal be used in Federation games as well.

On a pass, use the supplementary signal after the incomplete pass signal. The supplementary signal is used only to indicate the pass was incomplete solely because the receiver was out of bounds. If the receiver did not have possession of the ball as he was going out of bounds, give the incomplete pass signal only.

Another *Referee* recommendation is use of the pass juggled signal (palms up, arms alternately moved up and down). Again, if the pass would have been ruled incomplete because the receiver was out of bounds, only the incomplete pass signal should be used. The juggled pass signal indicates the receiver did not have control of the pass when he went out of bounds.

In the signal chart that follows, a triangle (▼) indicates the signal is not authorized and is a *Referee* recommendation.

Receiver off the line/backward pass

Fist extended at shoulder level.

11 players on field

Upraised thumb extended at shoulder level.

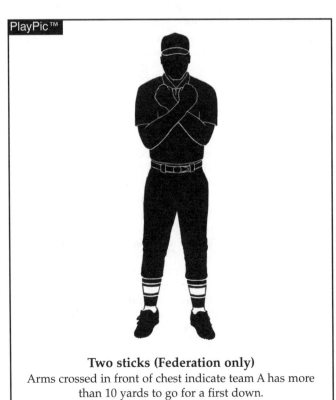

Two sticks (Federation only)

Arms crossed in front of chest indicate team A has more than 10 yards to go for a first down.

Snapper protection rules apply (Federation only)
Fourth down rules apply (NCAA only)

Rotate fists in front of chest.

**Play ended out of bounds; don't start clock
(Federation only)**
Signal from one official to referee; arms at sides pushed
toward sideline, palms facing away from field.

**Scoring kick wide/▼receiver out of bounds
(NCAA only)**
Arms extended in front of body,
then swept to the appropriate side.

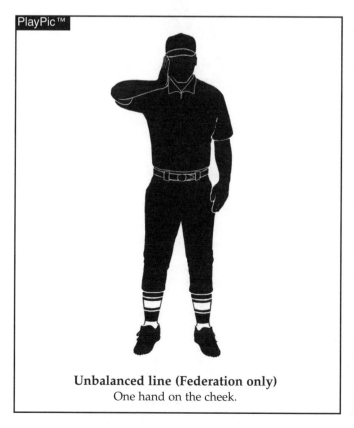

Unbalanced line (Federation only)
One hand on the cheek.

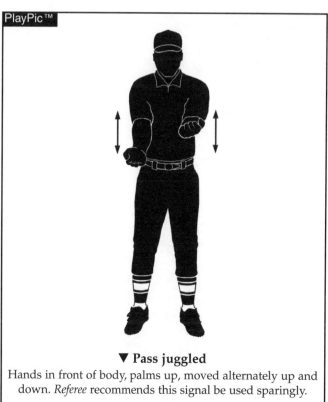

▼ Pass juggled
Hands in front of body, palms up, moved alternately up and
down. *Referee* recommends this signal be used sparingly.

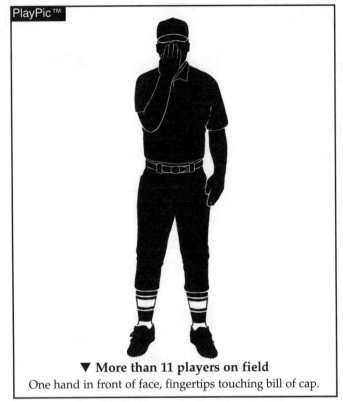

▼ More than 11 players on field
One hand in front of face, fingertips touching bill of cap.

▼ Less than 11 players on field
Palms of both hands flat against the chest.

Chapter 7

Penalty
Signaling
Sequences

The order of the penalty signals used by the referee is just as important as the clarity of the signals. Again using the language parallel, think of signal sequence as words in a sentence. The singular words, "Sequence important the is the of signals," makes little sense when thought of as individual words, but "The sequence of the signals is important," uses the same words and is easy to understand.

The key to quality signaling is remembering that it is a sequence of fluid movements. Take your time. Signals executed with separate and distinct motions ensure clarity; jumbled quickly together and the messages are lost. Also, remember to wait for the linesman to indicate the chains are in position and the rest of the crew is ready before giving the ready-for-play.

It is also important to face the proper direction when giving the signal. Most signals are given facing the pressbox. However, the signals for sideline interference and illegal forward pass or handing are given facing *away from* the pressbox.

Neither manual specifies that the ready-for-play signal is given before the start-the-clock signal when the clock starts on the ready. Try both and see what works best for you.

There are some differences between the Federation and NCAA signals because of differences in the rulebooks.

In **Federation** games:

• The signal for grasping the facemask is never preceded with the signal for a personal foul.

• The false start and encroachment signals are always preceded by the signal for a dead-ball foul.

In **NCAA** games:

• The signal for grasping the facemask is preceded with the signal for a personal foul if the foul is deemed not to have been incidental.

• The signal for roughing the kicker or holder is preceded with the signal for a personal foul. However, when the kicker or holder was run into rather than roughed, the signal for a personal foul is not used.

• The first down signal is given after the signal for a personal foul on the defense.

• The signals for false start, offensive encroachment, defensive offside or defensive encroachment are never preceded by the signal for a dead-ball foul.

By following these principles and using the correct, accepted signals you will effectively communicate your decisions to all involved.

MECHANICS ILLUSTRATED: LIVE-BALL FOULS

Most fouls in high school and collegiate football are live-ball fouls. That means signaling the penalty is a four-step process: foul signal, followed by a point toward the team that fouled, followed by an indication of the next down, followed by either the ready-for-play or start-the-clock signal.

In PlayPic A, team B has been called for pass interference. The referee gives the signal for pass interference (1), indicates which team has fouled (2) and signals that team A has been awarded a new series (3). The referee waits to be sure the chains have been moved and the other officials are in position. If the pass

was complete in spite of the interference and the runner was downed inbounds, the referee blows his whistle and simultaneously gives the start-the-clock signal (4). If the pass was incomplete or the play ended out of bounds, the referee gives the ready-for-play while simultaneously blowing his whistle (5).

In PlayPic B, team B has been called for pass interference, but team A scored a touchdown. The referee gives the signal for pass interference (1) and indicates which team has fouled (2). Because the penalty is declined by rule, the referee must signal the declination (3) and the result of the play — in this case, a touchdown (4).

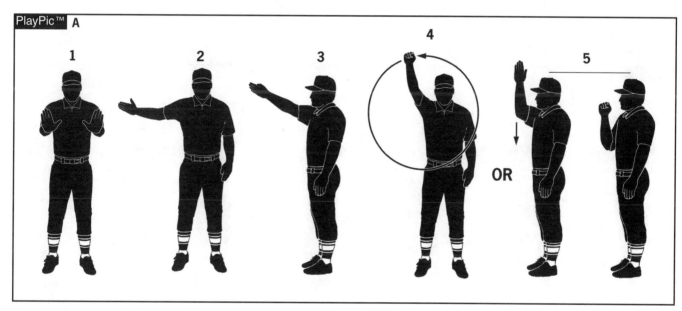

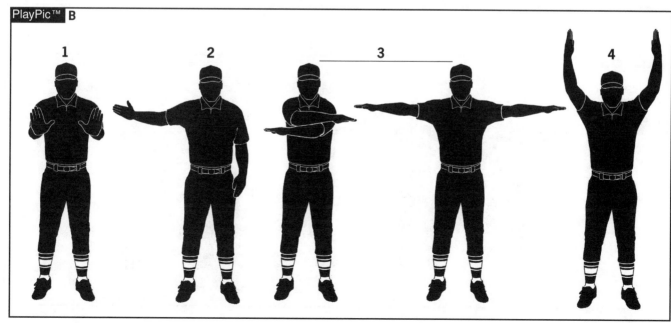

In PlayPic C, the defense has been called for roughing the passer. The referee first indicates the foul (1), followed by the fouling team (2). Because the penalty includes a first down, the referee signals that team A has been awarded a new series (3). If the pass was complete in spite of the foul and the runner was downed inbounds, the referee blows his whistle and simultaneously gives the start-the-clock signal (4). If the pass was incomplete or the play ended out of bounds, the referee gives the ready-for-play while simultaneously blowing his whistle (5).

Cases that involve an ejection add a step to the process. The referee must indicate the decision to the pressbox. PlayPic D illustrates the sequence for a live-ball foul for illegal helmet contact that results in an ejection. The referee first indicates the nature of the foul (1) and the fouling team (2). The ejection is then indicated (3). Because the penalty includes an automatic first down (NCAA only), the referee signals that team A has been awarded a new series (4); in Federation, the referee signals the next down. In this example, the penalty has given team A sufficient yardage for a first down. If the previous play ended inbounds, the referee blows his whistle and simultaneously gives the start-the-clock signal (5). If the previous play was an incomplete forward pass or if the play ended out of bounds, the referee gives the ready-for-play while simultaneously blowing his whistle (6).

MECHANICS ILLUSTRATED: DEAD-BALL FOULS

When a dead-ball foul has been called, the dead-ball signal must precede the signal for the nature of the foul. That means signaling the penalty is a four- or five-step process: the dead-ball signal, followed by the foul signal, followed by a point toward the team that fouled, followed by an indication of the next down, followed by either the ready-for-play or start-the-clock signal.

In PlayPic A, team B has been flagged for a personal foul that occurred during a dead-ball period. The referee begins with the dead-ball signal (1), followed by the signal for personal foul (2). He then indicates the team that fouled (3) and signals the next down. Because the penalty includes an automatic first down (NCAA only), the referee signals that team A has been awarded a new series (4); in Federation, the referee signals the next down. In this example, the penalty has given team A sufficient yardage for a first down. If the previous play ended inbounds, the referee blows his whistle and simultaneously gives the start-the-clock signal (5). If the previous play was an incomplete forward pass or if the play ended out of bounds, the referee gives the ready-for-play while simultaneously blowing his whistle (6).

Penalties for dead-ball fouls are rarely declined because the yardage is "free." However, on those rare occasions when a dead-ball foul is declined, the referee must indicate the declination after indicating which team fouled. In PlayPic B, team K is ready to attempt a try but team R has been called for encroachment (Federation) or because a team R player entered the neutral zone and contacted a team K player (NCAA). Team K declines the penalty because their kicker is more comfortable kicking from the present distance. In Federation only, the referee gives the signals for dead-ball foul (1) and encroachment/offside (2). He indicates which team has fouled (3), followed by the declination (4) and the signal for untimed down (5). The referee then gives the ready-for-play while simultaneously blowing his whistle (6).

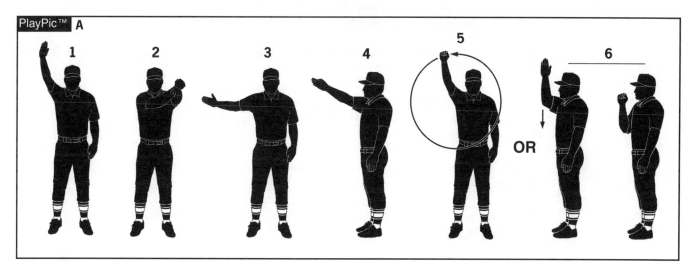

PlayPic™ A

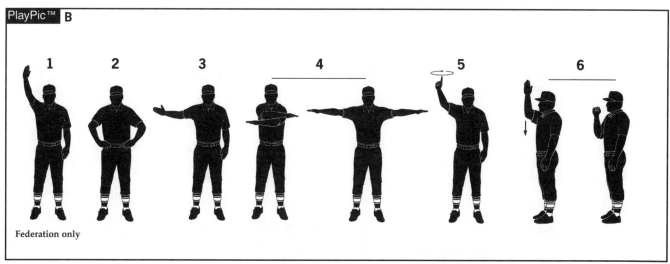

PlayPic™ B

Federation only

• The signals for sideline interference and illegal forward pass or handing are given facing away from the pressbox.

• Indicate that a foul occurred by dropping the flag in front of you and on the proper yardline; do not throw the flag at the offending player.

• When signaling to the pressbox, come to a complete stop and keep your head up.

• Pick out a spot halfway up the bleachers and focus on it to maintain good head height while giving signals.

Quiz

Without referring back, you should be able to answer the following true-false questions.

1. Positive body language can help ease and control a potential conflict.

2. In NCAA, the signal for dead-ball foul precedes the signal for false start.

3. When the live-ball foul is a specific personal foul such as clipping or roughing the passer, the signal for personal foul precedes the signal for the specific violation.

4. Signaling the penalty for a dead-ball foul is at least a five-step process.

5. Signaling an ejection to the pressbox should be avoided because it adds further tension to a contentious situation.

1. True 2. False 3. False 4. True 5. False

Chapter 8

Reporting Fouls

Fouls must be reported to the pressbox and both coaches. Additionally, all fouls must be communicated to all members of the officiating crew as each official has a role in penalty enforcement. Your signals and sequence speak a language. Using signals to report is just like talking to the pressbox and spectators, only you're using signals instead of words.

Notification

Once the flag is thrown, the official who threw it must ensure both the referee and linesman are aware as soon as possible after the play ends. The linesman will ensure the chains and box are not moved and the referee will prepare for the steps that follow. *Referee* recommendation: use three short blasts on the whistle after the ball is dead to bring the flag to the referee's attention.

The referee's first step in quality communication is to get an accurate report from the official who threw the flag. The referee must then move clear of the players, face the pressbox, stand stationary and indicate the foul and the offending team using the appropriate signal. In subvarsity games, youth games or games at which there is no public address announcer, *Referee* recommends giving the signal to both sidelines.

When wing officials throw a flag for a dead-ball foul prior to the snap, they should jog slowly toward the middle of the field to report the foul to the referee. Remember to practice good dead-ball officiating during the jog; if a player has crossed the neutral zone and contacted an opponent, the contacted opponent may try to retaliate.

Another technique to avoid is signaling the foul rather than reporting the foul to the referee. It's common in the NFL, but should not be practiced at other levels because another official may have a different foul. For instance, say the line judge throws a flag because a team B player entered the neutral zone and contacted the left guard but the umpire throws a flag because the snapper illegally moved the ball. If the line judge stays on the wing, gives the hands-on-hips signal and points to the defense but the penalty is assessed against the offense, the coach of the offensive team is certain to be upset. Instead of signaling from the wing, in this case the linesman, line judge and umpire should get together to discuss what each official has seen, then report their decision to the referee. The wing officials would then return to the sidelines to explain to the coaches what occurred.

Getting the explanation

Some referees simply want to hear the foul and offender, "No. 49 offense, illegal motion." Others prefer to be told what the reporting official saw, "No. 49 cut upfield too soon." It may make sense to use both techniques dependent upon the experience level of the crewmate. By getting more detail from newer officials, the referee can ensure there really was a foul. Be careful with movement fouls where the order of occurrence is a prime factor and be especially careful if offensive players on the end of line are involved — their movement is not as restricted as it is for the interior linemen who cannot move from a three-point stance.

On certain fouls, it is critical that the referee be told the status of the ball when the foul occurred or whether a player involved was an eligible receiver. Of course the guilty team must also be identified. The trend at many levels is to get away from referring to teams by jersey color. The pregame conference should include a discussion of how to report fouls.

Giving the explanation

Under NCAA rules, the referee is empowered to enforce a penalty without consulting a captain if the choice is obvious. In that case, announce it and proceed with enforcement or declination. If a captain objects or asks, explain the alternatives and conform to his choice.

Federation specifies the choices be presented on all penalties unless it is a double foul or the penalty is automatically declined. The foul should be explained to the captains along with the options. State the options briefly, but correctly, clearly and courteously. The umpire must listen to the referee's explanation to ensure the options are properly offered.

The wing official on the sideline of the penalized team should tell the coach the number of the guilty player and explain the foul in non-technical terms, e.g. "Your man in motion cut downfield too soon," instead of, "There was illegal motion." The other wing official need only tell the coach the nature of the foul.

Once the referee determines whether the penalty has been accepted or declined, he must inform other members of the crew. If the penalty is accepted, the umpire must understand where to walk from – the enforcement spot, how far to walk and which direction to walk. It's quite embarrassing to have the penalty enforced against the offended team and having to reverse tracks amid the inevitable protests.

The wing officials must be apprised so they can

keep their sideline informed. The wing on the offending team's sideline should tell the coach the number of the player who fouled; however, if the covering official didn't get the number, don't guess or make one up. If a non-existent number is reported, crew credibility is immediately destroyed.

Finally, the referee should again move clear of the players, face the pressbox, stand stationary and indicate the foul and the offending team using the appropriate signals.

Working with captains

When the referee and umpire meet with the coaches prior to the game, they should obtain the name and number of each captain. Communication between officials and captains can affect the flow of the game. Knowing when and in what depth to talk to captains can avoid unnecessary delay.

Under NCAA rules, the referee need not consult with the captain when the choice on a penalty is obvious. Federation rules require the options be explained to the captains for all penalties unless it is a double foul or the penalty is automatically declined.

There are several types of fouls that will always be accepted:

• Dead-ball fouls. Since the replay of a down is not in question, the distance is gratis. There are two exceptions when you should check with the captain: on a try and on a fourth-down play when the offense is just out of field goal range.

A foul by the defense on a try will move the ball to the 1-1/2 yardline. If team A is not considering going for two points, they may very well want to stick to their normal routine and kick from the spot they've practiced a thousand times. When the offense is just out of field goal range, teams will often intentionally incur a penalty for delay. The strategy is to have five more yards to put the punt out of bounds and avoid the touchback. Team B may prefer to decline the penalty and foil the strategy.

• Fouls after a change of possession. Certain fouls during kickoff, punt, interception and fumble returns are similar to dead-ball fouls in that there is no down to replay. The interests of the game are best served by immediately walking off those penalties. If there is more than one foul against the same team, you can easily figure out which penalty will yield the greatest benefit.

• Fouls that negate scores, turnovers and first downs.

• "Add on" or "tack-on" fouls. Examples of live-ball fouls that add yardage to the end of a play include a defensive facemask foul on a running play and roughing the passer on a completed pass.

• Loss of down/automatic first down. It would be most unusual for a team not to want a penalty that carries loss of down or an automatic first down. There are many other situations in which acceptance of the penalty is obvious, such as pass interference on an incomplete pass.

Declination of a penalty can also be an obvious choice. When a play results in a first down and the penalty would not, you can signal the refusal without discussion.

• Fouls must be reported to the pressbox and communicated to all members of the officiating crew.

• When a flag is thrown, the official who threw it must ensure both the referee and linesman are aware as soon as possible.

• Communication between officials and captains can affect the flow of the game.

• By getting more detail from newer officials, the referee can ensure there really was a foul.

• There are several types of fouls that will always be accepted.

Quiz

Without referring back, you should be able to answer the following true-false questions.

1. It is critical that the referee be told the status of the ball when the foul occurred or whether a player involved was an eligible receiver.

2. A defensive facemask foul on a running play is an example of a foul that has tack-on penalty enforcement.

3. The linesman will ensure the chains and box are not moved when a penalty flag has been thrown.

4. If the covering official didn't get the number of a player who fouled, he should make one up.

5. The umpire must listen to the referee's explanation to ensure the options are properly offered.

1. True 2. True 3. True 4. False 5. True

Chapter 9

Use of the
Penalty Flag

Correct penalty enforcement can be facilitated if the flag is thrown properly. There are two ways to throw the flag: into the air or carefully to a spot. The latter is used when a spot foul occurs. If it is possible for the spot of the foul will be the enforcement spot, you must get your flag as close to that spot as possible. If you're off target, you should relocate the flag as soon as possible after the play by picking it up and moving it definitively. The longer you delay making this correction, the more it will appear you are manipulating the situation. Also, attempting to kick it to the correct spot gives an underhanded appearance.

For dead-ball fouls or fouls simultaneous with the snap, the flag should be tossed into the air directly in front of the official.

A few techniques to avoid: slam-dunking the flag to the ground; looking angry when you toss it; holding the flag and waving it, instead of throwing it; or throwing it at the fouling player. On late hits, the latter looks confrontational, and worse yet, might hit the player in the face.

Covering the flag

In some areas, a technique called "covering a flag" is used. That involves having the official closest to the official who threw his flag also throwing his flag as a means of supporting his partner. The concept is the coach will think it is an acceptable call because two officials had it. The technique is both unnecessary and deceptive.

While there are some situations where the coverage will overlap two officials, many plays dictate each official maintain unique coverage. Further, if the two officials were to offer contradicting explanations of the foul, the crew's integrity would be severely diminished. Finally, excessive flags will contribute to an image of a "flag happy" crew.

MECHANICS ILLUSTRATED: THROWING THE PENALTY FLAG

How you throw your penalty flag depends on the type of foul, whether the ball is live or dead and your position on the field.

In PlayPic A, the referee sees the offensive lineman holding the pass rusher. Because the penalty may be enforced from the spot of the foul, it is important for the referee to throw his flag to the yardline on which the infraction was committed. The flag should be thrown so that it hits the ground on either side of the players; don't think of the player as a dart board and your flag as a dart. Throwing the flag in the direction of the players will help the referee observe the number of the offending player. Whether an overhand or underhand motion is used is up to the individual.

The same holds true for other officials when the spot of the foul will be used for enforcement. Don't stop officiating after throwing the flag, however.

In PlayPic B, a defensive player has committed a dead-ball foul by crossing the neutral zone and contacting a team A player. The flag should be thrown into the air in front of you and the stop-the-clock signal given. Again, don't stop officiating. The offensive lineman could take exception to the penalty and retaliate. Once you are confident the action has stopped, jog toward the center of the field and report the foul to the referee. Don't signal; the other wing official may well have a different view or another foul.

Line of scrimmage

Chapter 10

Use of the
Beanbag

The beanbag is perhaps the least understood tool an official has available.

The beanbag is used to mark spots, other than the spot of a foul, which may later be needed as a reference point. Back judges on five-man crews and line judges on four-man crews may have a need to mark multiple spots on the same play and should carry two beanbags.

Under no circumstances should the beanbag be used as a substitute for hustle. One common example of lazy officials using the beanbag instead of proper mechanics involves a play in which the runner is downed near or past a sideline. Some wing officials approach the players, throw their beanbag toward the spot and retrieve the ball from the runner. In that instance, the beanbag should be dropped (not thrown) only after the official has squared off to the spot and only if players need to be escorted back to the field from beyond the sideline.

The beanbag should be dropped on the correct spot and not thrown; however that won't always be practical. If the spot is in a side zone, then only the correct yardline is needed because any penalty enforcement would bring the ball back to the nearest hashmark. Here are the situations where the beanbag should be used and how the spot which is marked could be utilized:

Forward progress

In most situations, the wing officials mark the forward progress spot. If the covering official must leave that spot to recover the ball or observe ensuing action, the beanbag can be used to mark the dead-ball spot. That can happen both in the field of play and on the sideline. When a runner goes out of bounds, several players may continue into the bench area and tending to any possible extracurricular activity becomes the priority.

The beanbag is occasionally used to mark forward progress when a runner is driven back in the field of play. If the runner subsequently breaks free and continues his run the beanbag can be ignored; otherwise, the runner is credited with his original gain.

A quarterback sack presents a particular problem for crews of five or less. The wings have gone downfield with the receivers. The umpire is watching the blocking and has stepped up no farther than the line. The referee is far enough behind the play so he doesn't become part of it. The referee must take responsibility for marking the forward progress spot with his beanbag. To do that, he should step forward and drop the bag on the appropriate spot while keep an eye on the post-tackle activity.

Fumbles

For penalty enforcement, the basic spot on a running play is where the run ends. If the ball is fumbled, the run ends at the spot where possession was lost. Consequently, the spot of the fumble must be marked in the event a penalty occurs and that spot is needed. Technically, the spot is required only for fumbles beyond the neutral zone, but the habit of bagging all fumbles should be developed.

First touching/illegal touching

During both free and scrimmage kicks, there are times when it is improper for team K to touch a ball that has been kicked. Federation calls it "first touching" and NCAA calls it "illegal touching." That applies only when team K touches the ball when they are not entitled to possession.

On free kicks, if team K touches the ball before the ball crosses team R's free kick line (NCAA: restraining line) and before it is touched there by any team R player, the spot must be marked with the beanbag. For a scrimmage kick, the spot must be marked in Federation if team K touches the ball in the field of play beyond the line before team R touches it. Under NCAA rules, if team K touches a kick that has crossed the neutral zone before team R touches the ball, it is illegal touching.

The spot must be marked because team R may have the right to take the ball at that spot. Please see the appropriate rulebook for the exceptions.

Punts

Punts present several opportunities to use the beanbag. Under NCAA rules, the end of the kick is used for post-scrimmage kick enforcement and must always be marked. In Federation play, that spot is never used for penalty enforcement and need not be marked.

Punts are also an opportunity to witness the momentum exception. If a punt or other scrimmage kick is caught by a team B player between his five yardline and the goalline and his original momentum carries him into the end zone where the ball is declared dead in his team's possession or goes out of bounds in the end zone, the exception applies and the ball belongs to team B at the spot possession was obtained.

The Federation momentum exception also applies to a team B player who intercepts a forward pass or catches a free kick inside his five yardline. NCAA rules are similar, but also apply to the interception of backward passes and to the catch and recovery of fumbles, free kicks and scrimmage kicks.

It's important for officials to recognize a momentum

situation and to beanbag the spot where possession is gained. For the exception to apply, original momentum must be the cause of the ball entering the end zone. If the covering official judges the player voluntarily carried the ball across the goalline, regular rules apply and the play could result in a safety. The beanbagged spot might also be used to enforce a penalty that occurs after possession was obtained.

Out of bounds

The beanbag can also be used to mark the out of bounds spot on punts. On free kicks, if the ball is kicked out of bounds untouched, it is a foul and the spot can be marked with the flag. As an alternative, the spot can be marked with the beanbag while the flag is tossed high into the air.

The beanbag is useful when certain players go out of bounds during a play. If a player is pushed or blocked off the field, he may legally return and participate as long as he immediately reenters; that spot does not need to be marked. However in Federation, if a player of team A or team K goes out of bounds, before a change of possession, the spot should be marked. It is not a foul unless he returns and the return spot should then be marked with a flag. The beanbag will demonstrate the covering official was on top of the play.

Under NCAA rules, there are only two restrictions: (1) A kicking team player cannot go out of bounds during a kick down and return; and (2) an eligible receiver cannot touch a pass after returning until it is touched by an opponent. Again, the departure spot should be beanbagged and the foul flagged, if and when it occurs.

Finally, there are several situations in which use of a beanbag may seem appropriate, but is not necessary. The following spots are not used for enforcement purposes unless the momentum exception applies: interceptions, end of free kicks and fumble recoveries.

Chapter 11

Instructing the Chain Crew, Timer and Ballboys

No matter how well the four or five onfield officials function as a unit, cohesion can break down if auxiliary personnel such as timers, chain crew members or ballboys do not properly discharge their duties. Unfortunately, there is little the officials can do but grin and bear it when faced with sideline personnel who are incompetent, obstinate or have short attention spans. In extreme cases (such as refusal to obey officials, drunkenness, confrontations with visiting team personnel or constant criticism of officials' calls), game management should be asked to find replacements. Dishonesty that provides a "home-field advantage" is rare but not unheard of; because it is also extremely difficult to prove, accusations of cheating should be kept to an absolute minimum.

Most of the time, an officiating crew will simply acknowledge that some chain crews, timers and ballboys are better than others, just as some teams are better than others.

One way of increasing the chances for competence is a thorough pregame meeting. Here are some tips for instructing chain crews, timers and ballboys.

Chain crews
A four-person chain crew is preferable. If the crew consists of only three members, the person working the box can perform most of the duties involving the clip while the trail chain holder tends to the box. No one on the chain crew should double as a ballboy.

When a new series begins, the box is set on the spot where the linesman's downfield heel intersects with the sideline. The chains are then set according to the position of the box. Once the spot has been established, the box should be moved at least six feet away from the sideline. The six-foot spacing allows the chain crew some cushion. If players approach, the chain crew must retreat and drop the equipment. That protects the players and the chain crew.

Remind the box holder that all spots are taken from the forward point of the ball. At the start of a new series, the linesman will go to the sideline and mark the spot with the heel of his downfield foot. That ensures the correct spot is taken and, more importantly, the linesman can attest to what was done.

The box holder is not to change the down or move the box until the linesman echoes the referee's announcement of the next down. Let the box holder know what signals will be used to indicate the down (inexperienced chain crews may not know that a fist indicates fourth down).

Remind the box holder the box will be needed on trys. In games using collegiate rules, the box should not be moved after a missed field goal; when the snap is outside team B's 20 yardline, the ball is returned to the previous spot.

Although most chain holders understand not to move the chains unless directed by the linesman, the reminder needs to be offered. The chain holders should be shown the signal the linesman will use telling the crew to stay put and the signal that moves the crew. Many linesman use the "stop" signal (arm outstretched, palm up and facing the chain crew) to indicate stay put and a beckoning motion of the hand or arm as the signal to move.

If the linesman tells the crew to move, not seeing that a penalty marker is down, the crew should be told not to hesitate to point out the flag to the linesman.

When a first down is declared, the trail pole goes immediately behind the box so the officials' view of the box is not obstructed. The lead holder is responsible to ensure the chain is taut at all times. Instruct the chain crew that when the trail pole is set behind the box, the trail pole holder should step firmly on the chain; that ensures the chain will be taut and that the trail pole will not be displaced when the lead pole is pulled.

Once a first down is awarded to team A inside team B's 10 yardline, the chains are no longer needed and should be moved well away from the sideline.

A double-check procedure for the box is used at the higher levels of football. The box holder jots down the previous spot on a strip of tape placed attached to the pole. If the box is displaced for any reason, the note serves as a backup to ensure the box is returned to the proper yardline. An easier method is to give the box holder a golf tee that should be placed in the ground behind the box before every play.

The linesman's clip is a safety valve. If the chains are moved either in error or for safety reasons, the clip provides the exact chain location. The clip operator should be told exactly on what part of the line you want the clip placed: leading edge, middle of the line or the back edge. It doesn't matter as long as everyone is in sync.

The clip goes on the five yardline nearer the trail stake, the yardline is set on the clip and the clip is never removed until the stakes are in a new position.

Another tool the linesman can use is tape on the halfway point of the chain. The tape helps the linesman determine if team A will achieve a first down on a five-yard penalty, thus precluding the need for a measurement.

For instance, if the box is three links behind the tape and team B is flagged for a five-yard penalty, the linesman can check the tape and tell the referee, "They'll still be short." Conversely, if the box is slightly beyond the tape, the linesman can tell the referee, "It will be first down." If, during his pregame inspection of the chains, the linesman sees there is no tape on the chain, he should ask a trainer or team manager for a strip of tape about six inches long. The chain is folded in half and the tape wound around the links at the halfway mark.

The linesman should also carry an additional snap clip to aid in resetting the box after the first and third quarters. The chain crew should be informed of the procedures used at the end of the first and third quarters, for measurements and for "hurry-up" offenses. The latter points are covered in detail in Chapters 22 and 30 (Measurements) and Chapter 13 (Odds and Ends).

Timers

Unlike in basketball, the clock operator for a football game technically is not part of the officiating crew. Still, the timer serves an important role and can help make the difference between a smooth contest and an ugly one.

For five-man crews, the back judge is responsible for the clock and meets with the timer before the game. In a four-man crew, the line judge assumes clock responsibilities.

Before going to the pressbox to meet the timer in the pregame, the appropriate official must confirm with the game manager the starting time of the game and the length of halftime. That information should also be confirmed with the timer.

It is preferable to have the clock expire before the scheduled starting time. If coordinated properly, the introduction of starting lineups or other pregame ceremonies will be concluded so that the starting time will not be delayed. Example: Game time is 7:30 p.m. and the introductions and national anthem take roughly 10 minutes to complete. The clock should hit zero at 7:20 p.m. That system is preferable but is rarely used at most levels.

On free kicks, remind the timer to wait for the proper signal. From scrimmage, the clock will start either with the referee's ready or on the snap.

Remind the timer that five signals should cause him to stop the clock: stop the clock, incomplete pass, touchdown, touchback and safety.

The timer must observe the covering official on plays that end at the sideline. If the covering official gives the start-the-clock signal to indicate the ball is inbounds and then signals to stop the clock, the timer must understand that the sequence means the clock will next start on the ready. Also remind the timer to look for the stop-the-clock signal when the ball goes near a sideline, there is a change of possession or there is a first down, and that trys are always untimed.

Instruct the timer to wait for the referee's signal before starting the countdown for halftime. That signal is contingent upon both teams clearing the field. For Federation games, there is an additional three-minute warmup that immediately follows the intermission. That time should also start on the referee's signal so he can ensure both teams are on the field ready to loosen up.

Another item for prep games: If the regulation game ends in a tie and overtime is played, the timer will need to put three minutes on the clock (Federation rules mandate a three-minute break between the end of regulation play and the first overtime period) and again wait for the referee's signal. After that, the clock is not needed unless there is a second overtime (a two-minute break occurs in that case).

The timer should be asked how the referee will be able to communicate with the timer if the clock needs to be corrected. In some cases, assistant coaches in the pressbox communicate through headphones to coaches on the sideline. Using the coaches is one method of relaying information. Another is to have the referee signal the correct time with his fingers, like a basketball official reporting a foul to the scorer.

The CCA manual mandates that an onfield official time the game, while the Federation manual lists that as a duty only if there is no visible field clock. Those duties fall to the line judge in a four-man crew or the back judge in a five-man crew. *Referee* recommends having an official time the game as a backup. If the clock malfunctions during the game, the timer should be instructed to wait for a timeout or other break in the action before resetting the clock. The timer should communicate with the referee to obtain the correct time, then reset the clock.

Ballboys

Like a capable chain crew, good ballboys are hard to find. (*Referee* acknowledges that the person handling these duties might well be a ballgirl, ballwoman or ballman. For brevity's sake, the term "ballboy" is used throughout this book.)

Ballboys are rarely provided at games below the varsity level. Even in varsity games, there are occasions when only one ballboy will be available. Many ballboys are youngsters whose attention spans diminish as the game progresses. Accept it and prepare for it.

If two ballboys are available, appoint one to be responsible for each sideline. The ballboys keep up with the play at all times, normally mirroring the position of the wing official on their side of the field.

In addition each ballboy should be made responsible for the endline in field goal and try situations. One ball should be placed on the ground behind the goalpost. The ballboys then take a position well behind the posts in order to recover the ball after the kick. An official can pick up the ball behind the goalpost for use on the ensuing kickoff or snap.

If the ball becomes dead out of bounds or inbounds nearer the sideline than the hashmarks, the ballboys should give a ball as quickly as possible to the nearest official. If the dead ball goes out of bounds, or is dead because of an incomplete pass, the ballboy should then retrieve it. If the dead ball is inbounds, the ballboy should wait with the official covering the spot until it is no longer required and then take it off the field.

The CCA manual states that ballboys should not be allowed on the field. *Referee* recommends that in cases when an official needs to hold the spot and another official is not nearby to get a new ball, the ballboy should be instructed by the official to take the ball onto the field and give it to the umpire.

In inclement weather or muddy conditions the ballboys must ensure that their ball is kept dry and clean. It is the responsibility of game management to supply towels for that purpose.

Remind the ballboys that, for the purposes of the game, they are officials and must remain impartial. They must make no remarks to players and express no opinions on official rulings. Balls are not to be given to players. Players may not practice with nor interfere with the game balls.

• Instruct the ballboys to follow the wing official on their sideline.

• In field goal and try situations, one ball should be placed on the ground behind the goalpost. The ballboys then take a position well behind the posts in order to recover the ball after the kick.

• The timer should be asked how the referee will be able to communicate with the timer if the clock needs to be corrected.

Quiz

Without referring back, you should be able to answer the following true-false questions.

1. It is OK to have the down box operator double as a ballboy.

2. If the linesman tells the chain crew to move, but the chain crew sees that a penalty marker is down, the crew should point out the flag to the linesman.

3. The chains should remain on the sideline if a first down is awarded to team A inside team B's 10 yardline.

4. The timer should stop the clock when he sees one of the following five signals: stop the clock, incomplete pass, touchdown, touchback and safety.

5. The home team is required to have four persons on the chain crew.

1. False 2. True 3. False 4. True 5. False

Chapter 12

Reading and Understanding Keys

If you had the ability to know what someone was going to say before they said it, you'd avoid many uncomfortable situations. If you knew exactly which questions were going to be asked on a test before you took it, you'd be better prepared because you'd know what type of research and study you needed to complete.

Believe it or not, football officials have a kind of telepathy to help them determine what's going to happen before it occurs. These hints are called keys.

There are two basic types of keys. For the purpose of this chapter, let's call them "situational" and "positional" keys.

Situational keys (Four- and five-man crews)

Situational keys are partially based on the down, distance, score, time remaining, offensive and defensive formations and actions of players at the snap. For example, it's third down and 11. Team A trails by two points with 1:37 to play in the fourth quarter and has the ball on its own 44 yardline. Going without a huddle, team A lines up in a shotgun formation with trips on the right side of the formation. All of that adds up to a pass. That hunch is confirmed when, at the snap, the offensive linemen drop back to pass block, the quarterback retreats into the pocket and the receivers run pass patterns rather than block team B's linebackers and defensive backs.

Unfortunately, not all situational keys are that easy to read. However, with study and experience, keys can be used to make less obvious situations easier to discern.

In addition to down, distance and other game factors, offensive and defensive formations provide hints as to what type of play an official can expect in a given situation. Most teams using the wishbone formation, for instance, are predominantly running teams. Teams using four-receiver sets and shotgun formations pass more times than not.

Defense is more reactionary. Although teams use one defensive alignment such as a 4-3 (four down linemen and three linebackers) or 3-4 (three down linemen and four linebackers) as their base defense, the manner in which they deploy players will depend on what scouting or past experience has determined the opposing offense is likely to do in certain situations.

However, observing the safeties and cornerbacks can provide keys. When a defensive back approaches the line of scrimmage as the quarterback is calling signals he is showing blitz. Although teams sometimes fake a blitz, officials can use that key to prepare their coverage for the play.

The umpire and referee rely on linemen for their situational keys. Pulling linemen indicate a sweep or trap block. Retreating linemen indicate a pass. Charging linemen indicate a running play. When offensive linemen provide only passive resistance, allowing defensive linemen to penetrate the neutral zone, a screen pass often follows.

The referee observes the running backs and quarterback prior to the snap. Once the ball is snapped, he looks through the quarterback to the opposite side tackle. For instance, if the quarterback is right-handed and the referee is properly stationed to the quarterback's right, the key is the left tackle.

The umpire observes the snapper and the guards prior to the snap, then shifts his look to the opposite tackle after the snap. If the keys indicate a run, the umpire must determine the point of attack. A double team or a trap block often occur at the point of attack. Likewise, pulling guards often provide the interference for a sweep or reverse.

Wing officials (and the back judge in a five-man crew) key the eligible receivers that serve as their positional keys to discern their situational keys.

Positional keys (Five-man crew)

Positional keys are predetermined by the position you are working in the game. Positional keys deal more with the back judge and wing officials. For instance, in a five-man crew, the back judge's main positional key is the inside eligible receiver outside the tackle on the strong side of the formation (that will usually be the tight end or the slotback). At the snap, the back judge observes the actions of his key player. If that player moves into another official's coverage area, the back judge gives him up and shifts his attention to players who have entered his coverage area.

In order to determine positional keys, the officials must recognize the strength of the formation (strong side vs. weak side). Strength has nothing to do with the number (or size) of the offensive linemen on each side of the center. For the purposes of this book, the strong side is the side on which there are more eligible receivers outside of the tackle.

In regard to determining keys, it doesn't matter if a player is on or off the line of scrimmage. For instance, the player closest to the tackle is the back judge's key whether the player is a tight end (directly next to the tackle) or a wide out (split outside the tackle). If players are stacked, the player nearest the line of scrimmage is considered to be the widest. For example, if a wingback is stacked directly behind the tight end, the tight end is considered the widest and is the wing official's key.

The back judge has priority in determining keys, followed by the wing men. Wing officials should not key the same player as the back judge.

The positional keys:

• **Unbalanced formation** — The back judge keys on the wideout (or the flanker if the inside receiver is a tight end). The wing official on the strong side keys on the inside player of the formation, normally a flanker or wing back. The wing official on the weak side keys the end nearest his side, normally a wideout.

• **Balanced formation** — In a balanced formation, strength is always considered to be on the line judge's side. The back judge keys on the tight end or split end closest to the tackle. The wing officials key on receivers other than the back judge's key and any backs who move toward them at the snap.

• **Trips formation** — The back judge keys on the two widest receivers and the strong side wing official keys on the inside-most receiver. The weak side wing official keys on the end nearest him.

• **Double wing formation** — Strength is declared to the line judge's side. The back judge keys the inside receiver on the line judge's side. The line judge keys the outside receiver. The linesman has both receivers on his side.

• **Wishbone** — Another balanced formation, which means strength is declared to line judge's side. The back judge has the end on the line judge's side. The line judge keys the backs. The linesman keys the end on his side.

Motion (Five-man crew)

An offensive player in motion can affect positional keys. It is crucial that the back judge and wing officials know where the motion man is at the snap because the strength of the formation (and therefore the keys) may change.

Let's say team A lines up strong to the linesman's side. The back judge keys on the tight end or the split end nearest the tackle. The linesman keys on the flanker or wing back on his side. The line judge keys the wideout on his side. Now the flanker on the linesman's side goes in motion toward the line judge.

If the motion man gets to the line judge's side of the ball at the snap, the strength of the formation is now on the line judge's side and the keys change. The back judge now has the tight end or inside receiver on the line judge's side, the line judge has the motion man and the linesman has the end on his side of the line. Although the line judge is keying on the motion man's action after the snap, the linesman is responsible for watching to ensure the motion man does not cut

upfield before the snap. Legality of motion is always the responsibility of the official away from whom the player is moving.

If the motion man does not get to the line judge's side of the ball in this example, the keys do not change because the strength of the formation has not changed.

Positional keys (Four-man crew)

Positional keys are easier to determine in a four-man crew. Simply stated, the wing men key on the eligible receivers who line up on their sides of the field. When there is more than one eligible receiver on a particular side, the primary key is the eligible receiver on the end of the line of scrimmage (the tight end or split end). Any flanker, slot back or motion man is a secondary key.

Motion (Four-man crew)

Legality of motion is always the responsibility of the official away from whom the player is moving. Responsibility for observing the actions of key players after the snap changes when the players enter another official's coverage area. The motion man is a secondary key for the wing official.

READING FORMATIONS

Once you learn positional and situational keys, you can use the knowledge to read formations. When you understand what offensive players are trying to accomplish and why teams use certain formations, you will be better prepared to observe your key players.

As stated in the section on reading situational keys, some offensive formations and their purposes are easily identified. But most often, teams will operate out of a base offense. Three-receiver formations and two-tight end sets are variations of base offenses.

A few disclaimers: No attempt was made to identify every offensive set, every variation of the formation and every strategy teams employ when using the formation. In most cases, the strength of formation may be on either side of the line even though each formation is depicted only once. This section is intended to identify the most widely used formations and the most common fouls officials can expect to look for as players attempt to carry out their assignments.

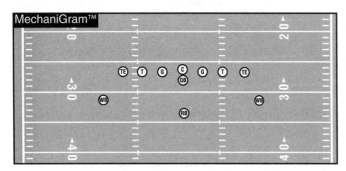

DOUBLE WING-T

A passing and running formation using the wingback as a motion man. Common plays include a quarterback bootleg in the direction opposite of the motion, runs between tackles and fake handoffs to the wingback in motion. The wingback and tight end will often double team, otherwise one-on-one blocking is used. The quarterback is a prime weapon in this offense. One wingback may initially set as running back, then shift to a wing. Watch for crackbacks by wingbacks. If the team uses a passing-dominated offense, every eligible receiver is a potential target.

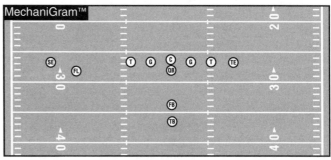

I FORMATION

A passing and running formation using the flanker as a motion man. Common plays include short, intermediate and deep pass patterns; running plays between the tackles; tosses to the fullback or tailback on isolation plays; and the triple option. Common blocking includes one-on-one blocking and trap blocks. Watch for chop blocks on double teams.

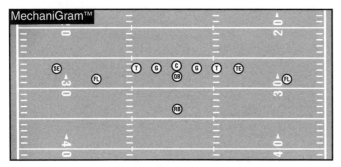

ONE-BACK PRO FORMATION

Primarily a passing offense that uses flankers as motion men. Common plays include draws and screen passes. Common blocking includes pass blocking and brush blocks on screen plays. Watch for the split end and flanker working pick plays and for linemen downfield if a screen pass is caught beyond the neutral zone.

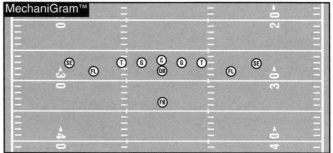

ONE BACK, DOUBLE SPLIT

A passing formation that rarely uses motion men. Common plays include deep and intermediate passes and traps or draws with the fullback carrying the ball. Pass blocking and trap blocking are often used. Watch for the quarterback lining up or shifting to shotgun formation and split ends and flankers working pick plays.

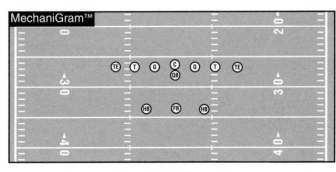

STRAIGHT T

A running formation on which motion is rare. Common plays include the inside belly, trap plays, dives and sweeps. Pulling guards and trap blocks are common, as are backs leading on sweeps. Watch for one tight end splitting wide in an effort to spread the defense. The quarterback will rarely keep the ball. Watch for illegal blocks on traps and sweeps.

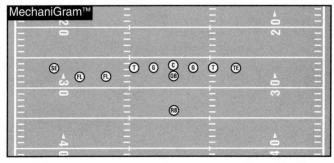

TRIPS

A passing formation that will often feature the outside flanker going in motion to the opposite side of the line. Common plays include deep and intermediate passes, shovel passes to backs and the hook and ladder. Pass blocking is most prevalent. Watch for the quarterback starting or shifting into shotgun formation and split ends and flankers working pick plays downfield. The tight end and running back may block or may run pass routes and the running back may shift to tight end position.

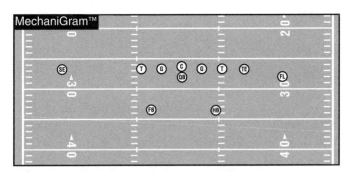

TWO-BACK PRO FORMATION

Passing or running formation that will feature the flanker as a motion man. Common plays include outside runs, backs used as pass receivers and screen passes. One-on-one blocking is most common although brush blocks are used on screen plays. Watch for chop blocks on double teams and linemen downfield if a screen pass is caught beyond the neutral zone.

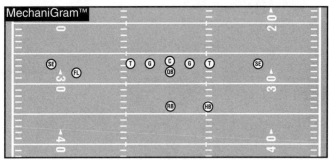

TWO-BACK, THREE-RECEIVER OFFSET I

A passing formation rarely using motion men Common plays include deep and intermediate passes. Pass blocking is most prevalent. Watch for backs blocking below the waist the quarterback lining up or shifting into the shotgun. The fullback usually stays in to block.

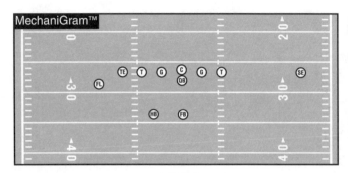

VEER

A running formation that features the flanker or tight end as potential motion men. Common plays include the triple option and sweeps. Pulling guards are common as are backs leading on sweeps. Plays are often run to the weak side. The quarterback will either keep the ball or pitch to a trailing back. Be alert for illegal blocks; muffs on backward passes, the flanker shifting to the line of scrimmage and the tight end shifting into backfield and possibly going in motion.

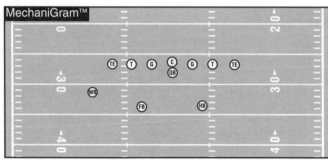

WING-T

Primarily a running offense. The wingback is a potential motion man. Common plays include a quarterback bootleg in the direction opposite of the motion, runs between the tackles, fake handoffs to the wingback in motion and wingback reverses or inside counter plays. The wingback and tight end will sometimes double team on blocks; otherwise one-on-one blocking is used. Watch for illegal crackbacks by the wingback.

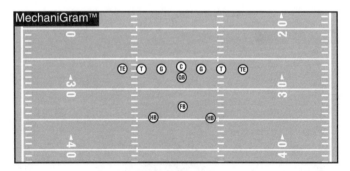

WISHBONE

Primarily a running formation that uses no motion men. The triple option and sweeps are common plays. Guards will pull and backs will be used as lead blockers. Tight ends are expected to block, not catch passes, except on third and long. The tight end may split in an effort to spread the defense. Be especially alert for illegal blocks on sweeps and muffs on backward passes.

WING OFFICIAL AND BACK JUDGE KEYS (FIVE-MAN CREW)

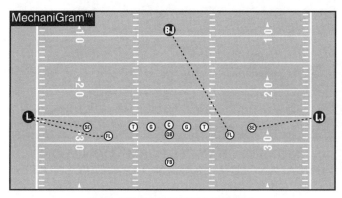

BALANCED FORMATION

In a balanced formation, strength is always considered to be on the line judge's side. The back judge keys on the tight end or split end closest to the tackle. The line judge keys on the split end while the linesman keys on the split end and flanker on his side. Either wing official may also have the back if he runs a pass route.

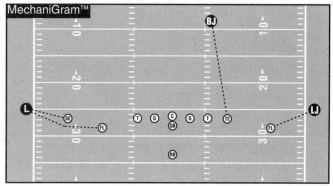

BALANCED FORMATION, STRENGTH DECLARED TO LINE JUDGE'S SIDE

In a balanced formation, strength is always considered to be on the line judge's side. The back judge keys on the tight end. The line judge keys on the flanker while the linesman has both the split end and flanker on his side. Either wing official may also have the back if he runs a pass route.

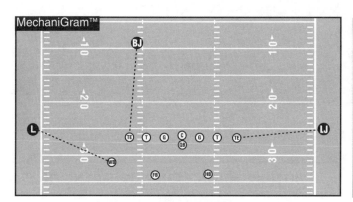

DOUBLE TIGHT ENDS, STRENGTH TO LINESMAN'S SIDE

This is primarily a running formation used on short yardage, but teams sometimes throw quick passes out of this formation. The back judge keys on the tight end on the strong side (the linesman's side in this case). The linesman keys on the wing back. The line judge keys on the tight end on his side. Either wing official may also have a back who runs a pass route.

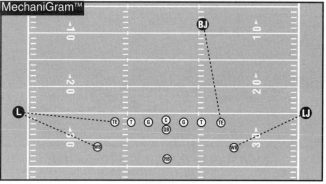

DOUBLE WING, DOUBLE TIGHT END FORMATION

Strength is declared to the line judge's side. The back judge keys the tight end on the line judge's side. The line judge keys on the wingback on his side. The linesman has the tight end and wideout on his side. Either wing official may also have the back if he runs a pass route.

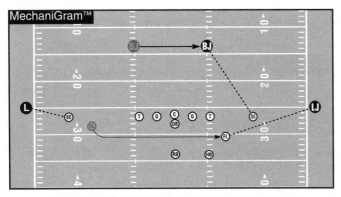

MOTION CHANGES FORMATION FROM UNBALANCED TO BALANCED; SPLIT END KEY

Strength was to the linesman's side, but motion changed the formation from unbalanced to balanced. In a balanced formation, strength is declared to the line judge's side. The back judge shifts position and keys on the strong side split end. The line judge keys on the flanker and the linesman keys on the split end on his side. Although the line judge is keying on the motion man's action after the snap, the linesman is responsible for watching to ensure the motion man does not cut upfield before the snap. Legality of motion is always the responsibility of the official away from whom the player is moving.

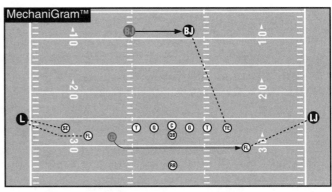

MOTION CHANGES FORMATION FROM UNBALANCED TO BALANCED; TIGHT END KEY

Strength was to the linesman's side, but motion changed the formation from unbalanced to balanced. In a balanced formation, strength is declared to the line judge's side. The back judge shifts position and keys on the strong side tight end. The line judge keys on the flanker and the linesman keys on the split end and flanker on his side. Although the line judge is keying on the motion man's action after the snap, the linesman is responsible for watching to ensure the motion man does not cut upfield before the snap. Legality of motion is always the responsibility of the official away from whom the player is moving.

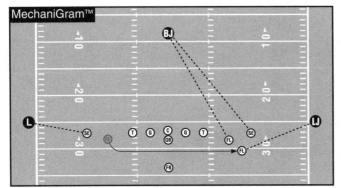

MOTION CHANGING STRENGTH

Motion by the flanker turned a balanced formation into a formation strong to the line judge's side. The back judge keys the flanker and the split end on the line judge's side. The line judge keys on the motion man and the linesman keys the end on his side of the line. Although the line judge is keying on the motion man's action after the snap, the linesman is responsible for watching to ensure the motion man does not cut upfield before the snap. Legality of motion is always the responsibility of the official away from whom the player is moving.

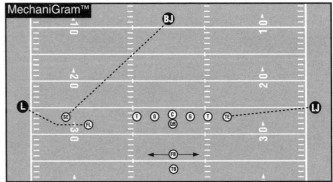

MOTION DOESN'T CHANGE STRENGTH

Strength is to the linesman's side. Even if the back goes in motion to the line judge's side, strength is not considered to have changed. The back judge keys the split end and the linesman keys on the flanker. The line judge keys on the split end. Either wing official may also have the back if he runs a pass route.

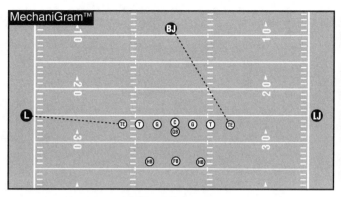

STRAIGHT T

This is primarily a running formation, but on passing downs teams sometimes move a tight end to split end. It's a balanced formation, so strength is declared to the line judge's side. The back judge keys on the tight end on the line judge's side. The linesman keys on the weak side tight end. The line judge has no formal key, but should observe the tackle on his side and strong side halfback. Either wing official may also have a back who runs a pass route.

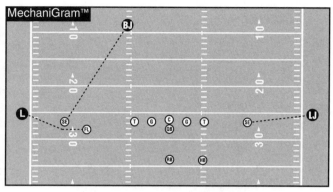

STRENGTH TO LINESMAN'S SIDE, WEAK SIDE SPLIT END

The back judge keys on the wideout and the linesman keys on the flanker. The line judge keys the split end. The fullback will likely stay in the backfield for pass protection, but the halfback may run a pass route. If the route is to the line judge's side, the line judge takes him.

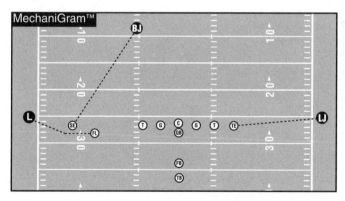

STRENGTH TO LINESMAN'S SIDE, WEAK SIDE TIGHT END

The back judge keys on the wideout and the linesman keys on the flanker. The line judge keys the tight end. The fullback will likely stay in the backfield for pass protection, but the tailback may run a pass route. If the route is to the line judge's side, the line judge takes him.

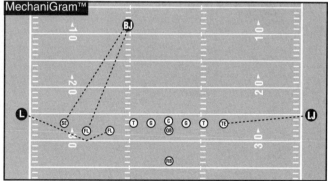

TRIPS TO LINESMAN'S SIDE

The back judge keys on the two widest receivers and the strong side wing official keys on the inside-most receiver. In this formation, that is the flanker, but it could be a tight end if the formation had only two wide receivers. The line judge keys on the end nearest him. Either wing official may also have the back if he runs a pass route. If the same formation were strong to the line judge's side, the line judge would key on the inside receiver and the back judge on the two widest receivers.

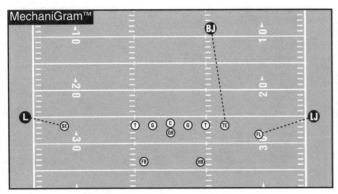

**UNBALANCED FORMATION,
STRENGTH TO LINE JUDGE'S SIDE**

The line judge keys on the flanker because the inside receiver is the tight end. The back judge keys on the tight end. The linesman keys on the wideout. Either wing official may also have a back running a pass route.

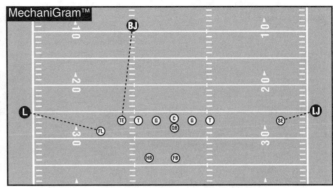

VEER

Although primarily a running formation, teams will occasionally throw to the flanker or split end. In this example strength is to the linesman's side. The back judge keys the tight end and the linesman keys the flanker. The line judge keys on the split end. The fullback's primary function is a blocker.

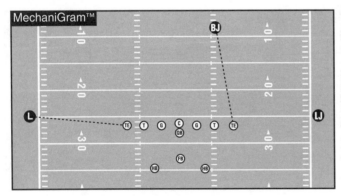

WISHBONE

A balanced formation, which means strength is declared to line judge's side. The back judge keys the tight end on the line judge's side. The line judge keys the backs. The linesman keys the tight end on his side.

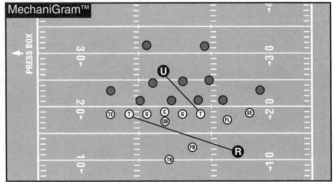

REFEREE AND UMPIRE KEYS

Regardless of the formation, the referee and umpire key on the opposite-side tackle. In all but the rarest cases, that means the referee keys on the left tackle and the umpire on the right tackle.

WING OFFICIAL KEYS (FOUR-MAN CREW)

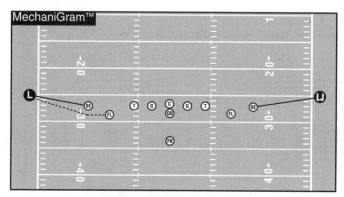

BALANCED FORMATION

In this balanced formation, there are two receivers outside of the tackles on either side of the formation. The wing officials' main key is the widest receiver (in this case, the split end); the flankers are secondary keys.

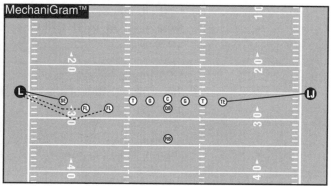

TRIPS TO LINESMAN'S SIDE

In a trips formation, the wing official on the strong side keys on the receiver on the end of the line (in this case the split end) and the two flankers are secondary keys. The line judge keys on the tight end, the only receiver on the line on his side of the formation.

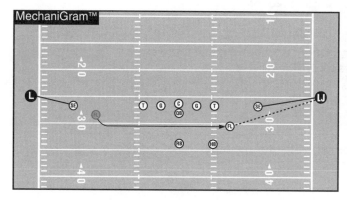

MOTION CHANGES FORMATION FROM UNBALANCED TO BALANCED

Strength was to the linesman's side, but motion changed the strength of the formation to the line judge's side. The split end remains the line judge's key and the motion man is a secondary key. However, the linesman observes the action of the motion man. Legality of motion is always the responsibility of the official away from whom the player is moving. The linesman's key is the split end.

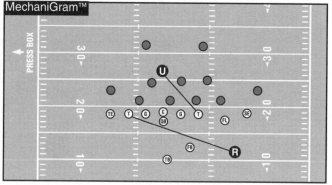

REFEREE AND UMPIRE KEYS

Regardless of the formation, the referee and umpire key on the opposite-side tackle. In all but the rarest cases, that means the referee keys on the left tackle and the umpire on the right tackle.

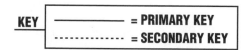

• Situational keys are partially based on the down, distance, score, time remaining, offensive and defensive formations and actions of players at the snap.

• Positional keys are predetermined by the position you are working in the game. Positional keys deal more with the back judge and wing officials.

• The strong side of a formation is the side on which there are more eligible receivers outside of the tackle.

• In regard to determining keys, it doesn't matter if a player is on or off the line of scrimmage.

Quiz

Without referring back, you should be able to answer the following true-false questions.

1. In a balanced formation, strength is always considered to be on the line judge's side.

2. It is crucial that the back judge and wing officials know where the motion man is at the snap because the strength of the formation may change.

3. In a four-man crew, when there is more than one eligible receiver on a particular side, the primary key is the inside receiver.

4. In a five-man crew, the back judge in a balanced formation favors the linesman's side.

5. Motion always changes the strength of the formation.

1. True 2. True 3. False 4. False 5. False

Chapter 13

Odds & Ends

Glance at the clock

Each time an official stops the clock, quickly glance at the clock to see the time. Before glancing, however, make sure players' actions are under control; you don't want to look away from the players if there's a potential problem among them.

All officials should glance. The non-covering official may have a better chance to glance more quickly since that official is not involved with action around the ball.

In addition, glance at the clock just after the referee gives the signal to start the clock. Obviously, the time that is on the clock when it is started should be the same as the time when the clock was stopped.

By gathering clock information, you are fully prepared if the clock malfunctions or if time is run off the clock — accidentally or intentionally. It takes some discipline to develop this good habit, but once accomplished, glancing at the clock becomes second-nature. Your efforts will pay off the first time you confidently — and correctly — handle a clock problem.

Whistle control

Think of the whistle as a communication tool. It's really just an extension of your voice and your signals. Blowing the whistle loudly has the same impact of you screaming; blowing the whistle softly equates to whispering. A "normal" whistle blow equates to talking in a normal tone of voice.

When stopping the clock, supplement your signal with a sharp, strong whistle blast. There's no need to blow the whistle many times with short blasts; that doesn't communicate anything of substance and draws unnecessary attention to yourself. If opposing players appear ready to square off, use your voice instead of your whistle.

When a team requests and is granted a timeout, use a slightly longer whistle while signaling the timeout. That longer whistle distinguishes a timeout from a normal whistle blast that stops the clock.

Contrary to the belief of coaches, players and spectators, the whistle does not make the ball dead (except for an inadvertent whistle). The whistle prevents a dead ball from becoming live (such as in a false start situation) or serves as a warning that the ball is already dead. You will encounter situations when a play ends and no whistles will be needed. If you don't have to blow the whistle to stop the clock and players unpile without incident, don't blow your whistle just for the sake of blowing it.

An axiom worth repeating: Don't blow the whistle if you don't see leather. You may well have been deceived by a fake or you may be unable to see a loose ball. Also, blow the whistle only when the play is in your coverage area. If you're a linesman and the play ends in the line judge's side zone, you should not blow your whistle.

An area of great debate among officials involves the use of finger whistles vs. a whistle on a lanyard (some officials, mostly umpires, use both). A finger whistle gives you an extra second or two to decide if you really want to blow the whistle. Detractors say using a finger whistle leads to a lot of signaling with one arm when two arms are called for (e.g. touchdown, stop the clock, etc.) If you choose a finger whistle, concentrate on blowing the whistle, then signaling.

If you use a lanyard, put the whistle in your mouth until the ball is snapped, then spit it out until you need to blow it. It may take some practice before you'll be able to grab the whistle and put it in your mouth while running, but that's what the off season is for.

Changing calls

Referee could publish another entire book on the philosophy of changing another official's call. There are definitely debatable pros and cons.

The first step in correctly changing a call is having the right attitude. Omit the word "overrule" from your vocabulary. You are not overruling your crewmate; you are helping your crewmate get the call right. That's a subtle yet critical difference. Officials who have an overruling attitude tend to makes calls out of their area and try to dominate the game. Officials who help their crewmates do so only in very rare instances. Maintaining the proper attitude with help prevent over-officiating.

When an incorrect call is made and the calling official agrees to make the change, the calling official signals the correct decision, not the helping official.

Following correct procedure, the helping official blows the whistle and simultaneously uses the stop-the-clock signal. The helping official then runs toward the calling official. That's an obvious indicator to the calling official that something may be amiss.

The helping official then asks the calling official, "Did you get a good look at the play?" That initiates a quick conversation about what happened. The helping official then tells the calling official what the helping official saw. The calling official makes the decision on how to handle it. If the calling official changes the call, only the calling official makes the new signal.

The helping official should never make the call, especially from the area where the helping official started the play and without talking to the calling official.

Here's an example: On a sweep toward the sideline, the linesman sees the runner fumble. The ball rolls toward a sideline and a team B player falls on the ball. The linesman gives the stop-the-clock signal and signals that team B has been awarded a new series. However, the linesman did not see that the ball went out of bounds before bouncing back onto the field, where the team B player recovered it. The referee, properly trailing the play, saw the entire play correctly.

The referee blows the whistle, signals to stop the clock (even though the clock is already stopped) and runs toward the linesman. The referee asks the linesman if he got a good look at the play. Both officials briefly state what they saw. If the linesman agrees that he did not see the ball go out of bounds, team A should again be given possession and the linesman should signal the next down. The referee helped the linesman get the play right.

When two officials cannot agree on what they saw or are unsure, the referee must become involved. The referee listens to each official in turn, the three arrive at a decision (the referee may be forced to break a tie vote) and the referee alone signals.

An example: The line judge and the umpire see a receiver slide on the ground and attempt to catch a low pass. Each has a good angle. The line judge believes he saw the ball hit the ground but the umpire is equally certain the ball was caught. They blow their whistles and make eye contact but neither signals. They get together and discuss what they saw. The referee should join the conversation and ask each what he saw and if the official is sure. If either backs down, the other official's call should prevail and the referee should give the appropriate signal. If neither backs down, the referee has to break the tie. *Referee* recommends ruling an incomplete pass in such cases; in this example, the referee would signal the pass incomplete.

Here are some general guidelines for changing calls. Each play, however, must be judged on the impact that a change has on the game.

• **Only obvious mistakes should be corrected.** We're only talking about a call that everyone in the park knows is wrong. The helping official must be 100 percent certain the calling official is wrong before offering the suggested change. "I think the receiver trapped the ball," is not acceptable. "I clearly saw the receiver trap the pass," is acceptable. The helping official must see the entire play clearly to offer an opinion. If you're 99 percent sure, that's not good enough.

Overall, you should only have to help an official change a call a few times a season. Any more than that and either you're over-officiating or your crewmate's not doing a very good job.

• **The change must have a positive impact on the game.** Do not change things just to change them. Think about the long-term ramifications of changing the call. Is it good for the game or will every judgment by any official from that moment forward be questioned by players and coaches who want an "overrule"?

• **Virtually any call can be discussed.** Whether it's a catch/no catch or facemask/no facemask, if an official who had a better angle can help his crew get the call right, the helping official owes it to his crewmate to initiate a discussion. Help is expected and commonly accepted.

• **Incorrect rule applications should be changed.** Rules applications are different from judgment calls. If you know your crewmate is getting a rule wrong (like including a loss of down on an ineligible downfield penalty), step in immediately and get it right.

Calling out of your area

Calling things out of your normal coverage area is a controversial practice. Officials who try to dominate the game by making calls over the whole field, regardless of coverage area responsibilities, are bad for the game. They over-officiate and are not always watching what they're supposed to be watching. They certainly are not fun to work with.

In rare instances, however, it's OK to call something that's not in your normal coverage area. There are two key factors: The play has got to be blatantly obvious and the call has to be "good for the game." What does that mean? If the penalty went uncalled, game control would suffer immensely.

Sometimes your crewmate's view is blocked on a play; sometimes, your crewmate just freezes for whatever reason and doesn't react to a play. Be ready to make a call out of your area if it's obvious and good for the game. You must, however, have seen the entire play clearly to make a call. That should rarely happen if you're watching what you're supposed to be watching, however.

Making a call out of your area should happen only a few times a season. If it happens more than that, you're either over-officiating or your crewmate's not doing a very good job.

Sideline decorum

Every official has his own idea of what conduct and language is acceptable and what is objectionable. For a crew to work efficiently, the entire crew must agree on what sort of conduct (outside of what is specifically covered in the rules) will merit a penalty. Because of the wide diversity of opinions on this topic, *Referee* will not recommend when a flag should or should not be thrown.

However, *Referee* does recommend that a wing official (since by their position on the sidelines, the wings are the main conduit between the coaches and the officials) answer, when time and the situation permit, any question that is asked in a sportsmanlike manner. If a coach asks the wing a question that only another official can answer (such as which player was guilty of a penalty), the wing official should say, "I'll try to find out for you, coach." When time allows, the wing should then make an effort to find out.

Reporting ejections

If a player is ejected, the referee and the wing official on the ejected player's side of the field report the ejection to the head coach. Although the referee does the actual reporting, involving another official provides a witness to the conversation.

If the referee is not the official ordering the ejection, he should find out exactly what the player did to cause the ejection. A thorough explanation from the calling official reduces the chances the calling official will be involved in the discussion with the coach. That reduces the amount of time the officials have to spend at the sideline in front of a coach who is likely upset over losing a player. At the same time, the opposite wing official should inform the opposing coach of the ejection.

The referee should keep the conversation brief. For example, "Coach, number 33 has been ejected because an official saw him punch an opponent." If the coach has not sent in a substitute for the ejected player, gently but firmly remind him to do so. Then, move away from the area and get the game moving again. Don't let the coach use the situation as a timeout to discuss strategy.

The calling official should record the number of the player ejected, the time of the ejection and the nature of the incident. All other officials should record the number of the ejected player and the time of the ejection. In some cases, it is the calling official's responsibility to write the report that will be sent to the proper authority (e.g. assigning agent, conference commissioner, etc.); otherwise, it is the referee's duty.

An incident report should be written as soon as possible after the game, while memories are still fresh. The report should include a detailed description of the incident, anything that the official or the player said (If profanity is used, use the correct words; for example, don't change "damn" to "darn") and anything else the official feels was noteworthy. Do not editorialize ("This was the worst incident I've seen in 20 years of officiating"), suggest punishment for the guilty party ("I think this player should be suspended for three weeks") or use hyperbole ("The player went nuts" does not explain the incident; "The player threw his helmet at me" describes the player's action).

The report should be filed with the proper authority within 24 hours of the incident. Keep a copy for your records.

Dealing with fights

Football is a physical game involving emotional players. Sometimes those emotions become misplaced and confrontations occur. Most of the time when two players square off in a combative manner, a firm verbal warning such as, "The play is over. Now get back to your huddles," is enough to quell a disturbance. But when that doesn't work (or the confrontation escalates before the official can reach it) and a fight breaks out, crews must have a plan in place to deal with the situation.

Getting in the middle of a skirmish and trying to separate three or more players is not recommended. If there are just two combatants, try to get between them and

keep it from escalating. If that fails, back off and start writing down numbers so the proper players will be penalized and ejected.

Don't push players away from each other; you don't know how players are going to react to contact.

If the fight goes into a sideline area, ask the coaches to help. The official who is nearest to the benches should urge players on the sidelines not to enter the field or join in the fight. Officials away from the fight should observe players on the field to ensure another fight does not break out and jot down numbers of players who leave the bench to join in the fight.

No matter what, maintaining composure is vital. By exuding calm through voice and body language, an official can maintain control.

Using "get-back" coaches

Linesmen and line judges can improve their chances of clean sidelines by having each head coach designate a "get-back coach." The get-back coach is usually an assistant coach who urges substitutes, trainers and other sideline personnel to stay in the team boxes.

The wing official should introduce himself to the get-back coach shortly before the game begins. If, in the excitement of the game, the get-back coach forgets his duties, a gentle reminder from the wing official usually does the trick.

"Hurry-up" offenses

Offensive teams trying to score before the end of the second or fourth quarters often accelerate their pace between plays by not huddling and calling signals at the line. This strategy is known as the no-huddle or "hurry-up" offense.

When a team employs the hurry-up, the officials also need to step up their pace. However, that should not come at the expense of skipping important between-downs duties.

The referee must be sure every official (especially the linesman) is in position and ready to go before blowing the ready-for-play. The umpire can help by straddling the ball and telling the offense, "Wait for the whistle," until the referee blows the ready. The chain crew must also be ready to move at a quicker rate. It is important that the linesman discuss the hurry-up in his pregame meeting with the chain crew. The linesman should ensure the box shows the correct down and is in position, then make eye contact with the referee to let the referee know the linesman is ready for the next play.

Team B must not be allowed to illegally conserve time by failing to quickly unpile. The penalties for such conduct are covered in the rulebooks, and crews should discuss in their pregame meeting under what circumstances those penalties will be called.

MECHANICS ILLUSTRATED: PREVENTING SIDELINE PROBLEMS

Wing officials have plenty to do when a ballcarrier winds up out of bounds. The tasks multiply when the play ends in or near a team area. An alert, hustling crew can give the covering official the help he needs while preventing potential problems.

In PlayPic A, the official is positioned correctly as the play proceeds downfield. He's close enough to observe the action but not so close he could become involved in the play.

As the tackler brings down the runner and the players tumble out of bounds (PlayPic B), the covering official marks the spot and gives the stop-the-clock signal. The official can use voice commands to let the players know an official is present and to encourage them to return to the field quickly and without incident. Phrases such as, "We're done," or, "That's all, fellas," are more effective than blasts on the whistle.

Regardless of the ferocity of the tackle or the reaction of sideline personnel, the presence of another official helps a crew maintain control of the game. In PlayPic C, a second official moves in and is ready to step between the runner and tackler. Depending on how far beyond the line of scrimmage the play ends, the back judge (five-man crew) or umpire (four-man crew) is the official most likely to provide the assistance.

If trouble does appear imminent, the covering official should drop his beanbag to mark the spot and help his crewmate quell the disturbance. In the event a fight breaks out immediately, marking the spot is secondary to the role of peacemaker.

At no time while players are out of bounds should officials turn their backs on the play. Never allow players who have crossed the sideline return to the field without an official accompanying them.

Chapter 14

Postgame

Postgame

POSTGAME REVIEW

After the game, it's a good idea to review what happened during the game. The postgame review is another important part of the learning process.

The first order of business immediately after the game is to relax. Officiating can be stressful and postgame relaxation helps get you back to normal.

At a reasonable time after the game, review the game with your crew. Some crews like to review before taking a shower and relaxing. Others like to wait until the postgame dinner. Do whatever is convenient and comfortable for you and your crew.

When reviewing the game, talk about:

Points of emphasis
Were the pregame points of emphasis handled effectively? Many times, rough play and sportsmanship are emphasized. Did you control the game effectively? Were dead-ball situations handled appropriately? If the points of emphasis were not handled properly, discuss remedies for your next game.

Tempo
Did you let the game come to you or did you assert yourself when you didn't need to? Did the game develop a flow? If not, is there anything you could have done to keep the game moving?

Sideline decorum
How did you handle the benches? Did you let the coaches go too far? Were you approachable?

Strange plays, rulings
Discuss and review any strange plays or rulings. If necessary, confirm your ruling with the rulebook and casebook. Make sure you've got the rule down so you can apply it correctly if it happens again. Discuss any unusual penalty enforcements and confirm they were handled properly.

Solicit constructive criticism
One of the ways to improve is to get opinions and advice from others. Your crew is a great source. Always ask if there's anything you could have done differently or better.

After asking, accept the constructive criticism. Don't be one of those referees who asks, "How'd I do?" expecting a shower of praise. If you don't want to know the truth, don't ask. Take the criticism offered, analyze the comments and apply the changes if you feel they're appropriate.

Be ready to offer a critique when asked. It's frustrating for an official who wants to learn to invite criticism only to hear, "You did a good job." There must be something that needs improving! You ought to be able to give your crew at least three things to think about after every game.

Write a journal
Consider keeping a journal during your season. Write down strange plays, your feelings about your performance, notes about your crew, things you did well and things you can improve on. The journal is a great way to look back during and after the season to see if there are patterns. If the same things keep appearing in your journal, you know there are things that need to be addressed.

Reviewing the journal is also a great way to start thinking about officiating before next season.

Notes

Crew of Five

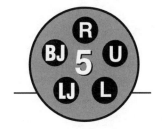

Chapter 15

Coin Toss

In most cases, the players' first contact with the officials will be at the coin toss. Discharging the coin toss duties professionally and efficiently will leave the captains with a positive first impression.

Do not use the coin toss as an opportunity to tell the captains how the game will be officiated. Let the captains know you will do your best to answer any questions they have during the game and that they will serve as the conduit between the officials and the other players.

The positioning and duties for coin tosses are further explained in Chapters 15 and 23.

General procedures

When the referee and umpire meet with the coaches prior to the game, they should obtain the name and number of each captain so they can be greeted by name. The coach may specify which captain will make decisions during the coin toss (that captain is known as the "speaking captain"). At about five minutes prior to game time, the referee and umpire go to their respective sidelines to greet the captains by name (refer to them by title, such as Captain Smith or Mr. Brown), shake their hands and ask them to remove their helmets. Having the captains remove their helmets and carry them to the center of the field allows full face-to-face contact during the toss.

The speaking captains should be positioned so they are closest to the referee when the group meets in the center of the field. For the sake of uniformity, it is preferable to have the referee face the scoreboard during the toss.

Referee recommendation: Regardless of the location of the pressbox, have the referee escort the home team captains while the umpire takes the visitors.

In Federation, the coin toss is normally conducted in the center of the field five minutes before the game. The state association may prescribe alternative procedures. The toss may be held at an earlier time off the field if both coaches agree. In such a case the results may be simulated in the center of the field three minutes before the game. The umpire goes to the sideline with the line-to-gain equipment and the referee to the opposite sideline. In most situations the visiting team is opposite the pressbox with the line-to-gain equipment on their sideline. When they reach the center of the field, the referee and umpire will be across from each other. The back judge remains on the hashmark on the side of the field with the chains; the line judge assumes a similar position on the opposite side. The linesman remains on his sideline.

In NCAA, the toss is normally conducted in the center of the field three minutes before the game. The referee goes to the sideline with the line-to-gain equipment and the umpire to the opposite sideline. In most situations the visiting team is opposite the pressbox with the line-to-gain equipment on their sideline. When they reach the center of the field, the referee and umpire will be next to each other. The back judge, on the side of the field with the chains, and line judge, on the opposite sideline, wait until the captains have been escorted to the middle of the field, then move to the numbers. The linesman stays on the sideline with the chains.

Players who are not involved in the toss should be kept out of the area between the top of the numbers on both sides of the field. Upon arrival in the center of the field, the umpire and referee should be directly facing each other and the captains stand so their backs are to their own sidelines. The captains are asked to introduce themselves to each other.

The referee should allow all captains to view both sides of the coin, identifying which side is heads and which is tails. *Referee* recommendation: Use a silver dollar or half-dollar; their size eases identification of heads and tails.

The referee explains the coin flip procedure: The visiting captain is instructed to call heads or tails while the coin is in the air. The coin will be caught by the referee and turned or not turned over. If the coin is dropped, the toss should be repeated. The referee may choose to have the captain declare heads or tails before the coin is flipped. The referee may also choose to have the coin hit the ground.

Once the winner is determined, the winner is offered his choice. *Referee* recommends that the captain of the team winning the toss should be offered choices in the following sequence: defer, receive or defend a goal. The order is that of the most likely selection and omits "kick." Kick is a valid choice, but one that, most likely, will get the captain in trouble. If the captain was told to pick kick, he will pick it whether or not it is offered.

If the choice is to defer, the referee immediately faces the pressbox, taps the shoulder of the deferring captain and signals the declination. The remaining choices are then presented to the other captain and the final selection is made by the deferring captain. If the winner of the coin toss does not defer, no signal is immediately given.

When the final selections are made, the captains are asked to put their backs to the goalline their team will defend and the referee gives the appropriate signal. If the choice is to kick or receive, only the first selection is signaled. If the choice is to defend a goal, two signals are given: pointing both arms toward the goalline being defended, followed by the appropriate signal for the other captain.

If at any time during the toss the referee errs or gives incorrect information (for instance, giving the wrong team an option), the umpire should speak up immediately.

When the toss is completed, the other officials join the referee and umpire in the center of the field and record the results of the toss. All officials simultaneously move to their kickoff positions.

The procedure is repeated before the second half. When the three-minute warmup period ends (NCAA: When the halftime intermission expires), the referee and umpire go to their respective sidelines and once again escort the captains to the center of the field while the other officials assume the same positions as for the pregame toss. The referee offers the choices to either the deferring captain of the loser of the pregame coin toss, as appropriate.

Overtime procedure

If overtime is necessary, the officials wait for the three-minute intermission to end (NCAA: No intermission is specified; the officials meet to review overtime rules and procedures). The referee and umpire go to their respective sidelines and once again escort the captains to the center of the field while the other officials assume the same positions as for the pregame toss. The coin toss is repeated with the visiting team again calling it. When the winner is determined, the options are explained. The winner may not defer, but may choose offense, defense or the goal to be used.

When the selections are completed, the captains of the team on offense are asked to face the goalline in the direction their team will advance and the opposing captains stand with their backs to that goalline. The referee then taps the shoulder of the captain of the team that won the toss and gives the first down signal in the appropriate direction.

OUTLINE

I. Referee:

1. About five minutes (or as directed by state association) before game time, escort to center of field captains of team whose team box is on side opposite line-to-gain equipment. Speaking captain should be closest to referee; referee faces scoreboard.

2. Have captains face each other with their backs to their respective sidelines.

3. After the umpire introduces the captains, introduce captains to each other and give them instructions.

4. In presence of umpire:

a. Instruct visiting captain to call toss while coin is in air (or before coin is tossed).

b. Inform captains if coin is not caught, you will toss again.

c. Inform captains if there is question about call, you will toss again.

d. After making toss and determining winner, place hand on captain's shoulder and have captain choose one of following options: Kick or receive, defend a goal or defer choice to second half.

e. If winner chooses not to defer and makes a choice, give opposing captain choice of remaining options.

f. If winner of toss defers, step toward pressbox and give penalty declined signal.

g. Opposing captain then given choice of options, followed by deferring captain's choice of remaining option.

5. Place captains in position facing each other with backs toward goal they will defend.

6. While facing in same direction as the first choosing captain, signal choice by:

a. Swing leg simulating kick.

b. Make catching motion simulating receiving.

c. If first choosing captain elected to defend a goal, point with both arms extended toward that goalline, then move to other captains and give appropriate signal for choice of other captain.

7. Dismiss captains.

8. Second-half choices:

a. Prior to beginning of second half, escort to center of field captains of team whose team box is on side opposite line-to-gain equipment.

b. Obtain second-half choices and give appropriate signals to pressbox.

c. Dismiss captains after any further instructions.

NOTES

1. If coin toss is held off field, results may be simulated at center of field three minutes prior to start of game or as directed by state association.

2. If coin toss is needed for overtime, repeat procedures with the following modifications:

a. Coin toss occurs after three-minute intermission.

b. Inform captains how many timeouts they have remaining for overtime period.

c. After making toss and determining winner, place hand on captain's shoulder and have captain choose one of following options (deferment no longer an option): Offense, defense or defend a goal.

d. Position offensive captain facing goal toward which ball will be advanced and give first down signal.

II. Umpire:

1. About five minutes (or as directed by state association) before game time, escort to center of field the captains of team whose team box is on side where line-to-gain equipment is located. Speaking captain should be closest to referee.

2. After introducing captains to referee, remain with referee to listen to instructions and record toss options.

3. Repeat choice of calling captain loudly enough for all captains and referee to hear. If there is a discrepancy in what you heard and what captain says he called, flip should be repeated.

4. Second-half choices:

a. On signal from referee, escort captains to center of field.

b. Remain with referee and captains and check on options given teams to ensure accuracy.

III. Linesman

1. Remain on side where line-to-gain equipment is located.

2. Obtain football of kicking team's choice.

3. Second-half choices:

    a. Remain on side where line-to-gain equipment is located.

    b. Review procedures and correct problems with line-to-gain crew.

    c. Indicate end of field line-to-gain crew will be on prior to kickoff.

    d. Assume same position at inbounds mark as prior to first half kickoff.

    e. Obtain football of kicking team's choice.

IV. Line judge

1. Remain at inbounds mark (Federation) or at the numbers (NCAA) on side opposite line-to-gain equipment to keep team members who are not involved in toss between you and sideline.

2. Second-half choices:

    a. Assume same position at inbounds mark as prior to first-half kickoff.

V. Back judge

1. Remain at inbounds mark (Federation) or at the numbers (NCAA) on side where line-to-gain equipment is located; keep team members who are not involved in toss between you and sideline.

2. Second-half choices:

    a. Remain on side where line-to-gain equipment is located.

    b. Assume same position at inbounds mark as prior to first half kickoff.

One of the things that makes a great official is a complete understanding of the game. That goes beyond rules and mechanics. Great referees anticipate plays. They always seem to be in the right place at the right time. It's not an accident or just luck. It's preparation and an understanding of the game. That puts them in the right spot at the right moment.

Studying the game

Part of that preparation is studying the game itself. Just what are the teams trying to do on the field? The novice or unprepared referee doesn't think beyond, "This team is trying to score more points than the other team."

The great referees think about offensive styles, defensive schemes, tempo and tendencies. For example, they'll know or recognize that Central High's motion men always go toward the wide side of the field. They use zone pass defense but double cover the widest receiver on obvious passing downs. They have a history of putting their best offensive lineman at left tackle and usually run the ball behind that tackle on short yardage situations. They isolate a fullback on a blitzing linebacker. They don't save onside kicks for obvious short free kick situations.

The different approaches are obvious: The more you know about the game and a team's tendencies, the better prepared you are.

Recognizing and knowing what coaches and players are trying to do elevates your game. When you have that knowledge, you can adjust your field coverage accordingly. In the section on Coverage Philosophy (page 20), you read how anticipation is critical to successful officiating. The obvious question is, how do you get better at anticipating plays? You study the game and the specific plays.

As the game of football becomes more complex, officials must be more aware of specific tendencies and strategies. When officials recognize offensive plays and defensive strategies, they make better field coverage adjustments.

Gaining the knowledge

How do you gain the knowledge about specific plays and teams? One way is to talk to other officials. If you know referees who have had a team you're about to officiate, ask them questions about style and tempo. Another way is to carefully watch the players during the pregame warmup.

The most common: Learning and adjusting while the game is in progress. You must develop the ability to see what's happening on the field and adjust accordingly.

Regardless of position, you're not just watching a bunch of players move. Learn to watch specific, orchestrated offensive and defensive plays while on the field. Then, make the necessary adjustments.

For most referees who don't have an extensive playing or coaching background, it takes time to develop those skills. Practice while watching other games (on TV or in person). See what's happening on the field and recognize the offensive plays and defensive schemes. Think about what is likely to happen once you've recognized the play.

Here's an example of how a well-schooled official thinks on the field. Central High, leading by five points with 1:40 remaining in the game, has the ball on its own 17 yardline. It's third down and six yards to go. The clock is running and West High is out of timeouts. The seasoned official realizes Central will likely not pass. Why not? Because an intercepted pass could be returned for the go-ahead touchdown or would at worst put West in prime scoring position. An incomplete pass would stop the clock, something West cannot do since it is out of timeouts.

What is more likely is that Central will use up as much of the 25-second count as possible before running a simple handoff. Central will bring its punt team onto the field and snap the ball after again letting most of the play clock expire. On the punt, West will either forsake a return by putting nine or more men on the line of scrimmage in hopes of blocking the punt, or allow Central to get off the kick and try to set up a long return.

Anticipating all of that action, the officials adjust their field coverage accordingly. An official who doesn't understand the game or recognize specific plays will be caught by surprise; a well-schooled official is prepared.

Reading the case studies

Remember the old "chalk talk" when you were a player? The coach frantically drew circles and lines and pounded the chalk until it became a fine white dust, all the while yelling something like, "If we block this play properly, it's a touchdown!" *Football Officials Guidebook* case studies take the chalk talk a giant step forward.

We've created game-specific plays for officials. We've inserted the officials and diagrammed their movements. The result: *Football Officials Guidebook* teaches officials to recognize specific offensive and defensive plays, help them adjust basic field positioning to properly officiate each play and shows exactly where each official should be looking. It's a referee chalk talk for the new millennium.

Case studies are included in the chapters on free kicks, scrimmage plays, goalline plays, scoring kicks and scrimmage kicks. Each includes actual game plays showing the movements of players and officials. Text accompanies each frame, so officials know where to go and what they're trying to see.

Combined with the chapters on positional and formation keys, you'll understand how to officiate a play from beginning to end.

Use these case studies to learn what plays look like and what you're supposed to do once you recognize them. As you become a student of the game, your officiating will dramatically improve.

One note: The case studies do not depict every conceivable play or variation on the play. For the sake of brevity, a play was depicted only once (e.g. there is a case study for a sweep to the linesman's side of the field but not to the line judge's side of the field).

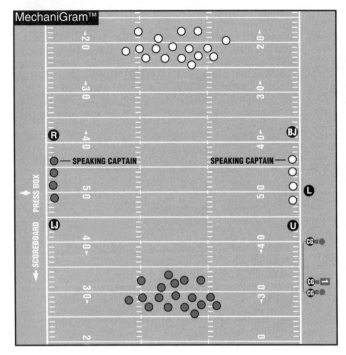

Action on the field: Captains at sideline; teams warming up.

Referee: At midfield on sideline opposite line-to-gain equipment.

Umpire: At midfield on sideline with line-to-gain equipment.

Linesman: On sideline.

Line judge: At midfield across field from umpire.

Back judge: At midfield across field from referee.

Action on the field: Introduction of captains.

Referee: Escorts captains to middle of field. Instructs captains to introduce themselves. Explains coin flip procedure.

Umpire: Monitors referee's discussion with captains; if necessary, corrects referee.

Linesman: On sideline.

Line judge: Escorts captains as far as hashmark. Prevents players not involved in coin toss from entering area where toss is being conducted.

Back judge: Escorts captains as far as hashmark. Prevents players not involved in coin toss from entering area where toss is being conducted.

KEY

 Referee Umpire Line Judge Linesman Back Judge Chain Gang Ballboy Coach ○ Offense ● Defense ● Football Possession of football

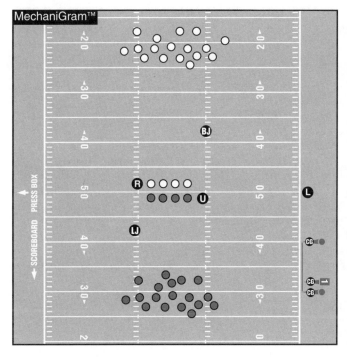

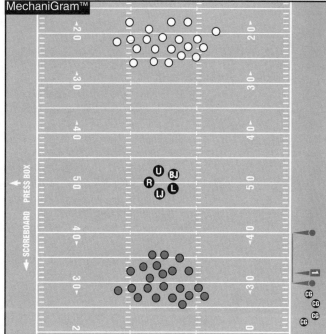

Action on the field: Coin toss winner determined.

Referee: Conducts toss and obtains choices from captains. If toss winner chooses to defer, referee should step away from group and signal that choice to pressbox. Asks captains to turn with backs to goal they will defend and signals toss winner's choice to pressbox. Moves to other set of captains and signals toss loser's choice to pressbox.

Umpire: Monitors referee's discussion with captains; if necessary, corrects referee. Records choices. Moves to other set of captains for referee's signal.

Linesman: On sideline.

Line judge: Prevents players not involved in coin toss from entering area where toss is being conducted.

Back judge: Prevents players not involved in coin toss from entering area where toss is being conducted.

Action on the field: Final phase.

Referee: Meets with remaining officials in center of field to confirm results of toss. Hustles to position for kickoff.

Umpire: Meets with remaining officials in center of field to confirm results of toss. Hustles to position for kickoff.

Linesman: Meets with remaining officials in center of field to confirm results of toss. Hustles to position for kickoff.

Line judge: Meets with remaining officials in center of field to confirm results of toss. Hustles to position for kickoff.

Back judge: Meets with remaining officials in center of field to confirm results of toss. Hustles to position for kickoff.

Movement | Previous position | Current position (stopped) | Previous position | Current position (still moving)

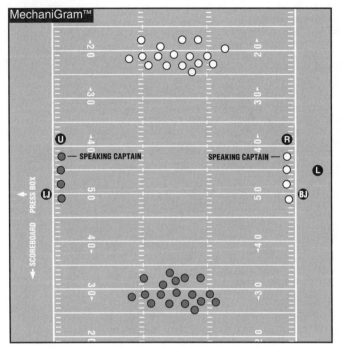

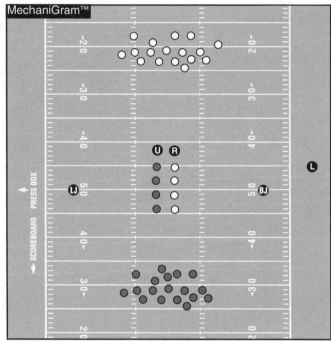

Action on the field: Starting positions.

Referee: At midfield on sideline with line-to-gain equipment.

Umpire: At midfield on sideline opposite line-to-gain equipment.

Linesman: On sideline.

Line judge: At sideline on umpire's side of field.

Back judge: At sideline behind referee.

Action on the field: Introduction of captains.

Referee: Escorts captains to middle of field. Instructs captains to introduce themselves. Explains coin flip procedure.

Umpire: Monitors referee's discussion with captains; if necessary, corrects referee.

Linesman: On sideline.

Line judge: Remains at sideline until captains have reached center of field, then moves to numbers.

Back judge: Remains at sideline until captains have reached center of field, then moves to numbers.

KEY

 Referee Umpire Line Judge Linesman Back Judge Chain Gang Ballboy Coach ○ Offense ● Defense ◗ Football ⊗ Possession of football

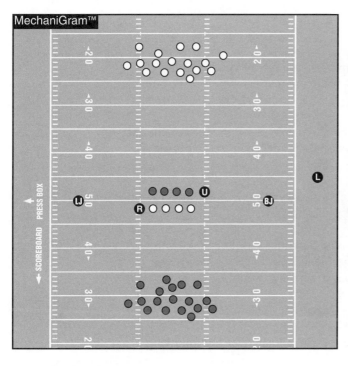

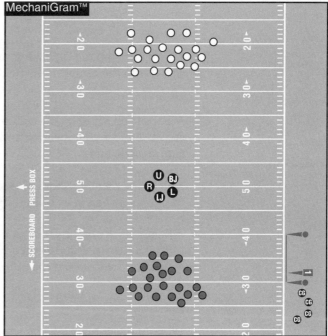

Action on the field: Coin toss winner determined.

Referee: Conducts toss and obtains choices from captains. If toss winner chooses to defer, referee should step away from group and signal that choice to pressbox. Asks captains to turn with backs to goal they will defend and signals toss winner's choice to pressbox. Moves to other set of captains and signals toss loser's choice to pressbox.

Umpire: Monitors referee's discussion with captains; if necessary, corrects referee. Records choices. Moves to other set of captains for referee's signal.

Linesman: On sideline.

Line judge: Prevents players not involved in coin toss from entering area where toss is being conducted.

Back judge: Prevents players not involved in coin toss from entering area where toss is being conducted.

Action on the field: Final phase.

Referee: Meets with remaining officials in center of field to confirm results of toss. Hustles to position for kickoff.

Umpire: Meets with remaining officials in center of field to confirm results of toss. Hustles to position for kickoff.

Linesman: Meets with remaining officials in center of field to confirm results of toss. Hustles to position for kickoff.

Line judge: Meets with remaining officials in center of field to confirm results of toss. Hustles to position for kickoff.

Back judge: Meets with remaining officials in center of field to confirm results of toss. Hustles to position for kickoff.

• Find out who the "speaking captains" are before you bring the captains to the center of the field and have them stand closest to the referee.

• If the team winning the coin toss chooses to defer, the referee should step away from the meeting and signal that decision to the pressbox before proceeding.

• Keep the meeting short. The coin toss is not the time for speeches or discussions of rules or officiating philosophy.

• Remind the captains they (not non-captains) should speak to an official if there are questions or problems and that the officials will speak to the captains if the officials are having trouble with a player.

Quiz

Without referring back, you should be able to answer the following true-false questions.

1. According to the Federation manual, the linesman should conduct his meeting with the chain crew during the coin toss.

2. If the referee gives incorrect information to the captains, the umpire should wait until after the coin toss to point out the error to the referee.

3. If a team's first choice is to defend a goal, the referee should indicate the choice by pointing with both arms in the direction the team will be going.

4. The team winning the toss before an overtime period is not allowed to defer its choice.

5. The officials should not meet in the middle of the field after the toss is completed.

1. True 2. False 3. True 4. True 5. False

Chapter 16

Free Kicks

Officials must realize that teams employ strategies for handling kickoffs, and those strategies should be recognized and officiated.

The kicking team is concerned about containment; that is, not permitting openings in coverage to let a kick returner escape for a long gain. For that purpose, kicking teams adopt two basic strategies. One planned procedure is to have players run straight down the field in imaginary lanes so as to cover the whole area of a runback in a systematic or blanket fashion. The second strategy is retaining one or two players behind the flow of teammates to act as safety valves, final pursuers in case a runner escapes from the first wave of pursuit.

Receiving teams, on the other hand, knowing that kickers stream downfield in lanes, try to open a pre-selected hole where blockers can wedge apart onrushing defenders, much the same as opening a hole in the line on regular scrimmage downs. As a result, receiving team members will often collapse into a makeshift offensive line around their own 25 or 30 yardline, intent on blocking for a runner as they would on a regular play.

Receivers form this makeshift line for two reasons. One, if players strung out across the field (as the ball is kicked) try to block onrushing kickers, it is relatively easy for kicking team players to avoid those blocks by feinting and sidestepping. Two, even if the receivers make contact, it is hard to sustain those open-field blocks, and the kicking team pursuers are likely to free themselves readily on the rebound and continue in their containment lanes. Literally, they'll just bump and charge.

Seeing the receiving team's wedge, kicking team players frequently leave their lanes to converge on the spot where receivers are trying to create an opening. Those convergent spots are where officials should focus their vision, because that is where most of the contact between opponents will take place. In real life, many officials watch the ball and the runner when they could service the game better by observing instead the blocking setup and the kicking team's pursuit.

General procedures

In Federation, the linesman and line judge simultaneously move toward the center of the field once the players are on the field. The linesman, who handles the ball, should not give the ball to the kicker until team K has 11 players on the field. All officials can ensure that team personnel are in their team boxes. The linesman should remind the kicker not to kick the ball until the referee has sounded his whistle.

The line judge reminds team R that all blocks must be above the waist. After identifying the free kick lines for their respective teams, the linesman and line judge turn toward each other, ensure that the other is ready, then simultaneously jog off to their sidelines, the linesman on team R's restraining line and the line judge on team K's restraining line.

In NCAA, the umpire handles the ball and waits in the middle of the field for the kicking team, and reminds the kicker not to kick the ball until the referee has sounded the ready. The umpire should be behind the kicker for the kickoff.

The referee's starting position is on the side of the field on which the chains are stationed. The referee sets up near the hashmark on team R's five yardline (NCAA: At the sideline on or near team R's 10 yardline). The back judge's position is on the side of the field opposite the referee, on team R's 20 yardline (NCAA: Directly across from the referee). The umpire in Federation should be on the same side of the field as the referee, at about team R's 30 yardline.

Each official, when in position and ready for the kick, should raise an arm as a ready signal for the referee. The referee blows his whistle and gives the ready for play signal once he sees a signal from each official.

The line judge and linesman watch for infractions involving their respective free kick lines. The covering official signals the clock to start if he sees the ball is touched other than first touching by team K (NCAA: If the clock is to start with the kick, the umpire gives the signal and the referee echoes the signal; otherwise the covering official signals the clock to start if he sees the ball is touched other than first touching by team K). The covering official is also responsible for signaling the clock to stop if the runner is downed in his area or if the ball goes out of bounds.

All officials not responsible for the runner must look for illegal blocks. If the kick goes out of bounds, the covering official is responsible for either dropping a beanbag (if team R caused the ball to go out of bounds) or a penalty marker (if team K caused the ball to go out of bounds). Officials trailing the runner must clean up after the play.

Coverage zones

According to Federation mechanics, if the kick is down the middle of the field, the referee stays with the runner to about team's R 25 yardline. If the return is to the referee's left and as wide as the hashmark, the back judge picks up coverage and stays with the runner to team R's 35 yardline, where the line judge takes over. If the kick is to the referee's right and as wide as the hashmark, the umpire takes up the coverage at about team R's 20 yardline and stays with the runner to about team R's 45 yardline, where he gives up coverage to the linesman.

If the kick is outside either hashmark, the umpire or back judge is responsible for the initial coverage of the runner. The referee cleans up behind the play, but must move cautiously in case team R runs a reverse or the runner reverses his field.

After the ball is kicked, the line judge and linesman drift downfield, maintaining coverage of their respective sidelines. Neither should go beyond team R's 45 yardline in case the runner breaks off a long return and enters either the line judge's or linesman's coverage area.

On kicks inside team R's five yardline, the referee is responsible for determining whether the momentum exception applies and whether the kick is to be ruled a touchback.

The CCA theory is to keep the play boxed in between the linesman, referee, line judge and back judge, while the umpire acts as a safety valve in case the runner breaks off a long return.

By maintaining a position near their respective sideline, the linesman, referee, line judge and back judge are able to keep play boxed in. All officials observe action in front of the runner when the runner is not in their general area.

The referee takes the ball only if it is in his side zone; if not, the back judge is responsible. On kicks inside team R's five yardline, either the referee or back judge (depending on which side zone the ball is kicked to) is responsible for determining whether the momentum exception applies and whether the kick is to be ruled a touchback. The official who does not make that determination is responsible for action in front of the deep receivers. If a touchback occurs, the referee and back judge should move quickly toward the middle of the field to prevent late hits.

Free kicks after a safety
In both Federation and NCAA, the coverage areas and mechanics are the same for the free kick that follows a safety.

In Federation, the linesman should be at team K's 20 yardline, the line judge at team K's 30 yardline and the position of the remaining officials is adjusted accordingly.

In NCAA, the umpire remains behind the kicker, the line judge should be at team K's 20 yardline, the linesman at team K's 30 yardline and the position of the remaining officials is adjusted accordingly.

CHALK TALK: FEDERATION FREE KICK POSITIONING AND COVERAGE ZONES

Referee: Starting position is on the side of the field on which the chains are stationed, near the hashmark on team R's five yardline. Once he sees a ready signal from each official, the referee blows his whistle and gives the ready for play signal.

If the kick is down the middle of the field, the referee stays with the runner to about team's R 25 yardline. If the kick is outside either hashmark, the referee cleans up behind the play, but must move cautiously in case team R runs a reverse or the runner reverses his field.

On kicks inside team R's five yardline, the referee is responsible for determining whether the momentum exception applies and whether the kick is to be ruled a touchback.

Umpire: Starting position is on the same side of the field as the referee, at about team R's 30 yardline. When in position and ready for the kick, the umpire should raise an arm as a ready signal for the referee.

If the kick is outside the hashmark on his side of the field, the umpire is responsible for the initial coverage of the runner. The umpire takes up the coverage at about team R's 20 yardline and stays with the runner to about team R's 45 yardline, where he gives up coverage to the linesman.

Linesman: The linesman and line judge move simultaneously toward the center of the field once the players are on the field. The linesman should not give the ball to the kicker until team K has 11 players on the field and should remind the kicker not to kick the ball until the referee has sounded his whistle. After identifying team K's free kick line, the linesman turns toward the line judge. After ensuring that the other is ready, they simultaneously jog off to their sidelines; the linesman is on team K's restraining line. When in position and ready for the kick, the linesman should raise an arm as a ready signal for the referee.

The linesman watches for infractions involving the free kick line. After the ball is kicked, the linesman drifts downfield, maintaining coverage of his respective sideline. He should not go beyond team R's 45 yardline in case the runner breaks off a long return and enters the linesman's coverage area. If the umpire has initial coverage of the runner, he stays with the runner to about team R's 45 yardline, where he gives up coverage to the linesman.

Line judge: The line judge and linesman move simultaneously toward the center of the field once the players are on the field. After identifying team R's free kick line, the line judge reminds team R that all blocks must be above the waist. The linesman and line judge turn toward each other, ensure that the other is ready, then simultaneously jog off to their sidelines; the line judge is on team R's restraining line. When in position and ready for the kick, the line judge should raise an arm as a ready signal for the referee.

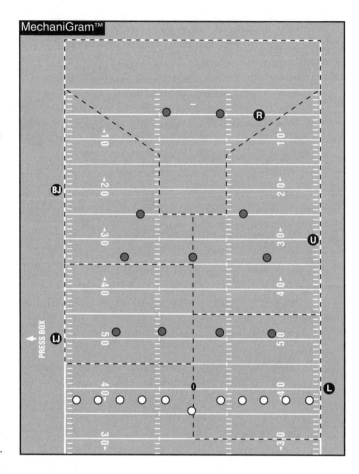

The line judge and linesman watch for infractions involving their respective free kick lines. After the ball is kicked, the line judge drifts downfield, maintaining coverage of his respective sideline. He should not go beyond team R's 35 yardline in case the runner breaks off a long return and enters the line judge's coverage area.

If the back judge has initial coverage of the runner, he stays with the runner to about team R's 35 yardline, where the line judge takes over.

Back judge: Starting position is on the side of the field opposite the referee, on team R's 20 yardline. When in position and ready for the kick, the back judge should raise an arm as a ready signal for the referee.

If the return is to the referee's left and as wide as the hashmark, the back judge picks up coverage and stays with the runner to team R's 35 yardline, where the line judge takes over. If the kick is outside his hashmark, the back judge is responsible for the initial coverage of the runner.

All officials: Any official not responsible for the runner must look for illegal blocks. If the kick goes out of bounds, the covering official is responsible for either dropping a beanbag (if team R caused the ball to go out of bounds) or a penalty marker (if team K caused the ball to go out of bounds). Officials trailing the runner must clean up after the play.

CHALK TALK: NCAA FREE KICK POSITIONING AND COVERAGE ZONES

Referee: Starting position is on the side of the field on which the chains are stationed, at the sideline on or near team R's 10 yardline. If the clock is to start with the kick, the referee echoes the umpire's signal.

The referee takes the ball only if it is in his side zone. By maintaining a position near the sideline, the deep officials are able to keep play boxed in.

On kicks to his side inside team R's five yardline, the referee is responsible for determining whether the momentum exception applies and whether the kick is to be ruled a touchback. If the kick is toward the referee's side, the referee is responsible for action in front of the deep receivers. If a touchback occurs, the referee should move quickly toward the middle of the field to prevent late hits.

Umpire: The umpire handles the ball, waits in the middle of the field for the kicking team, and reminds the kicker not to kick the ball until the referee has sounded the ready. The umpire should be behind the kicker for the kickoff. When in position and ready for the kick, the umpire should raise an arm as a ready signal for the referee. If the clock is to start with the kick, the umpire gives the signal and the referee echoes it.

After the ball is kicked, the umpire shouldn't move beyond the 50 yardline. The umpire acts as a safety valve in case the runner breaks off a long return.

Linesman: Starting position is on team R's restraining line. When in position and ready for the kick, the linesman should raise an arm as a ready signal for the referee. The linesman watches for infractions involving the free kick line.

After the ball is kicked, the linesman drifts downfield, maintaining coverage of his sideline. By maintaining a position on the sideline, the deep officials are able to keep play boxed in.

Line judge: Starting position is on team K's restraining line. When in position and ready for the kick, the line judge should raise an arm as a ready signal for the referee. The line judge watches for infractions involving the free kick line.

After the ball is kicked, the line judge drifts downfield, maintaining coverage of his sideline. By maintaining a position on the sideline, the deep officials are able to keep play boxed in.

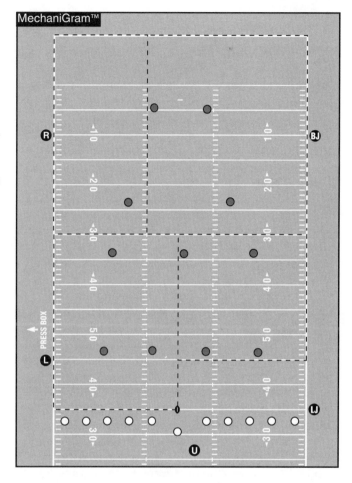

Back judge: Starting position is on the side of the field opposite the referee, directly across from the referee. When in position and ready for the kick, the back judge should raise an arm as a ready signal for the referee.

The back judge has coverage of the runner from the opposite hashmark to his sideline. By maintaining a position on the sideline, the deep officials are able to keep play boxed in.

On kicks to his side inside team R's five yardline, the back judge is responsible for determining whether the momentum exception applies and whether the kick is to be ruled a touchback. If the kick is toward the referee's side, the back judge is responsible for action in front of the deep receivers. If a touchback occurs, the back judge should move quickly toward the middle of the field to prevent late hits.

All officials: If the clock is not to start with the kick, the covering official signals the clock to start if he sees the ball is touched (other than first touching by team K).

All officials observe action in front of the runner when the runner is not in their general area.

ONSIDE KICKS

Although an onside kick is one of the oldest tricks used in football, its use is relatively rare. Crews may not see an onside kick more than once or twice each season. Because of the scarcity of its use, officials can get caught off-guard on a short free kick. Proper positioning in obvious onside kick situations will help prevent miscoverage of a seldom-used but critical play.

General procedures

In Federation, all officials except the umpire and back judge maintain their normal positions. The umpire moves to team R's free kick line while the back judge moves five yards downfield from the line judge. If the deepest receivers move closer to the spot of the kick, the referee may move forward accordingly.

The umpire, back judge, linesman and line judge should have their beanbags in hand to mark the spot if team K first touches the kick and should be prepared to blow the ball dead if a prone player from either team recovers the kick regardless of whether it has traveled 10 yards.

In NCAA, the decision to assume short free kick position is made by the referee. The linesman and umpire are positioned the same as for a conventional free kick. The back judge replaces the line judge on team K's restraining line; the line judge moves 10 yards upfield and across the field from the linesman. The referee moves into the center of the field and near the yardline of the deepest receiver.

If the kick travels to or beyond team R's 45 yardline, the line judge moves toward the ball and assumes his regular free kick responsibilities ahead of the runner in his area.

Alternate coverage

When a deliberate short kick is anticipated, a five-man crew has several options about where to place that extra crew member, all of which can be readily defended. If your association or assigning agency allows experimentation, here are some alternatives:

One choice is to put the line judge, linesman, umpire and back judge on the respective restraining lines. Such coverage should easily account for any kick touched by either team before the ball has traveled 10 yards.

A second choice would be to place the umpire near the sideline and about 20 yards from team K's restraining line, ordinarily near team R's 40 yardline. That would place an official in an ideal position to rule on kicks that elude team R's front line. Once the ball

moves past team R's free kick line only two issues need to be decided: Who possesses the ball, or who last touched it before it went out of bounds.

Because a kick going out of bounds should be marked with a beanbag (the flag indicating the foul should be tossed upward, not at the spot), and because first-touching by the kickers must also be designated, officials should have their beanbags at the ready, if not in their hands.

A third choice would be stationing the umpire in the middle of the field, about 10 to 15 yards behind team R's free kick line, once again, to rule on possession should the ball bounce or loop into that area. In such a case, the umpire could actually operate as a rover, moving to the exact spot of recovery.

The referee should probably remain near the goalline, because sometimes teams that look like they're going to dribble a short kick will instead pound a line drive downfield, hoping that a hard-to-handle ricochet will be recovered.

It is customary in onside kick situations for the kickoff to take place at the hashmark, with the bulk of kicking team players lined up on the open side of the field, to increase the pressure on receivers and to increase the odds for a kicking team recovery.

Sometimes, though, a kicking team will fake a kick toward the middle of the field and instead aim the kick at the lone player near the sideline, figuring that the receivers will bunch the opposite way and leave that area vulnerable. Officials must be alert for such a strategy.

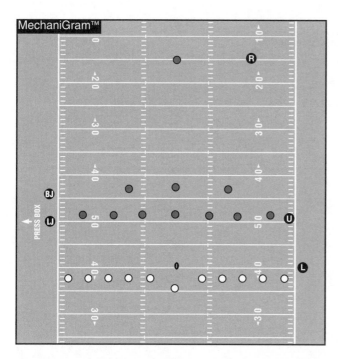

CHALK TALK: FEDERATION ONSIDE KICK POSITIONING

Referee: Starting position is on the side of the field on which the chains are stationed, near the hashmark on team R's 10 yardline.

Umpire: Starting position is on the same side of the field as the referee, on team R's free kick line. The umpire should have his beanbag in hand to mark the spot if team K first touches the kick and should be prepared to blow the ball dead if a prone player from either team recovers the kick regardless of whether it has traveled 10 yards.

Linesman: Starting position is on team R's restraining line. The linesman should have his beanbag in hand to mark the spot if team K first touches the kick and should be prepared to blow the ball dead if a prone player from either team recovers the kick regardless of whether it has traveled 10 yards.

Line judge: Starting position is on team K's restraining line. The line judge should have his beanbag in hand to mark the spot if team K first touches the kick and should be prepared to blow the ball dead if a prone player from either team recovers the kick regardless of whether it has traveled 10 yards.

Back judge: Starting position is on the side of the field opposite the referee, five yards downfield from the line judge. The back judge should be prepared to blow the ball dead if a prone player from either team recovers the kick regardless of whether it has traveled 10 yards.

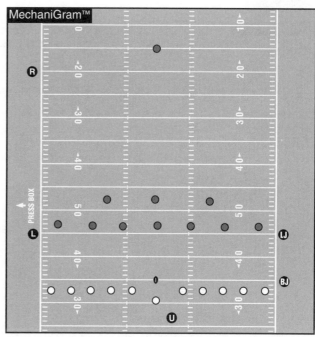

CHALK TALK: NCAA ONSIDE KICK POSITIONING

Referee: Starting position is on the side of the field on which the chains are stationed, in the center of the field and near the yardline of the deepest receiver.

Umpire: Starting position is behind the kicker.

Linesman: Starting position is on team R's restraining line, on the side of the field where the chains are location. The linesman should have his beanbag in hand to mark the spot if team K first touches the kick and should be prepared to blow the ball dead if a prone player from either team recovers the kick regardless of whether it has traveled 10 yards.

Line judge: Starting position is on team R's restraining line on the side of the field opposite the linesman. If the kick travels to or beyond team R's 45 yardline, the line judge moves toward the ball and assumes his regular free kick responsibilities ahead of the runner in his area.

Back judge: Starting position is on the side of the field opposite the referee, on team K's restraining line. The back judge should have his beanbag in hand to mark the spot if team K first touches the kick and should be prepared to blow the ball dead if a prone player from either team recovers the kick regardless of whether it has traveled 10 yards.

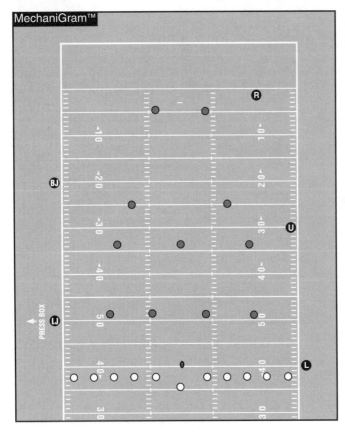

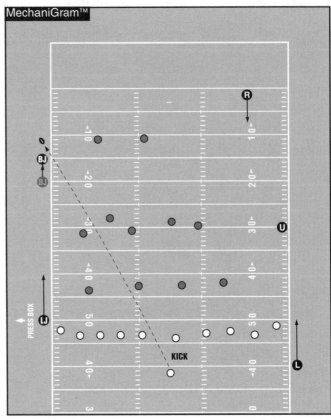

Action on the field: Starting positions.

Referee: Near team R's five or 10 yardline inside sideline on linesman's side of the field.

Umpire: At team R's 30 yardline on linesman's side of the field.

Linesman: On sideline at team K's restraining line on sideline with chains.

Line judge: On sideline opposite chains at team R's 20 yardline.

Back judge: On sideline opposite chains at team R's restraining line.

Action on the field: Ball kicked out of bounds in back judge's side zone.

Referee: Observes action in his area.

Umpire: Observes players in his area.

Linesman: Watches for infractions involving free kick line and contact involving players nearest him including kicker.

Line judge: Watches for infractions involving free kick line and contact involving players nearest him.

Back judge: Observes action in his area. Moves into position to judge which team caused kick to go out of bounds. Gives stop-the-clock signal when ball is out of bounds.

KEY

Referee	Umpire	Line Judge	Linesman	Back Judge	Chain Gang	Ballboy	Coach	Offense	Defense	Football	Possession of football

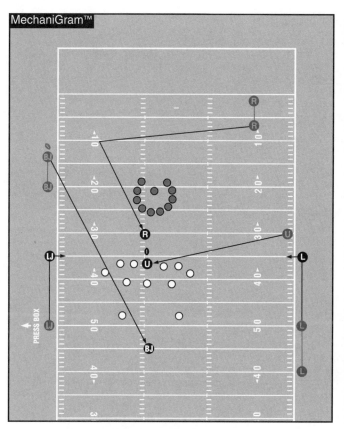

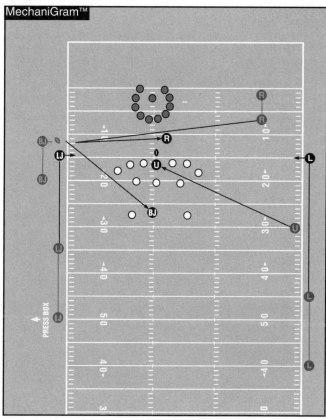

Action on the field: Team R chooses to take ball at its own 35 yardline.

Referee: Observes action in his area. Communicates result of play with back judge. Obtains choice from team R captain. Signals team K's foul and points toward team R's 35 yardline, where ball will next be put in play. (If team R chooses a rekick after enforcement, returns to position for rekick.)

Umpire: Observes action in his area. Moves to hashmark at team R's 35 yardline, to set ball for new series. (If team R chooses a rekick after enforcement, returns to position for rekick.)

Linesman: Observes action in his area. Moves to team R's 35 yardline, where team R will begin new series, assists chain crew in setting chains. (If team R chooses a rekick after enforcement, walks off penalty and returns to position for rekick.)

Line judge: Observes action in his area. Moves downfield to team R's 35 yardline, where new series will begin. (If team R chooses a rekick after enforcement, returns to position for rekick.)

Back judge: Observes action in his area. Communicates result of play with referee. Moves to position for start of new series.

Action on the field: Team R caused the ball to go out of bounds.

Referee: Observes action in his area. Communicates result of play with back judge. Signals new series will begin at spot where kick went out of bounds.

Umpire: Observes action in his area. Moves to hashmark where new series will begin and sets ball.

Linesman: Observes action in his area. Moves to spot where new series will begin and assists chain crew in setting chains.

Line judge: Observes action in his area. Moves downfield to spot where new series will begin.

Back judge: Communicates result of play with referee. Holds spot until umpire arrives at hashmark to set ball for new series. Moves to position for start of new series.

Movement	Previous position → Current position (stopped)	Previous position → Current position (still moving)	

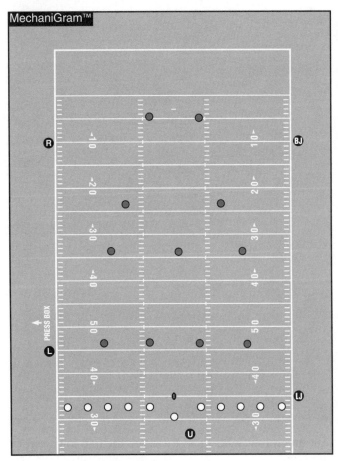

MechaniGram™ (left)

MechaniGram™ (right)

Action on the field: Starting positions.

Referee: On sideline opposite the back judge in front of the deepest receiver.

Umpire: In middle of the field behind kicker.

Linesman: On sideline at team R's restraining line on sideline with chains.

Line judge: On sideline at team K's restraining line on side opposite linesman.

Back judge: On sideline opposite the chains in front of the deepest receiver.

Action on the field: Ball kicked out of bounds in back judge's side zone.

Referee: Observes action in his area.

Umpire: Watches for infractions involving free kick line. When ball is kicked, gives start-the-clock signal if clock is to start with the kick. Observes contact involving kicker. .

Linesman: Watches for infractions involving free kick line and contact involving four team K players nearest him from the time ball is kicked until players reach team R's restraining line.

Line judge: Watches for infractions involving free kick line and contact involving four team K players nearest him from the time ball is kicked until players reach team R's restraining line.

Back judge: Observes action in his area. Moves into position to judge which team caused kick to go out of bounds. Gives stop-the-clock signal when ball is out of bounds.

KEY

Referee   Umpire   Line Judge   Linesman   Back Judge   Chain Gang   Ballboy   Coach   Offense   Defense   Football   Possession of football

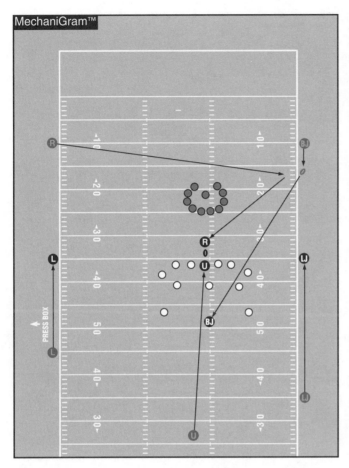

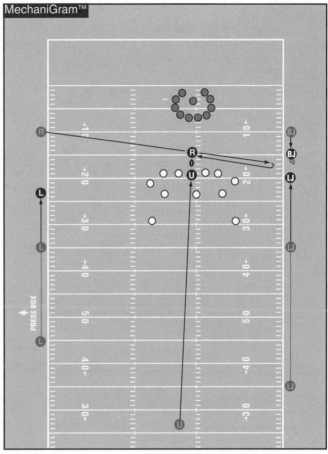

Action on the field: Team R chooses to take ball at its own 35 yardline.

Referee: Observes action in his area. Communicates result of play with back judge. Obtains choice from team R captain. Signals team K's foul and points toward team R's 35 yardline, where ball will next be put in play. (If team R chooses a rekick after enforcement, returns to position for rekick.)

Umpire: Observes action in his area. Moves to hashmark at team R's 35 yardline, to set ball for new series. (If team R chooses a rekick after enforcement, walks off penalty and returns to position for rekick.)

Linesman: Observes action in his area. Moves to team R's 35 yardline, where team R will begin new series, assists chain crew in setting chains. (If team R chooses a rekick after enforcement, returns to position for rekick.)

Line judge: Observes action in his area. Moves downfield to team R's 35 yardline, where new series will begin. (If team R chooses a rekick after enforcement, returns to position for rekick.)

Back judge: Observes action in his area. Communicates result of play with referee. Moves to position for start of new series.

Action on the field: Team R caused the ball to go out of bounds.

Referee: Observes action in his area. Communicates result of play with back judge. Signals new series will begin at spot where kick went out of bounds.

Umpire: Observes action in his area. Moves to hashmark where new series will begin and sets ball.

Linesman: Observes action in his area. Moves to spot where new series will begin and assists chain crew in setting chains.

Line judge: Observes action in his area. Moves downfield to spot where new series will begin.

Back judge: Communicates result of play with referee. Holds spot until umpire arrives at hashmark to set ball for new series. Moves to position for start of new series.

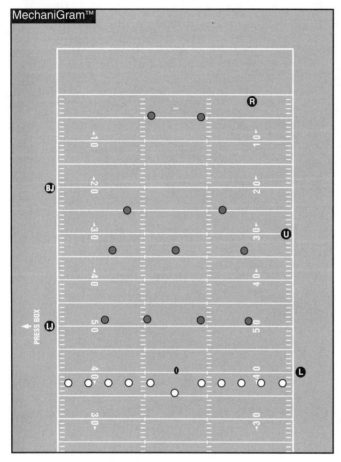

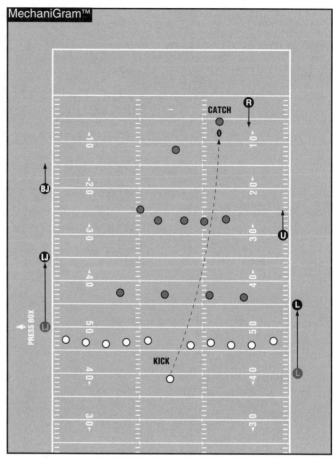

Action on the field: Starting positions.

Referee: Near team R's five or 10 yardline inside sideline on linesman's side of the field.

Umpire: At team R's 30 yardline on linesman's side of the field.

Linesman: On sideline at team K's restraining line on sideline with chains.

Line judge: On sideline opposite chains at team R's 20 yardline.

Back judge: On sideline opposite chains at team R's restraining line.

Action on the field: Receiver catches kick.

Referee: Observes catch. Signals clock to start when ball is caught by receiver. Moves to stay ahead of receiver and observes action of runner during return.

Umpire: Observes players in his area. Retreats slowly in case runner enters coverage area.

Linesman: Watches for infractions involving free kick line and contact involving players nearest him including kicker while moving downfield no farther than team R's 45 yardline.

Line judge: Watches for infractions involving free kick line and contact involving players nearest him while moving downfield no farther than team R's 45 yardline.

Back judge: Retreats slowly and observes action in his area.

KEY

R Referee	**U** Umpire	**LJ** Line Judge	**L** Linesman	**BJ** Back Judge	**CG** Chain Gang	**BB** Ballboy	**C** Coach	○ Offense	● Defense	▮ Football	⊗ Possession of football

MechaniGram™

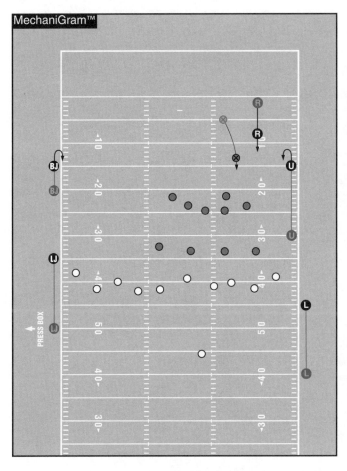

MechaniGram™

PRESS BOX

PRESS BOX

Action on the field: Runner advances.

Referee: Gives up coverage of runner to umpire. Observes action in front of runner (halo concept).

Umpire: Continues to move downfield. Takes coverage of runner when runner enters area (about team R's 15 yardline).

Linesman: Observes action in front of runner.

Line judge: Observes action in front of runner.

Back judge: Pivots and moves upfield with runner. Observes action in front of runner.

Action on the field: Runner continues advance and is downed.

Referee: Moves slowly downfield trailing runner. Observes players. When certain no penalty flags are down, signals new series for team R.

Umpire: Blows whistle and gives stop-the-clock signal when receiver is downed. Squares off and holds spot until back judge mirrors; spots ball for next down.

Linesman: Observes players. When referee signals possession for team R, instructs chain crew to set chains for new series.

Line judge: Observes players. Moves behind back judge, releasing him from spot, and mirrors spot until umpire sets ball.

Back judge: Observes players. Squares off and mirrors spot until umpire sets ball or back judge releases him.

Movement | Previous position Current position (stopped) | Previous position Current position (still moving)

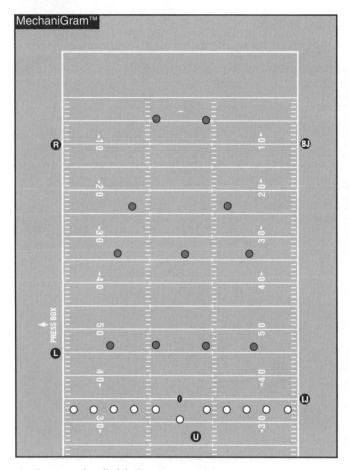

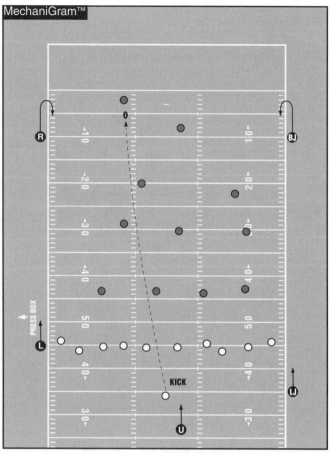

Action on the field: Starting positions.

Referee: On sideline opposite the back judge in front of the deepest receiver.

Umpire: In middle of the field behind kicker.

Linesman: On sideline at team R's restraining line on sideline with chains.

Line judge: On sideline at team K's restraining line on side opposite linesman.

Back judge: On sideline opposite the chains in front of the deepest receiver.

Action on the field: Receiver catches kick.

Referee: Observes catch. Signals clock to start when ball is caught by receiver if clock is to start on touching by team R. Moves to stay ahead of receiver and observes action of runner during return.

Umpire: Watches for infractions involving free kick line. When ball is kicked, gives start-the-clock signal if clock is to start with the kick. Observes contact involving kicker. Moves slowly downfield.

Linesman: Watches for infractions involving free kick line and contact involving four team K players nearest him from the time ball is kicked until players reach team R's restraining line. Moves slowly downfield.

Line judge: Watches for infractions involving free kick line and contact involving four team K players nearest him from the time ball is kicked until players reach team R's restraining line. Moves slowly downfield.

Back judge: Retreats slowly and observes action in his area.

KEY

 Referee Umpire Line Judge Linesman Back Judge Chain Gang Ballboy Coach ◯ Offense ⬤ Defense ◗ Football ⊗ Possession of football

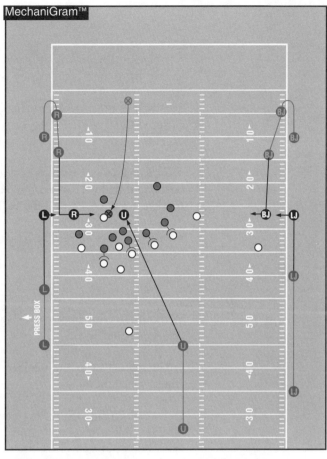

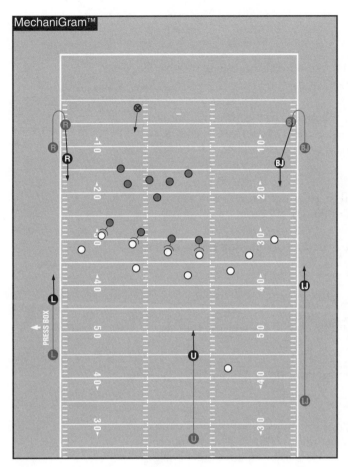

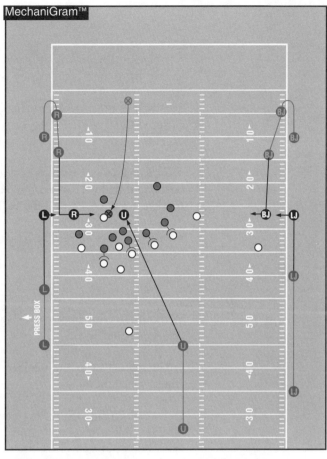

Action on the field: Runner advances.

Referee: Moves slowly upfield and observes runner and action around runner.

Umpire: Moves slowly downfield and observes action in front of runner.

Linesman: Moves slowly downfield and observes action in front of runner.

Line judge: Moves slowly downfield and observes action in front of runner.

Back judge: Moves slowly upfield and observes action in front of runner.

Action on the field: Runner advances and is downed.

Referee: Moves upfield. Sounds whistle and gives stop-the-clock signal when runner is downed. Observes players. Squares off and holds spot until umpire arrives to set ball. When certain no penalty flags are down, signals new series for team R.

Umpire: Moves downfield and observes players. Hustles to hashmark where ball will be put in play to start new series.

Linesman: Moves downfield and observes players. When referee signals possession for team R, instructs chain crew to set chains for new series.

Line judge: Moves downfield and observes players. Moves behind back judge, releasing him from spot, and mirrors spot until umpire sets ball.

Back judge: Moves upfield and observes players. Squares off and mirrors spot until umpire sets ball or back judge releases him.

• In obvious onside kick situations, the officials on the restraining lines should have their beanbags in their hands and ready to be dropped.

• Although the referee moves up when the deepest receiver moves closer to the free kick lines, he must be ready to retreat if team K executes a conventional kick instead of an onside kick.

• If a free kick goes out of bounds, the covering official should drop a beanbag if team R caused the ball to go out of bounds or a penalty marker if team K caused the ball to go out of bounds.

• Officials' eyes should be focused on the players, not on the ball in flight.

Quiz

Without referring back, you should be able to answer the following true-false questions.

1. The referee's starting position is on the side of the field on which the chains are stationed.

2. On kicks inside team R's five yardline in NCAA mechanics, the referee alone is responsible for determining whether the momentum exception applies and whether the kick is to be ruled a touchback.

3. In Federation mechanics, the line judge and linesman should never cover a kick beyond team R's 45 yardline.

4. The covering official should blow the ball dead if a prone player from either team recovers the kick regardless of whether it has traveled 10 yards.

5. In NCAA, the decision to assume short free kick position is made by the umpire.

1. True 2. False 3. True 4. True 5. False

Chapter 17

Plays from Scrimmage

In some ways a five-man crew can be looked upon as four-plus-one, because the wing officials remain essentially as they would if they were stationed in a four-man lineup. The back judge becomes an extra pair of eyes looking at things that weren't keenly noticed in a four-man crew (such as what wideouts and split receivers are up to when they filter into the defensive secondary). Of course a deep official is a virtual necessity on long plays such as passes or punts.

In many ways, though, a back judge can become an integral member of a unified quintet, operating as pure helper much of the time — on runs that end out of bounds runs, for instance — and functioning in synchrony with wing officials, as long as they are adept at communicating to the back judge what their coverages will be and what his are supposed to be.

When an offense spreads players across the field and uses an unbalanced line, the defense is forced to also spread forces. That gives offensive players favorable blocking angles, plus an opportunity to generate velocity in blocking. Velocity means that some players can get a running start before they encounter the person they are trying to knock out of the way. Significant pass route capabilities are also possible, because the potential receivers are already out there toward the sidelines, where they can speed downfield and execute a variety of routes in order to free themselves to catch passes.

Those are all the advantages in creating combinations of the attack, and those advantages are what officials must officiate. Teams do things to confuse defenders, and their moves sometimes confuse officials as well.

The important thing is that officials should recognize those things and make mental adjustments for anticipating plays; that means communicating with each other to assure proper coverage once the snap takes place.

Factors such as formation, game situation and player characteristics (i.e. right-handed or left-handed quarterback) will cause variations in positioning.

Referee: The referee's position is on the passing-arm side of the quarterback, approximately 10 to 12 yards deep in the offensive backfield and wide enough to see the opposite-side tackle and all of the backs. The referee is responsible for observing the huddle to ensure team A is not violating substitution rules, identifying eligible receivers in the backfield, observing shifts and watching for false starts and other pre-snap violations by the offense.

By keying on the opposite-side tackle, the referee can determine if the play is a run or pass. If the tackle fires out or pulls, the play is likely a run; if the tackle retreats, the play is likely a pass or draw.

On a running play, the referee focuses on the ball, the runner and the blocking around the runner. If the play goes to the opposite side, the referee should move toward or parallel to the line of the scrimmage and maintain a position approximately in line with the runner.

Overaggressiveness is not be avoided in case the play is a reverse. If the play is to the referee's side, the referee moves behind the play and is responsible for the runner until he crosses the neutral zone or turns upfield. The referee should watch the handoff or the pitchout, see the runner head outside the free clipping/free blocking zone, and watch to see that no one contacts the quarterback before drifting along to follow the play. He will not have much to observe besides the quarterback because little significant action is likely to take place behind the runner, and the runner himself is being watched by the appropriate wing official.

On passing plays, the referee observes blocking by the backs as the quarterback drops back. The referee should move to maintain the 10- to 12-yard distance between himself and the quarterback (e.g. if the quarterback drops back seven yards, the referee retreats seven yards).

Once the pass has been released, the referee shouts "Gone!" to help prevent roughing the passer but continues to observe the passer. By maintaining spacing between himself and the quarterback, the referee will widen his field of vision. The wider view allows the referee to determine if the pass is forward or backward (using the extended arm signal to indicate a backward pass) yet continue to focus attention on the passer. If the flight of the pass is altered because the passer's arm is hit by a defender, the referee must determine whether the resultant loose ball is a forward pass or a fumble. If the referee rules the play to be an incomplete pass, he must blow his whistle and signal emphatically. If the play results in a fumble, the referee must beanbag the spot where possession was lost and continue officiating.

The referee is also responsible for ruling on intentional grounding and can work with the umpire to determine whether a passer was beyond the line of scrimmage when the pass was thrown. The referee should move to the spot of the pass and observe the location of the passer's feet. If the passer is clearly beyond the line, a penalty marker should be dropped. In cases that are too close for an immediate determination, a beanbag should be dropped. At the end of the play, the referee can compare the spot of the beanbag and the location of the down box in order to make the call.

On runs that end out of bounds behind the neutral zone, the referee is responsible for marking the spot. He also must beanbag the spot of a muff, fumble or quarterback sack in the offensive backfield.

Although the CCA manual dictates that the back judge times the game as well as the 25-second clock when there is no visible 25-second clock, *Referee* recommends that the referee handle the 25-second clock. Even with a multiple-mode watch, it would be difficult to expect one man to handle both of those chores.

Umpire: Until the referee blows the ready for play signal, the umpire should stand with his feet straddling the ball.

After the signal, the umpire moves to a position three to eight yards behind team B's line and between the defensive ends. The CCA manual advises the umpire to line up on the side opposite the tight end. *Referee* recommends that position because it decreases the number of players who will charge off the line toward the umpire. The position should be varied so that the umpire does not limit the movement or vision of the linebackers or defensive backs.

The umpire must be able to see the ball from the time the snapper handles the ball until the time it is snapped and is responsible for ensuring that team A has five players numbered 50 to 79 on the offensive line. The umpire should listen for defenders interfering with the offense's snap count. Umpires also help count the offense. Umpires definitely should relay information about the down and distance to fellow crew members; identify the offensive formation; observe the snapper for snap infractions and look for false starts by offensive linemen.

It is crucial for umpires to determine the point of attack because of the potential for holding, chop blocks and other fouls. The umpire must read the interior line because the screen of defenders and the offensive line will prevent his getting a good look at backfield players. He shouldn't look at backfield people anyway, because his responsibility at the snap is to judge the legality of play at the line of scrimmage. Stand-up blocking will tell him that a pass or draw is forthcoming.

The umpire must then observe the blocking to find the point of attack. For example, if the right tackle blocks down (to his right) and the center joins the right guard on a double-team block taking their man to their left, the point of attack most likely is the gap between the tackle and guard. When the hole opens, the umpire should move away from it (to avoid interfering with the defensive pursuit) and laterally (thus turning his head toward the blockers in front of the runner and the tackling efforts of the defense).

The most challenging play for the umpire is one on which the point of attack is aimed at him. An umpire who is lazy or is not paying attention can find himself inadvertently making the tackle, accidentally throwing a block or becoming sandwiched between opposing players. Not only is that poor officiating, it's dangerous.

Referee recommends that umpires blow their whistles only when they see the runner's knees have touched the ground and that he is still in possession of the ball. The collegiate manual also specifies the umpire should take the progress spot from the nearest wing official, a practice *Referee* strongly endorses. Because the umpire is parallel rather than perpendicular to the play, the umpire's position makes it next to impossible to determine the spot. The umpire should get the spot from the covering wing official (or, when the situation dictates, from the referee).

Plays that end in a side zone may require the umpire to move outside the hashmark and toward the sideline in order to clean up behind the play. When play swings around to one side, the umpire should turn his attention to the blocking ahead of the runner and should prepare to cross outside the hashmark if the runner is downed in the side zone near the sideline. The umpire can help get the ball back to the hashmark and set it at the progress spot. He should not automatically halt at the hash and rely on other officials to get him the ball.

On pass plays, the umpire must step up and reach the line of scrimmage. That takes the umpire out of short pass routes and puts him in a position to judge ineligibles downfield and passes thrown from beyond the line of scrimmage.

If a pass is first touched by a team B player, the umpire gives the tipped ball signal; that lets the other officials know that pass interference restrictions are lifted. If a forward pass is caught, touched, batted, muffed or strikes an ineligible team A player, the umpire must know whether the action occurred behind or beyond the neutral zone for purposes of penalty enforcement.

When the pass is thrown, the umpire pivots to follow the flight of the ball. The umpire has catch/trap responsibility if the receiver is facing the umpire.

The umpire should have one rubber band-type of device on each hand. One is for keeping track of downs; the other is for keeping of track of the position of the ball relative to the hashmarks. That will help the umpire return to the correct previous spot after an incomplete pass or penalty. If, for instance, the umpire uses his right hand to determine ball position, the thumb indicates the ball was last snapped from the left hash; index finger, between the left upright and the left hash; middle finger, middle of the field; ring finger, between the right upright and the right hash; and pinkie, right hash.

Linesman and line judge: The linesman and line judge straddle the line of scrimmage on their respective side of the field. The Federation manual dictates that, except in goalline or short-yardage situations, neither should be closer than nine yards outside the widest offensive player. The CCA manual places the wingmen at least seven yards outside the widest offensive player and never inside the top of the numbers. *Referee* recommends a compromise between the manuals. Working on the sideline is strongly encouraged because it affords a wide-angle view of the action and prevents the official from interfering in the play. In short-yardage (e.g. fourth down and a half-yard to go) or goalline situations (when the ball is snapped at or inside team B's eight yardline), the wings may choose to "pinch" the ends. However, even when pinching, a wing official should never allow a team A player to get behind him.

Before the snap, the wing officials identify the eligible receivers on their side of the field, assist the referee in monitoring substitutions, count to ensure team A has at least seven players on the line of scrimmage and assist the umpire in checking the legality of uniform numbers of offensive linemen and receivers. If the receiver nearest the official is in the offensive backfield, the wing uses the extended arm signal to alert the opposite wing. Legality of motion is always the responsibility of the official away from whom the player is moving, even if the player reverses his motion. Obvious infractions should be flagged by either official regardless of which way the motion man is moving.

The wing officials' keys vary. But looking through receivers to the tackles allows the linesman and line judge to ascertain if the play is a run or pass. Be alert for illegal crackback blocks, especially by motion men.

Because they will mark forward progress the vast majority of the time, the line judge and linesman must be especially alert for quick-hitting running plays into the line. On runs to the opposite side of the field, the off wing must clean up after the play but be careful not to venture too far into the middle of the field in case team A runs a reverse or a fumble forces the flow of the play back toward the off wing.

Another major blunder occurs when a wing official reacts too slowly to a run to his side of the field and is unable to stay out of the way of the action (or worse, turns his back to the action). If that happens, *Referee* recommends that the covering wing back up to the sideline (beyond if necessary) and toward the offensive backfield, then turn and follow the play as it flows downfield.

The covering wing official is responsible for team B's goalline when the ball is snapped at or inside team B's 10 yardline; goalline coverage outside team B's 10 yardline is the responsibility of the back judge. The wing officials should communicate with the back judge to confirm the transfer of goalline coverage.

Pass coverage for the wing officials is made easier by the presence of the back judge. With a fifth official deep in the defensive backfield, the wings are able to concentrate on the short and intermediate pass routes.

After identifying the eligible receivers before the snap, the wing officials watch initial contact between receivers and defenders. Remember that interference restrictions for team A begin at the snap; for team B, the restrictions begin when the pass is in the air. Be especially alert for pick plays when receivers run short crossing patterns.

The wingmen have to follow receivers downfield. When a wing official sees receivers move purposefully off the line of scrimmage, he must trace their paths visually, making sure to see any defenders' contact against the receivers, reading the routes so as to get to the place where the pass arrives and making sure the receivers do not block downfield. But the deep officials also have to know for sure that the play is really a pass.

Therefore, wing officials should look back at some point to see if a passer is truly setting up to pass. They should do this after traveling no more than five to 10 yards downfield (about two seconds into the play). They should look back only if receivers are running free, i.e., not being bumped by

defenders. If contact by defenders is imminent, the wing officials should look at that before checking the offensive backfield to see about the quarterback and his intentions.

On quick passes in the flat, the wings must be ready to rule if the pass is forward or backward. If the pass is backward and is caught, the extended arm signal is directed toward the offensive backfield. If the pass is backward and muffed, the covering official must drop a beanbag at the spot of the muff, but no signal is given. No signal is needed if a forward pass is complete, but an incomplete forward pass should be signaled as such.

If the play is not a screen or a similar short pass, the wing official should drift cautiously five to seven yards downfield, maintaining a position about halfway between the line of scrimmage and the deepest receiver on his side. If the pass is to the wing's coverage area, the wing official must move quickly to get the best possible angle to observe the attempted catch. If the receiver's back is to the official, preventing a good look, eye contact with the official who has a clearer view is crucial. The official with the unobstructed view should then make the call. *Referee* recommendation: when in doubt, a pass is incomplete.

On pass plays near the sidelines, wing officials have a better chance of determining whether or not a receiver has made a catch if their focus is parallel with the line rather than perpendicular to it. By maintaining a look parallel with the sideline, the official can see if the receiver keeps a foot inbounds and whether or not the receiver controlled the pass. The technique is called "looking down the gun barrel." Watch the receiver's feet first; if the player has been unable to get one foot inbounds before going out of bounds (a technique known as "dotting the i"), it doesn't matter if the receiver secured control of the pass because the pass will be ruled incomplete. In order to get that look, the official must avoid being too close to the action. Maintaining proper distance will allow the official to see the feet first, then the ball, with a minimum of head movement.

The Federation does not authorize the official to use supplementary signals such as the pass juggled (hands palm up and alternately moved up and down) or the possession gained out of bounds signal (sweeping motion with both arms) to indicate why the pass was incomplete. Use those signals only if your association or assigning agency allows their use.

Wing officials have responsibility for the passer if he scrambles past the line of scrimmage. They must be especially alert if the passer heads for the sideline. If the quarterback is tackled out of bounds the wing official must rule on the legality of the contact. Dead-ball officiating is especially important if the tackle is made in the team area. If the runner is driven out of bounds less than five yards past the scrimmage line, the covering wing official can handle the play and supervise players outside the sideline after marking the out of bounds spot with a beanbag.

When a play is more than a five-yard gain and the runner heads across the sideline, the covering wing official marks the spot while keeping an eye on players; the referee or back judge must hustle to the spot and escort the players back to the field.

Back judge: The back judge's starting is position is 15 to 20 yards past the line of scrimmage (NCAA: 18 to 22 yards) and always deeper than the deepest defender. Width varies on ball position and offensive formation (See Chapter 12, Keys). If back judges can cover ground swiftly, playing deeper than the manuals prescribe is not a detriment. As a general rule, it is better to be separated from players a considerable distance at the start of plays than it is to be too close.

The back judge is responsible for the 25-second count, whether or not a visible 25-second clock is used. The CCA manual mandates that the back judge also time the game; the Federation makes that duty mandatory only where there is no field clock. *Referee* recommends having the back judge time the game as a back up in case the stadium clock malfunctions, but even with a multiple-mode watch, it would be difficult to expect one man to handle both of those chores. Therefore, *Referee* recommends that the referee handle the 25-second clock.

When the ball is snapped, the back judge keys on the tight end or the end on the strong side if the formation does not include a tight end. Because he is an eligible receiver, the end will likely move forward whether the play is a pass or a run. A quick glance at the tackle next to the end will allow the back judge to discern pass or run.

Offenses do not always run to the strong side of the formation. Therefore, it is vital that the back judge be mobile enough to keep the runner between himself and either wing official (if the play goes outside the tackles) or the umpire (on runs between the tackles).

When the run ends in a loss of yardage or a minimal gain, the back judge moves toward the line of scrimmage and observes the actions of players — especially those away from the pile. Known as "the accordion" because of the movement toward, then away from, the line, that movement by the back judge acts as a deterrent to dead-ball fouls.

The back judge has a large role to play on wide running plays. It is important for the back judge to determine whether the play is a run or a pass, because then he'll see those blocks by the split end and slotback, and he'll be able to establish their legality. The slotback is a prime candidate for throwing an illegal crackback block.

After the back judge notes interior blocking, his sequence of viewing should take his concentration toward the blocking ahead of the runner, or to the runner himself if the runner should advance more than 10 yards downfield.

When a play is more than a five-yard gain and the runner heads across the sideline, the back judge should

sweep out of bounds to protect players, with the covering wing official retaining a spot but also keeping an eye on players. On a play gaining considerably more than 10 yards, the wing official maintains the spot while the back judge escorts the players who went out of bounds back to the field. If a confrontation between opponents occurs, the wing may drop a beanbag to mark the spot and assist the back judge in separating the players.

The back judge is responsible for team B's goalline until the ball is snapped at or inside team B's 10 yardline; goalline coverage then is the responsibility of the covering wing official. When the ball is snapped at or inside team B's 10 yardline, the back judge's starting position is on the endline. The wing officials should communicate with the back judge to confirm the transfer of goalline coverage.

On pass plays, the back judge must retreat far enough so he is always deeper than the deepest receiver. In order to do that, the back judge may have to turn his attention away from his key and concentrate on the receivers running deeper patterns. The mechanic is comparable to a defense switching from man-to-man to zone coverage.

When the pass in flight, the back judge must quickly determine the intended receiver and get into the best possible position to observe the play. Both the offensive and defensive players must be observed for possible interference.

The Federation does not authorize the official to use supplementary signals such as the pass juggled (hands palm up and alternately moved up and down) or the possession gained out of bounds signal (sweeping motion with both arms) to indicate why the pass was incomplete. Use those signals only if your association or assigning agency allows their use.

More on pass coverage
Except for sideline receptions on curl and buttonhook passes, wherein one individual must pass judgment, all pass reception situations require the judgment of two or more officials (back judge, umpire and sometimes even the opposite wing). That means officials should make momentary eye contact with one another when a pass is thrown to the center of the field, to be sure of agreement on incompletions and receptions and to help one another with interference calls. The customary approach is for any official who sees an incompletion to signal immediately and vigorously, particularly if the call needs to be sold. Any official who wishes to wave off a pass does not need to look at (or consult) fellow officials. The inquisitive look between downfield officials on an apparent pass reception is only for affirmation.

Interference is different. You throw your flag and ask questions later. "Do you have defensive interference? I've got offensive interference!" Officials must talk things out before reporting to the referee if two flags are tossed on the play.

Referee: Starting position is on the passing-arm side of the quarterback, approximately 10 to 12 yards deep and at least as wide as the tight end. The referee is responsible for observing the huddle to ensure team A is not violating substitution rules, identifying eligible receivers in the backfield, observing shifts and watching for false starts and other pre-snap violations by the offense.

On a running play, the referee focuses on the ball, the runner and the blocking around the runner. If the play goes to the opposite side, the referee should move toward or parallel to the line of the scrimmage and maintain a position approximately in line with the runner. If the play is to the referee's side, the referee moves behind the play and is responsible for the runner until he crosses the neutral zone or turns upfield. The referee should watch the handoff or the pitchout, see the runner head outside the free clipping/free blocking zone, and watch to see that no one contacts the quarterback before drifting along to follow the play.

On passing plays, the referee initially observes blocking by the backs as the quarterback drops back. The referee should move to maintain the 10- to 12-yard distance between himself and the quarterback (e.g. if the quarterback drops back seven yards, the referee retreats seven yards).

The referee is also responsible for ruling on intentional grounding and can work with the umpire to determine whether a passer was beyond the line of scrimmage when the pass was thrown. The referee should move to the spot of the pass and observe the location of the passer's feet. If the passer is clearly beyond the line, a penalty marker should be dropped. In cases that are too close for an immediate determination, a beanbag should be dropped. At the end of the play, the referee can compare the spot of the beanbag and the location of the down box in order to make the call.

On runs that end out of bounds behind the neutral zone, the referee is responsible for marking the spot. He also must beanbag the spot of a muff or fumble and may have to beanbag a quarterback sack in the offensive backfield.

Umpire: Starting position is three to eight yards behind team B's line and between the defensive ends (NCAA: approximately a yard behind and to the side of or between the linebackers). The umpire must be able to see the ball from the time the snapper handles the ball until the time it is snapped and is responsible for ensuring that team A has five players numbered 50 to 79 on the offensive line. The umpire should listen for defenders interfering with the offense's snap count. observe the snapper for snap infractions and observe the guards for false starts.

The umpire must observe the blocking to find the point of attack. When the hole opens, the umpire should move away from it (to avoid interfering with the defensive pursuit) and laterally (thus turning his head toward the blockers in front of the runner and the tackling efforts of the defense).

Plays that end in a side zone may require the umpire to move outside the hashmark and toward the sideline in order to clean up behind the play. When play swings around to one side, the umpire should turn his attention to the blocking ahead of the runner and should prepare to cross outside the hashmark if the runner is downed in the side zone near the sideline. The umpire can help get the ball back to the hashmark and set it at the progress spot. He should not automatically halt at the hash and rely on other officials to get him the ball.

On pass plays, the umpire must step up and reach the line of scrimmage. If a pass is first touched by a team B player, the umpire gives the tipped ball signal. When the pass is thrown, the umpire pivots to follow the flight of the ball. The umpire has catch/trap responsibility if the receiver is facing the umpire.

The umpire can work with the referee to determine if the passer was beyond the line of scrimmage when the pass was thrown. The umpire should move to the spot of the pass and observe the location of the passer's feet. If the passer is clearly beyond the line, a penalty marker should be dropped. In cases that are too close for an immediate determination, a beanbag should be dropped. At the end of the play, the referee can compare the spot of the beanbag and the location of the down box in order to make the call.

Linesman and line judge: Starting position is straddling the line of scrimmage not closer than nine yards (NCAA: at least seven yards) outside the widest offensive player. Working on the sideline is strongly encouraged.

Before the snap, the wing officials identify the eligible receivers on their side of the field, assist the referee in monitoring substitutions, count to ensure team A has at least seven players on the line of scrimmage and assist the umpire in checking the legality of uniform numbers of offensive linemen and receivers. If the receiver nearest the official is in the offensive backfield, the wing uses the extended arm signal to alert the opposite wing.

On runs to the opposite side of the field, the off wing must clean up after the play but be careful not to venture too far into the middle of the field in case team A runs a reverse or a fumble forces the flow of the play back toward the off wing.

The covering wing official is responsible for team B's goalline when the ball is snapped at or inside team B's 10 yardline; goalline coverage outside team B's 10 yardline is the responsibility of the back judge. The wing officials should communicate with the back judge to confirm the transfer of goalline coverage.

On passes, the wing officials watch initial contact between receivers and defenders. The wingmen have to

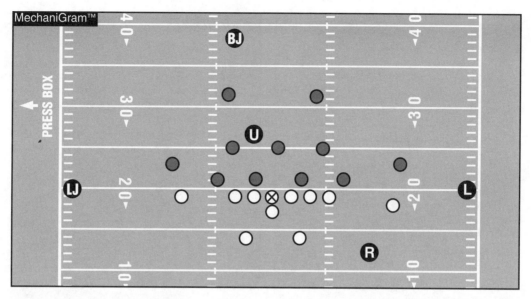

follow receivers downfield; the wing should use a shuffle step because it allows the official to watch the action without looking over a shoulder. After traveling no more than five to 10 yards downfield (about two seconds into the play), wing officials should look to see if a passer is truly setting up to pass.

On quick passes in the flat, the wings must be ready to rule if the pass is forward or backward. If the play is not a screen or a similar short pass, the wing official should shuffle step cautiously five to seven yards downfield, maintaining a position about halfway between the line of scrimmage and the deepest receiver on his side. If the pass is to the wing's coverage area, the wing official must move quickly to get the best possible angle to observe the attempted catch.

Wing officials have responsibility for the passer if he scrambles past the line of scrimmage. They must be especially alert if the passer heads for the sideline. If the quarterback is tackled out of bounds the wing official must rule on the legality of the contact. If the runner is driven out of bounds less than five yards past the scrimmage line, the covering wing official can handle the play and supervise players outside the sideline after marking the out of bounds spot with a beanbag. When a play is more than a five-yard gain and the runner heads across the sideline, the covering wing official marks the spot while keeping an eye on players; the referee or back judge must hustle to the spot and escort the players back to the field.

A play gaining considerably more than 10 yards may find the covering wing official policing activity past the sidelines. The covering wing official and the back judge should work together to be sure the ball is properly spotted and off-the-field activity is monitored.

Back judge: Starting position is favoring the strong side of the formation, 15 to 20 yards (NCAA: 18 to 22 yards) beyond the line of scrimmage and deeper than the deepest defender. The back judge is responsible for the 25-second clock, whether or not a visible clock is used.

When the ball is snapped, the back judge keys on the tight end or the end on the strong side if the formation does not include a tight end.

When the run ends in a loss of yardage or a minimal gain, the back judge moves toward the line of scrimmage and observes the actions of players — especially those away from the pile.

On wide running plays, it is important for the back judge to determine whether the play is a run or a pass and observer blocks by the split end and slotback. After noting interior blocking, the back judge observes blocking ahead of the runner, or to the runner himself if the runner advances more than 10 yards downfield.

When a play is more than a five-yard gain and the runner heads across the sideline, the back judge should sweep out of bounds to protect players. A play gaining considerably more than 10 yards may find the back judge covering the out-of-bounds spot, with the covering wing official policing activity past the sidelines.

On pass plays, the back judge must retreat far enough so he is always deeper than the deepest receiver. When the pass in flight, the back judge must quickly determine the intended receiver and get into the best possible position to observe the play. Both the offensive and defensive players must be observed for possible interference.

The back judge is responsible for team B's goalline until the ball is snapped at or inside team B's 10 yardline; goalline coverage then is the responsibility of the covering wing official. When the ball is snapped at or inside team B's 10 yardline, the back judge's starting position is on the endline. The wing officials should communicate with the back judge to confirm the transfer of goalline coverage.

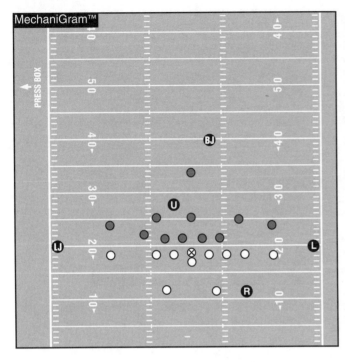

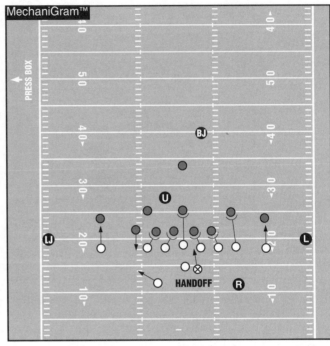

Action on the field: Starting position.

Referee: On the passing-arm side of the quarterback, approximately 10 to 12 yards deep and at least as wide as the tight end.

Umpire: Three to eight yards behind team B's line and between the defensive ends (NCAA: approximately a yard behind and to the side of or between the linebackers).

Linesman: Straddles the line of scrimmage not closer than nine yards (NCAA: at least seven yards) outside the widest offensive player.

Line judge: Straddles the line of scrimmage not closer than nine yards (NCAA: at least seven yards) outside the widest offensive player.

Back judge: Favoring the strong side of the formation, 15 to 20 yards (NCAA: 18 to 22 yards) beyond the line of scrimmage and deeper than the deepest defender.

Action on the field: Handoff to a back.

Referee: Reads blocking of left tackle and reads run. Observes handoff and action around quarterback after handoff.

Umpire: Reads blocking of center and right guard and reads run. Determines point of attack and observes blocking there.

Linesman: Reads blocking of right tackle and reads run. Observes blocking.

Line judge: Reads blocking of left tackle and reads run. Observes blocking.

Back judge: Reads blocking of tight end and reads run. Observes blocking.

KEY

| |  | | | | | |

R Referee **U** Umpire **LJ** Line Judge **L** Linesman **BJ** Back Judge **CG** Chain Gang **BB** Ballboy **C** Coach ○ Offense ● Defense Football ⊗ Possession of football

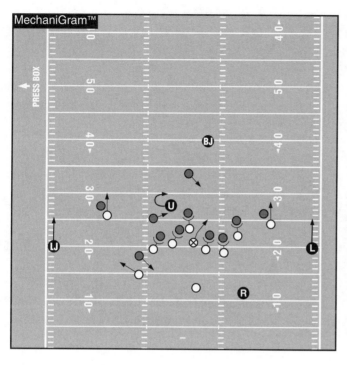

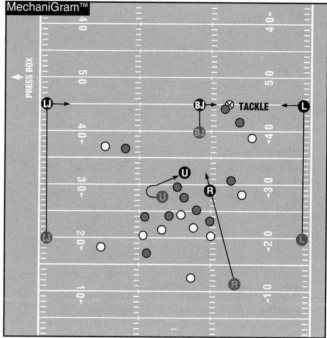

Action on the field: Runner advances.

Referee: Moves slowly downfield and observes action behind runner.

Umpire: Steps back to avoid interfering with play and pivots to observe play. Observes action around runner.

Linesman: Moves slowly downfield and observes action in front of runner.

Line judge: Moves slowly downfield and observes action in front of runner.

Back judge: Observes action in front of runner.

Action on the field: Runner continues advance and is downed.

Referee: Moves slowly downfield and observes players behind the ball in his area. If first down has been achieved and no penalty markers are down, signals linesman to have chain crew move the chains.

Umpire: Moves downfield and observes action behind runner. Observes players in his area.

Linesman: Moves quickly downfield and observes action around runner until runner enters back judge's coverage area. Observes players. Squares off to mark spot of forward progress. If first down has been achieved, gets signal from referee and instructs chain crew to move to spot. Assists chain crew in setting chains for new series.

Line judge: Observes action in front of runner on his side of the field. Squares off to mirror spot of forward progress. Observes players in his area.

Back judge: Moves into position to observe runner when runner enters coverage area. Blows whistle when runner is downed. (If first down is achieved, also gives stop-the-clock signal.) Squares off to mark spot of forward progress. Observes players. Maintains spot until linesman arrives to mirror spot.

Movement	Previous position Current position (stopped)	Previous position Current position (still moving)	

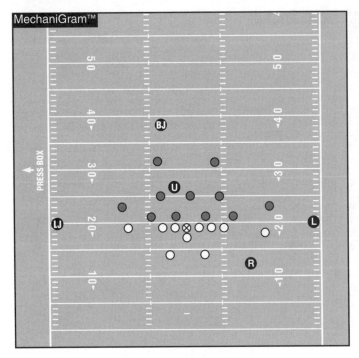

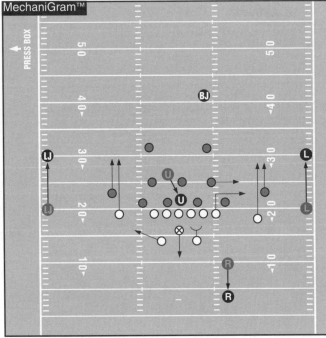

Action on the field: Starting position.

Referee: On the passing-arm side of the quarterback, approximately 10 to 12 yards deep and at least as wide as the tight end.

Umpire: Three to eight yards behind team B's line and between the defensive ends (NCAA: approximately a yard behind and to the side of or between the linebackers).

Linesman: Straddles the line of scrimmage not closer than nine yards (NCAA: at least seven yards) outside the widest offensive player.

Line judge: Straddles the line of scrimmage not closer than nine yards (NCAA: at least seven yards) outside the widest offensive player.

Back judge: Favoring the strong side of the formation, 15 to 20 yards (NCAA: 18 to 22 yards) beyond the line of scrimmage and deeper than the deepest defender.

Action on the field: Quarterback drops back.

Referee: Keys on opposite-side tackle; reads pass when tackle retreats. As quarterback drops back, moves back to maintain distance between himself and quarterback. Observes blocking by backs.

Umpire: Observes presnap adjustments and legality of snap. Keys on center and guards; reads pass when linemen retreat. Steps up to the line of scrimmage and observes blocking.

Linesman: Identifies the eligible receivers on his side of the field. Uses extended arm signal to alert line judge that end is in offensive backfield. After snap, observes initial blocking, then moves slowly downfield and watches initial contact between receivers and defenders.

Line judge: Identifies the eligible receivers on his side of the field. After snap, observes initial blocking, then moves slowly downfield and watches initial contact between receivers and defenders.

Back judge: Keys on tight end and tackle; reads pass when tackle retreats. As receivers move downfield, moves back to maintain distance between himself and receivers. Watches initial contact between receivers and defenders.

KEY

| **R** Referee | **U** Umpire | **LJ** Line Judge | **L** Linesman | **BJ** Back Judge | **CG** Chain Gang | **BB** Ballboy | **C** Coach | ○ Offense | ● Defense | Football | ⊗ Possession of football |

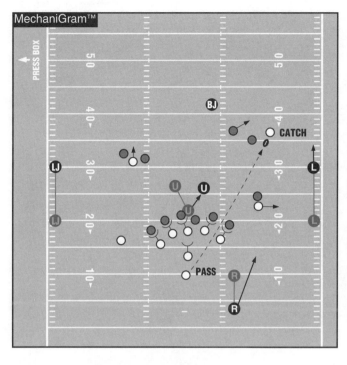

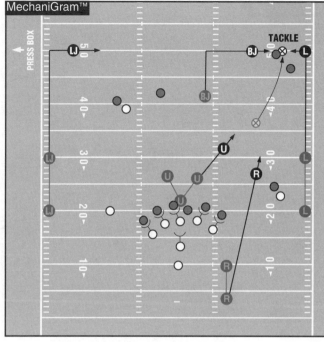

Action on the field: Pass thrown to and caught by receiver.

Referee: Observes passer. Moves downfield with flow of play.

Umpire: Pivots to follow flight and moves in direction of the ball.

Linesman: Moves downfield and maintains position about halfway between line of scrimmage and deepest receiver on his side, then moves quickly to get angle to observe attempted catch.

Line judge: Moves downfield and maintains position about halfway between line of scrimmage and deepest receiver on his side.

Back judge: Determines intended receiver and pivots to get angle and observe attempted catch.

Action on the field: Runner advances and is downed.

Referee: Moves slowly downfield and observes players in front of the ball.

Umpire: Moves slowly downfield and observes players in front of the ball. Once spot is established, hustles to hashmark to set ball for next down.

Linesman: Continues to move downfield. Blows whistle when receiver is downed. Squares off to mark spot of forward progress. Stops clock if first down has been achieved.

Line judge: Moves downfield and observes players behind the ball in his area. Practices dead-ball officiating.

Back judge: Moves downfield and observes players in his area. Squares off to mark spot of forward progress. Echoes stop-the-clock signal if first down has been achieved.

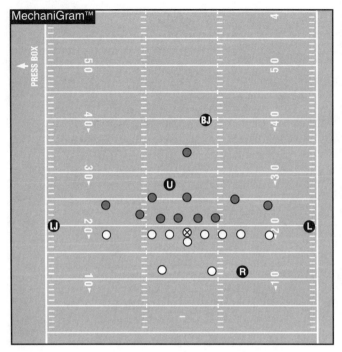

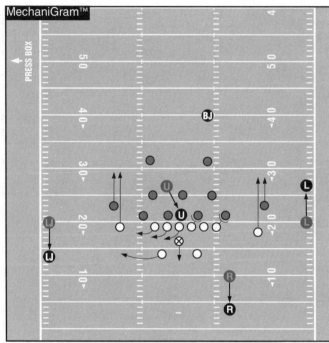

Action on the field: Starting position.

Referee: On the passing-arm side of the quarterback, approximately 10 to 12 yards deep and at least as wide as the tight end.

Umpire: Three to eight yards behind team B's line and between the defensive ends (NCAA: approximately a yard behind and to the side of or between the linebackers).

Linesman: Straddles the line of scrimmage not closer than nine yards (NCAA: at least seven yards) outside the widest offensive player.

Line judge: Straddles the line of scrimmage not closer than nine yards (NCAA: at least seven yards) outside the widest offensive player.

Back judge: Favoring the strong side of the formation, 15 to 20 yards (NCAA: 18 to 22 yards) beyond the line of scrimmage and deeper than the deepest defender.

Action on the field: Quarterback drops back.

Referee: Keys on opposite-side tackle; reads screen or draw when tackle pulls. As quarterback drops back, moves back to maintain distance between himself and quarterback. Observes blocking by backs.

Umpire: Observes presnap adjustments and legality of snap. Keys on center and guards; reads screen or draw when linemen pull. Steps up to the line of scrimmage and observes blocking.

Linesman: Identifies the eligible receivers on his side of the field. Uses extended arm signal to alert line judge that end is in offensive backfield. After snap, observes initial blocking, then uses shuffle step to move slowly downfield. Watches initial contact between receivers and defenders.

Line judge: Identifies the eligible receivers on his side of the field. After snap, observes initial blocking; reads screen or draw when tackle pulls. Moves into offensive backfield to cover receiver out of backfield.

Back judge: Keys on tight end and tackle; reads run when tackle fires out.

KEY

 Referee Umpire Line Judge Linesman Back Judge Chain Gang Ballboy Coach ○ Offense ● Defense Football Possession of football

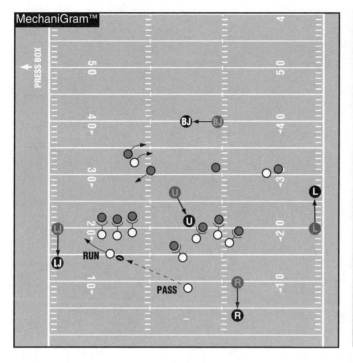

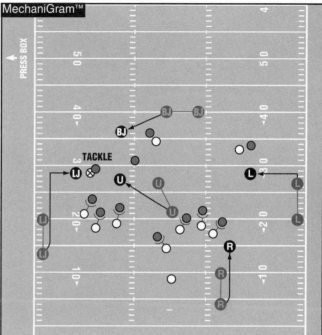

Action on the field: Pass thrown to and caught by back.

Referee: Observes passer. Looks to line judge for either backward pass signal, incomplete pass signal or no signal (complete forward pass).

Umpire: Observes blocking.

Linesman: Moves downfield and observes action of players in his area.

Line judge: Rules on whether pass is backward or forward (punches pass if backward). Observes action in front of runner.

Back judge: When position of ball is established, moves toward line judge's sideline and observes action in front of runner.

Action on the field: Runner advances and is downed.

Referee: Moves slowly downfield and observes players in his area.

Umpire: Pivots toward play and moves slowly downfield. Observes players in front of the ball. Moves to hashmark to set ball for next play.

Linesman: Moves downfield and observes players in his area. Squares off to mark spot of forward progress.

Line judge: Blows whistle when receiver is downed. Squares off to mark spot of forward progress. Stops clock if first down has been achieved.

Back judge: Moves toward play and observes players around pile.

Movement | Previous position | Current position (stopped) | Previous position | Current position (still moving)

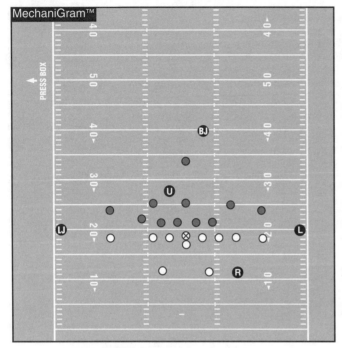

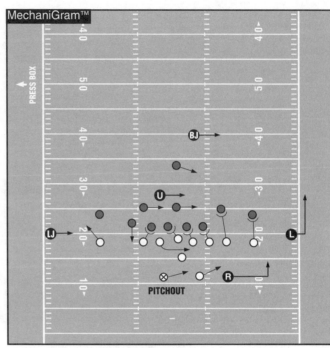

Action on the field: Starting position.

Referee: On the passing-arm side of the quarterback, approximately 10 to 12 yards deep and at least as wide as the tight end.

Umpire: Three to eight yards behind team B's line and between the defensive ends (NCAA: approximately a yard behind and to the side of or between the linebackers).

Linesman: Straddles the line of scrimmage not closer than nine yards (NCAA: at least seven yards) outside the widest offensive player.

Line judge: Straddles the line of scrimmage not closer than nine yards (NCAA: at least seven yards) outside the widest offensive player.

Back judge: Favoring the strong side of the formation, 15 to 20 yards (NCAA: 18 to 22 yards) beyond the line of scrimmage and deeper than the deepest defender.

Action on the field: Pitchout to back.

Referee: Reads blocking of left tackle and reads run. Moves with flow of play. Observes runner and action around runner.

Umpire: Reads blocking of center and right guard and reads run. Determines point of attack and observes blocking there. Moves with flow of play. Observes blocking and action in front of runner.

Linesman: Looks through end, reads blocking of right tackle and reads run. As flow comes to his side, steps across sideline to prevent interfering with play. Observes blocking and action in front of runner.

Line judge: Looks through end, reads blocking of pulling left tackle and reads sweep to opposite side. Moves slowly toward play. Observes blocking and action of players not involved in flow of play.

Back judge: Reads blocking of tight end and reads run. Moves with flow of play. Observes blocking and action in front of runner.

KEY

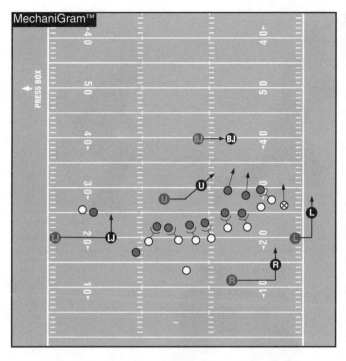

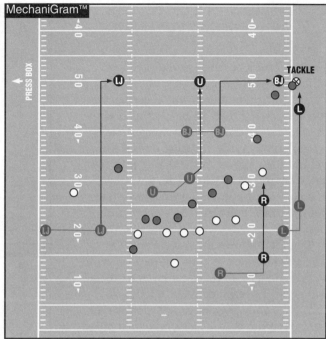

Action on the field: Runner advances.

Referee: Gives up coverage of runner to linesman. Moves slowly downfield trailing flow and cleans up after the play.

Umpire: Pivots and moves with flow of play. Observes blocking and action in front of runner.

Linesman: Takes coverage of runner and moves quickly up sideline to stay ahead of runner. Observes runner and action around runner.

Line judge: Moves slowly downfield and cleans up after the play.

Back judge: Moves toward play. Observes blocking and action in front of runner.

Action on the field: Runner continues advance and goes out of bounds.

Referee: Moves slowly downfield and observes players in front of the ball. If first down has been achieved and no penalty markers are down, signals linesman to have chain crew move the chains.

Umpire: Moves slowly downfield and observes players in front of the ball. Once spot is established, hustles to hashmark to set ball for next down.

Linesman: Gives up coverage of runner when runner enters back judge's coverage zone (halo concept). Moves down sideline and observes action behind the runner. Blows whistle and gives stop-the-clock signal when runner steps out of bounds. Hustles to dead-ball spot to prevent post-play action. If first down has been achieved, gets signal from referee and instructs chain crew to move to spot. Assists chain crew in setting chains for new series.

Line judge: Moves downfield with flow of play and cleans up after the play. Squares off to mirror spot of forward progress. Observes players in his area.

Back judge: Takes coverage of runner when runner enters coverage area (halo concept). Squares off to mark spot of forward progress. Observes players. Holds spot until umpire arrives to set ball for new series.

Movement | Previous position | Current position (stopped) | Previous position | Current position (still moving)

MECHANICS ILLUSTRATED: SIDELINE PASS COVERAGE

On pass plays near the sidelines, wing officials have a better chance of determining whether or not a receiver has made a catch if their focus is parallel with the line rather than perpendicular to it.

In PlayPic A, the covering official is behind the receiver as the player tries to catch a pass. From this angle, the official has no way of knowing if the player had control of the ball when he stepped out of bounds.

PlayPic B shows the correct position. The official's gaze is directed parallel with the sideline. From this position the official can see if the receiver keeps a foot inbounds and whether or not the receiver controlled the pass. The technique is called "looking down the gun barrel."

To properly rule on the play, officials must look at the receiver's feet first. If the player has been unable to get a foot inbounds before making the catch (a technique called "dotting the i"), it doesn't matter if the receiver secured control of the pass; the pass will be ruled incomplete. In order to get that look, the official must avoid being too close to the action. Maintaining proper distance will allow the official to see the feet first, then the ball, with a minimum of head movement.

PlayPic C illustrates how two officials working the sideline can communicate before making their ruling. The officials need only make eye contact and nod "yes" to indicate a legal catch or "no" to confirm an incomplete pass. If there is disagreement, both officials should give the stop-the-clock signal but no other signal. They then confer to share information before arriving at a consensus.

MECHANICS ILLUSTRATED: WIDE RUNS THAT END OUT OF BOUNDS

When the ball goes out of bounds, some officials think their work on that play is over. On the contrary, it is just the beginning.

In addition to determining forward progress and stopping the clock, covering officials must keep an eye on the ballcarrier and any other players in the vicinity. An unseen (and unpenalized) personal foul gives players the impression that anything goes outside the boundaries of the field.

Proper coverage on out-of-bounds plays begins when the ball is still inbounds. On sweep plays or quick sideline passes, linesmen and line judges should allow the play to pass them (PlayPic A). Trail the play by a minimum of five yards (PlayPic B). Allow more space if the defensive pursuit is coming from behind the runner.

Trailing in this manner may make you uncomfortable if you feel you are always supposed to be "right on top of the play." But letting the play get by you widens your field of vision, allows you a better view of the action and decreases the chance you will be injured yourself. Keeping your distance also means you'll have a better chance to see a clip or other illegal block, and provide a good look at the runner's feet to see if he steps out of bounds.

When the ballcarrier steps or is taken out of bounds, sound your whistle and get to the spot. Move quickly but cautiously. Be sure to make a one-quarter turn, facing away from the field, and direct your attention to the pile (PlayPic C). You'll need to be doubly alert if the ballcarrier and tacklers have landed in or near the team box; more people in the area means more potential trouble.

Hold your position and wait for the referee or the back judge (five-man crew) to retrieve the ball or obtain a different one from the ballboy. You shouldn't leave this position until the area is cleared of players. Don't mark the spot with a beanbag and retrieve the ball yourself. The beanbag should only be used to mark a spot only if a fight breaks out and you need to intervene.

Once the players have unpiled and are headed back to their respective huddles, turn around and give the umpire a spot from which he can mark the ball.

While the wing official is facing away from the field and the referee and back judge are helping on the sideline, it is important for the umpire and opposite wing official to observe all other players and substitutes. Players not involved in the action must be observed.

• By keying on the opposite-side tackle, the referee can determine if the play is a run or pass.

• Referee recommends that the umpire favor the side opposite the tight end because it decreases the number of players who will charge off the line toward the umpire.

• On runs to the opposite side of the field, the off wing must clean up after the play.

• Dead-ball officiating is especially important if the tackle is made in the team area.

• It is vital that the back judge be mobile enough to keep the runner between himself and either wing official (if the play goes outside the tackles) or the umpire (on runs between the tackles).

Quiz

Without referring back, you should be able to answer the following true-false questions.

1. If the quarterback drops back as if to pass, the referee should move toward the line of scrimmage.

2. The umpire must straddle the ball until the offensive team approaches the line of scrimmage.

3. If the right tackle blocks down (to his right) and the center joins the right guard on a double-team block taking their man to their left, the point of attack most likely is the gap between the center and guard.

4. If a wing official is "pinching" on a short-yardage play, it is OK if a team A player gets behind the official.

5. The back judge is responsible for team B's goalline until the ball is snapped at or inside team B's 10 yardline.

1. False 2. False 3. False 4. False 5. True

Chapter 18

Goalline Plays

Plays that begin at or inside team B's 10 yardline present an excellent opportunity for officials to work in tandem. Because the back judge is closer to the line than on normal plays, he can act as a second man in the middle on a running play. Close to the goalline, it is not necessary, or even sensible, for the back judge to play on the offensive team's strong side. Consequently, the back judge can take the tackle and guard on his side. The umpire can watch his own side of the line and step to the goal for inside help on a sweep.

If the play does turn out to be a pass, the back judge has only to step back a pace or two to the endline, and both wings should be at the goalline for complete coverage.

On passes into the corner of the end zone, the back judge and covering wing official have to coordinate judgments. What could be a complicated procedure is relatively simple. If either has the receiver out of bounds (or over the endline), there is no need to look at the other official. A look and a nod means, "I've got a successful catch for a score." If it's no good, there's no need to verify; signal the pass incomplete without looking to the crewmate.

The touchdown signal is given only by an official who actually sees the ball in possession of a runner break the plane of the goalline. Mirroring the signal is dangerous; if the covering official is incorrect, the crew will find it difficult to overcome two officials making a mistake. If the covering official is correct, there is no need for a second signal.

Referee recommendation: Have the wing officials "pinch" the ends (move closer than normal to the widest player) in goalline situations. The mechanic should be used only when the ball is snapped at or inside team B's eight yardline and when the wings are quick and alert enough to avoid being trapped inside if team A runs wide or throws a screen or a pass in the flat. It is also crucial that the wings allow no team A player to line up behind them; the wing should always be outside the widest offensive player.

General procedures

Minor adjustments in positioning take place in goalline situations. The Federation manual places the back judge on the endline instead of the usual 15 to 20 yards beyond the line; the other officials are in the same positions as for a regular scrimmage play. In NCAA, the umpire lines up approximately a yard behind and to the side of or between the linebackers. Since the linebackers will likely be closer to the line, the umpire

will also be closer to the line than his normal position. The back judge is positioned on the endline anytime the snap is on or inside team B's 10 yardline.

When the snap is at or inside team B's five yardline, the wings move immediately to the goalline and work back toward the ball if the runner is downed short of the goalline. The Federation manual advises wingmen to release slowly downfield at the snap and stay ahead of the runner to the goalline when the snap is between team B's 10 and five yardlines.

The referee must be especially aware of attempts by team A to gain an advantage. Such acts as a rolling start (in which the quarterback walks up behind the snapper and, without stopping, puts his hands under center and immediately receives the snap) and helping the runner must be penalized.

Because the umpire is parallel rather than perpendicular to the play, the umpire's position makes it next to impossible to determine the spot or rule whether a touchdown has been scored. The umpire should get the spot from the covering wing official.

Other short-yardage situations

Similar principles apply on short-yardage situations (e.g. fourth down and inches to go). The wings may choose to pinch the ends in those situations as well. However, the wings should move with the runner rather than moving immediately to a spot as they do when the goalline is involved.

CHALK TALK: FEDERATION GOALLINE POSITIONING AND COVERAGE

Referee: Starting position is on the passing-arm side of the quarterback, approximately 10 to 12 yards deep and at least as wide as the tight end. The referee must be especially aware of attempts by team A to gain an advantage. Such acts as a rolling start (in which the quarterback walks up behind the snapper and, without stopping, puts his hands under center and immediately receives the snap) and helping the runner must be penalized.

On a running play, the referee focuses on the ball, the runner and the blocking around the runner. If the play goes to the opposite side, the referee should move toward or parallel to the line of the scrimmage and maintain a position approximately in line with the runner. If the play is to the referee's side, the referee moves behind the play and is responsible for the runner until he crosses the neutral zone or turns upfield. The referee should watch the handoff or the pitchout, see the runner head outside the free clipping/free blocking zone, and watch to see that no one contacts the quarterback before drifting along to follow the play.

On passing plays, the referee observes blocking by the backs as the quarterback drops back. The referee should move to maintain the 10- to 12-yard distance between himself and the quarterback (e.g. if the quarterback drops back seven yards, the referee retreats seven yards).

The referee is also responsible for ruling on intentional grounding and can work with the umpire to determine whether a passer was beyond the line of scrimmage when the pass was thrown. The referee should move to the spot of the pass and observe the location of the passer's feet. If the passer is clearly beyond the line, a penalty marker should be dropped. In cases that are too close for an immediate determination, a beanbag should be dropped. At the end of the play, the referee can compare the spot of the beanbag and the location of the down box in order to make the call.

On runs that end out of bounds behind the neutral zone, the referee is responsible for marking the spot. He also must beanbag the spot of a muff or fumble and may have to beanbag a quarterback sack in the offensive backfield.

Umpire: Starting position is three to eight yards behind team B's line and between the defensive ends.

On runs, the umpire must observe the blocking to find the point of attack. When the hole opens, the umpire should move away from it (to avoid interfering with the defensive pursuit) and laterally (thus turning his head toward the blockers in front of the runner and the tackling efforts of the defense).

On pass plays, the umpire must step up and reach the line of scrimmage. If a pass is first touched by a team B

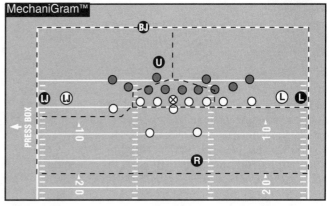

⟪LJ⟫ ⟪L⟫ = *Referee* recommendation

player, the umpire gives the tipped ball signal. When the pass is thrown, the umpire pivots to follow the flight of the ball. The umpire has catch/trap responsibility if the receiver is facing the umpire.

Linesman and line judge: Starting position is straddling the line of scrimmage. *Referee* recommendation: Have the wing officials pinch the ends in goalline situations. The mechanic should be used only when the ball is snapped at or inside team B's eight yardline and when the wings are quick and alert enough to avoid being trapped inside if team A runs wide or throws a screen or a pass in the flat.

When the snap is at or inside team B's five yardline, the wings move immediately to the goalline and work back toward the ball if the runner is downed short of the goalline. When the snap is between team B's 10 and five yardlines, wingmen should release slowly downfield at the snap and stay ahead of the runner to the goalline.

On passes into the corner of the end zone, the back judge and covering wing official have to coordinate judgments. If either has the receiver out of bounds or over the endline, the covering official should signal the pass incomplete. In cases when the pass is not definitely incomplete, the covering officials must make eye contact. A nod means, "I've got a successful catch for a score." If the officials concur, both should signal the touchdown.

Back judge: Starting position is on the endline, favoring the strong side of the formation.

The back judge can act as a second man in the middle on a running play. On passes, he need only step back a pace or two to the endline, and both wings should be at the goalline for complete coverage.

On passes into the corner of the end zone, the back judge and covering wing official have to coordinate judgments. If either has the receiver out of bounds or over the endline, the covering official should signal the pass incomplete. In cases when the pass is not definitely incomplete, the covering officials must make eye contact. A nod means, "I've got a successful catch for a score." If the officials concur, both should signal the touchdown.

CHALK TALK: NCAA GOALLINE POSITIONING AND COVERAGE

Referee: Starting position is on the passing-arm side of the quarterback, approximately 10 to 12 yards deep and at least as wide as the tight end. The referee must be especially aware of attempts by team A to gain an advantage. Such acts as a rolling start (in which the quarterback walks up behind the snapper and, without stopping, puts his hands under center and immediately receives the snap) and helping the runner must be penalized.

On a running play, the referee focuses on the ball, the runner and the blocking around the runner. If the play goes to the opposite side, the referee should move toward or parallel to the line of the scrimmage and maintain a position approximately in line with the runner. If the play is to the referee's side, the referee moves behind the play and is responsible for the runner until he crosses the neutral zone or turns upfield. The referee should watch the handoff or the pitchout, see the runner head outside the free clipping/free blocking zone, and watch to see that no one contacts the quarterback before drifting along to follow the play.

On passing plays, the referee observes blocking by the backs as the quarterback drops back. The referee should move to maintain the 10- to 12-yard distance between himself and the quarterback (e.g. if the quarterback drops back seven yards, the referee retreats seven yards).

The referee is also responsible for ruling on intentional grounding and can work with the umpire to determine whether a passer was beyond the line of scrimmage when the pass was thrown. The referee should move to the spot of the pass and observe the location of the passer's feet. If the passer is clearly beyond the line, a penalty marker should be dropped. In cases that are too close for an immediate determination, a beanbag should be dropped. At the end of the play, the referee can compare the spot of the beanbag and the location of the down box in order to make the call.

On runs that end out of bounds behind the neutral zone, the referee is responsible for marking the spot. He also must beanbag the spot of a muff or fumble and may beanbag a quarterback sack in the offensive backfield.

Umpire: Starting position is approximately a yard behind and to the side of or between the linebackers.

On runs, the umpire must observe the blocking to find the point of attack. When the hole opens, the umpire should move away from it (to avoid interfering with the defensive pursuit) and laterally (thus turning his head toward the blockers in front of the runner and the tackling efforts of the defense).

On pass plays, the umpire must step up and reach the line of scrimmage. If a pass is first touched by a team B player, the umpire gives the tipped ball signal. When the pass is thrown, the umpire pivots to follow the flight of the

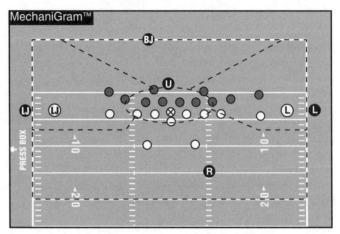

$\textcircled{\text{LJ}}$ $\textcircled{\text{L}}$ = *Referee* recommendation

ball. The umpire has catch/trap responsibility if the receiver is facing the umpire.

Linesman and line judge: Starting position is straddling the line of scrimmage. *Referee* recommendation: Have the wing officials pinch the ends in goalline situations. The mechanic should be used only when the ball is snapped at or inside team B's eight yardline and when the wings are quick and alert enough to avoid being trapped inside if team A runs wide or throws a screen or a pass in the flat.

When the snap is at or inside team B's five yardline, the wings move immediately to the goalline and work back toward the ball if the runner is downed short of the goalline. When the snap is between team B's 10 and five yardlines, wingmen should release slowly downfield at the snap and stay ahead of the runner to the goalline.

On passes into the corner of the end zone, the back judge and covering wing official have to coordinate judgments. If either has the receiver out of bounds or over the endline, the covering official should signal the pass incomplete. In cases when the pass is not definitely incomplete, the covering officials must make eye contact. A nod means, "I've got a successful catch for a score." If the officials concur, both should signal the touchdown.

Back judge: Starting position is on the endline, favoring the strong side of the formation.

The back judge can step up and act as a second man in the middle on a running play. On passes, the back judge has only to step back a pace or two to the endline, and both wings should be at the goalline for complete coverage.

On passes into the corner of the end zone, the back judge and covering wing official have to coordinate judgments. If either has the receiver out of bounds or over the endline, the covering official should signal the pass incomplete. In cases when the pass is not definitely incomplete, the covering officials must make eye contact. A nod means, "I've got a successful catch for a score." If the officials concur, both should signal the touchdown.

MECHANICS ILLUSTRATED: GOALLINE COVERAGE

Many scores occur during plays in which the ball is snapped on or inside the 10 yardline. It behooves officials to be at the goalline as soon as possible so they can make decisions based on what they've seen rather than on guesswork.

In PlayPic A, the wing official is straightlined because he is so far behind the play he cannot tell if the ball has broken the plane of the goalline or if the runner's knee has touched down the ground. PlayPic B illustrates the proper position.

Getting to the goalline is paramount, but linesmen and line judges should not get in the way of the play. Get as far as out of bounds as space allows. The position in PlayPic B gives the covering official a wide-angle view of the action, allowing him to see all of the key elements.

The wingmen have the best opportunity to view this specific play, in which the runner's knees, the sideline and the goalline are all involved. In the middle of the field, a hustling back judge (five-man crew) can anticipate the play and make the call.

The referee should employ these theories when the offense has the ball deep in its own territory. In PlayPic C, the quarterback is scrambling with a defender in pursuit. If the rusher catches the quarterback, the referee will be able to rule on a fumble that may be caused by the contact, whether or not the quarterback was tackled for a safety or advanced the ball completely out of the end zone and, if the quarterback gets off a pass, whether or not he was roughed.

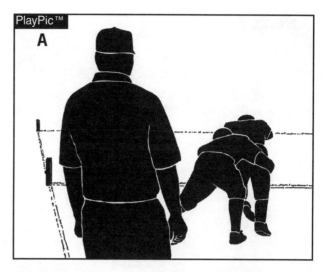

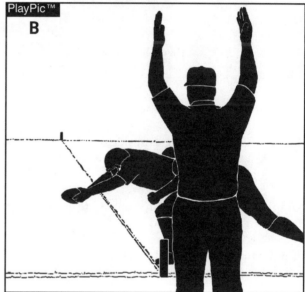

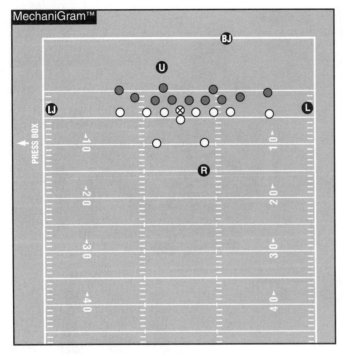

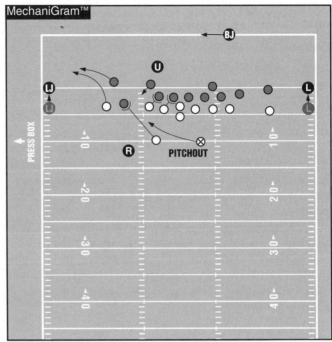

Action on the field: Starting position.

Referee: On the passing-arm side of the quarterback, approximately 10 to 12 yards deep and at least as wide as the tight end.

Umpire: Three to eight yards behind team B's line and between the defensive ends.

Linesman: Straddles the line of scrimmage. May choose to pinch end, but not so far inside as to get trapped.

Line judge: Straddles the line of scrimmage. May choose to pinch end, but not so far inside as to get trapped.

Back judge: On the endline, favoring the strong side of the formation.

Action on the field: Pitchout to back, sweep left.

Referee: Reads blocking of left tackle and reads run. Moves with flow of play. Observes runner and action around runner.

Umpire: Reads blocking of center and right guard and reads run. Determines point of attack and observes blocking there. Moves with flow of play. Observes blocking and action in front of runner.

Linesman: Moves immediately to goalline at snap. Observes initial blocking.

Line judge: Moves immediately to goalline at snap. Observes initial blocking.

Back judge: Reads blocking of tight end and reads run. Moves with flow of play. Observes blocking and action in front of runner.

KEY

Referee	Umpire	Line Judge	Linesman	Back Judge	Chain Gang	Ballboy	Coach	Offense	Defense	Football	Possession of football

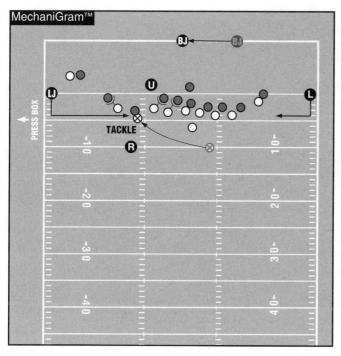

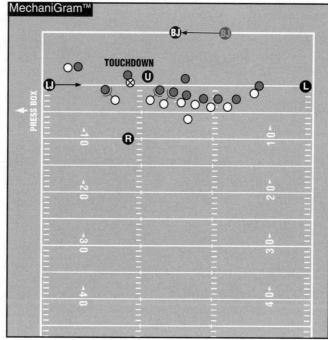

Action on the field: Runner stopped short of goalline.

Referee: Observes action.

Umpire: Observes blocking and action in front of runner.

Linesman: Officiates back to the ball and squares off to mirror line judge's spot.

Line judge: Officiates back to the ball to observe contact on runner and squares off to indicate forward progress. Blows whistle when runner is downed.

Back judge: Moves with flow of play and observes action.

Action on the field: Runner scores.

Referee: Observes action. When line judge signals touchdown (if no flags are down), turns to pressbox and mirrors signal.

Umpire: Observes action.

Linesman: Observes action.

Line judge: Observes runner. When ball in possession of runner breaks plane of goalline, moves toward runner while straddling goalline, blows whistle and signals touchdown.

Back judge: Moves with flow of play and observes action.

Movement → Previous position U → Current position U (stopped) Previous position U → Current position U (still moving)

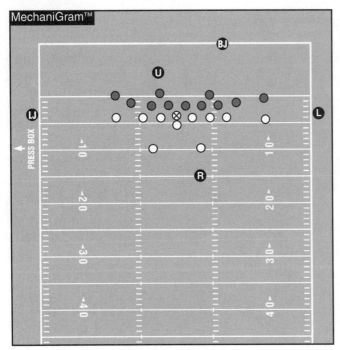

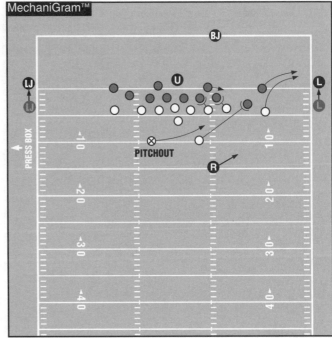

Action on the field: Starting position.

Referee: On the passing-arm side of the quarterback, approximately 10 to 12 yards deep and at least as wide as the tight end.

Umpire: Approximately a yard behind and to the side of or between the linebackers.

Linesman: Straddles the line of scrimmage at least seven yards outside the widest offensive player. May choose to pinch end, but not so far inside as to get trapped.

Line judge: Straddles the line of scrimmage at least seven yards outside the widest offensive player. May choose to pinch end, but not so far inside as to get trapped. Uses extended arm signal to alert linesman that end is in offensive backfield.

Back judge: On the endline, favoring strong side of the formation.

Action on the field: Pitchout to back, sweep right.

Referee: Reads blocking of left tackle and reads run. Moves with flow of play. Observes runner and action around runner.

Umpire: Reads blocking of center and right guard and reads run. Determines point of attack and observes blocking there. Moves with flow of play. Observes blocking and action in front of runner.

Linesman: Moves toward goalline at snap. Observes initial blocking.

Line judge: Moves toward goalline at snap. Observes initial blocking.

Back judge: Reads blocking of tight end and reads run. Moves with flow of play. Observes blocking and action in front of runner.

KEY

Referee	Umpire	Line Judge	Linesman	Back Judge	Chain Gang	Ballboy	Coach	Offense	Defense	Football	Possession of football

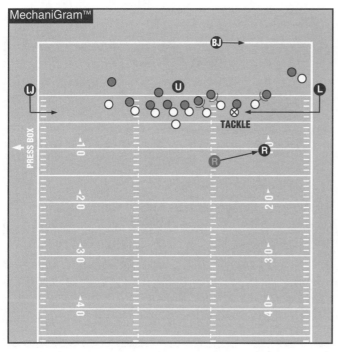

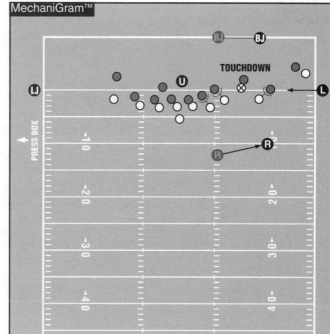

Action on the field: Runner downed short of goalline.

Referee: Observes action.

Umpire: Observes blocking and action in front of runner.

Linesman: Blows whistle when runner is downed and squares off to indicate spot.

Line judge: Squares off to mirror linesman's spot.

Back judge: Observes action.

Action on the field: Runner scores.

Referee: Observes action. When linesman signals touchdown (if no flags are down), turns to pressbox and mirrors signal.

Umpire: Observes action.

Linesman: Observes runner. When ball in possession of runner breaks plane of goalline, blows whistle and signals touchdown.

Line judge: Observes action.

Back judge: Observes action.

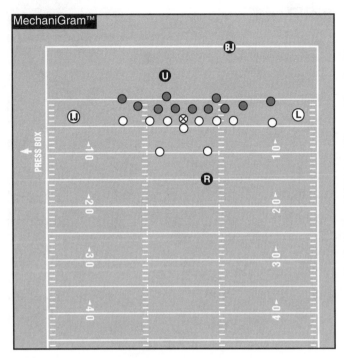

MechaniGram™

ⓊⓁ = *Referee* recommendation

Action on the field: Starting position.

Referee: On the passing-arm side of the quarterback, approximately 10 to 12 yards deep and at least as wide as the tight end.

Umpire: Approximately a yard behind and to the side of or between the linebackers.

Linesman: Straddles the line of scrimmage pinching the end, but not so far inside as to get trapped.

Line judge: Straddles the line of scrimmage pinching the end, but not so far inside as to get trapped.

Back judge: On the endline, favoring strong side of the formation.

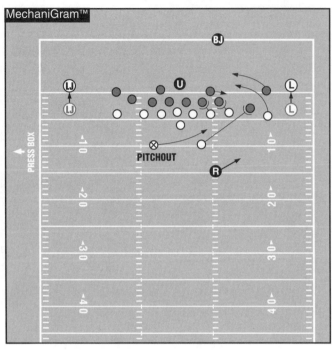

MechaniGram™

PITCHOUT

ⓊⓁ = *Referee* recommendation

Action on the field: Pitchout to back, sweep right.

Referee: Keys blocking of left tackle and reads run. Moves with flow of play. Observes runner and action around runner.

Umpire: Keys blocking of center and right guard and reads run. Determines point of attack and observes blocking there. Moves with flow of play. Observes blocking and action in front of runner.

Linesman: Uses extended arm signal to alert linesman that end is in offensive backfield. Moves toward goalline at snap. Observes initial blocking.

Line judge: Moves toward goalline at snap. Observes initial blocking.

Back judge: Keys blocking of tight end and reads run. Moves with flow of play. Observes blocking and action in front of runner.

KEY

Ⓡ	Ⓤ	Ⓛ	Ⓛ	Ⓑⓙ	Ⓒⓖ	Ⓑⓑ	Ⓒ	○	⬤	◖	⊗
Referee	Umpire	Line Judge	Linesman	Back Judge	Chain Gang	Ballboy	Coach	Offense	Defense	Football	Possession of football

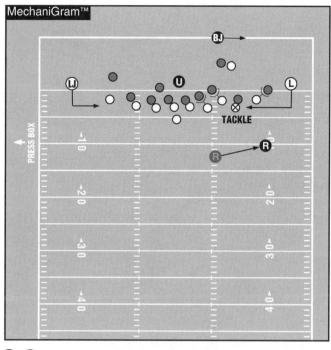

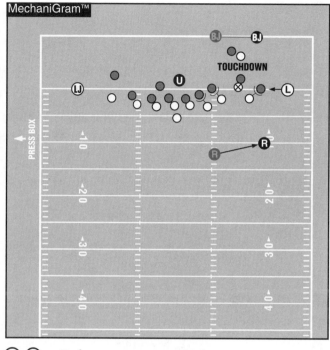

(LJ) (L) = *Referee* recommendation

(LJ) (L) = *Referee* recommendation

Action on the field: Runner downed short of goalline.

Referee: Observes action.

Umpire: Observes blocking and action in front of runner.

Linesman: Blows whistle when runner is downed and squares off to indicate spot.

Line judge: Squares off to mirror linesman's spot.

Back judge: Observes action.

Action on the field: Runner scores.

Referee: Observes action. When linesman signals touchdown (if no flags are down), turns to pressbox and mirrors signal.

Umpire: Observes action.

Linesman: Observes runner. When ball in possession of runner breaks plane of goalline, blows whistle and signals touchdown.

Line judge: Observes action.

Back judge: Observes action.

• The back judge can observe the tackle and guard on his side while the umpire can watch his own side of the line and step to the goal for inside help on a sweep.

• Have the wing officials "pinch" the ends only when the ball is snapped at or inside team B's eight yardline.

• Use eye contact on passes into the corner of the end zone. A look and a nod means, "I've got a successful catch for a score."

Quiz

Without referring back, you should be able to answer the following true-false questions.

1. Only the official who actually sees a player score a touchdown should signal.

2. When the snap is at or inside team B's 10 yardline, the wings move immediately to the goalline.

3. The back judge is responsible for goalline coverage when the ball is snapped at or inside team B's five yardline.

4. The umpire is responsible for forward progress spots anytime the ball is snapped at or inside team B's five yardline.

5. The referee must be especially aware of a rolling start and helping the runner.

1. True 2. False 3. False 4. False 5. True

Chapter 19

Scrimmage
Kicks

Some crews are still under the mistaken assumption that a weak or inexperienced official can be "hidden" at the back judge spot. That myth is propagated because, in many games, the back judge will have nothing but routine calls and the crew escapes unscathed. But there are plenty of crews whose ratings and coverage have suffered because the back judge was ill-equipped to handle key situations and make "home run" calls.

The back judge needn't be an Olympic-caliber sprinter (although speed is certainly is a plus). More than physical ability, the back judge has to have good judgment, understand the keys and know the mechanics of the position.

Many of the crucial judgment calls occur on scrimmage kicks. Among the decisions the back judge may have to make on a punt play: Was the fair catch signal valid? Was the receiver was given an unmolested opportunity to catch the kick? Did a receiver touch a bouncing kick? Did it touch the receiver? Does the momentum exception apply? Did the ball break the goalline plane? Was a new force or impetus imparted on the ball before it went into the end zone? Only a well-schooled, hustling back judge can make those calls correctly.

The back judge also has to be prepared to work with wing officials when a punt goes out of bounds. Perhaps the toughest call involves a kick near the intersection of the goalline and sideline. The back judge can determine if the ball broke the plane of the goalline (resulting in a touchback), but not if the ball went out of bounds first. Conversely, the respective wing official is too far away to tell if the ball broke the plane.

When such a play occurs, the back judge and wing official must get to the ball as quickly as possible. Stop the clock but give no other signal. Make eye contact to let the crewmate know you need to get together to compare notes. If the officials agree that the play resulted in a touchback, both should give the touchback signal. If it's decided the ball went out of bounds before breaking the plane of the goalline, the wing official should stand at the spot and give the first down signal to indicate a new series will begin for team R at the spot.

Referee: The referee's position is three to four yards in front of and five to yards outside the punter (NCAA: In front of the kicker, wider than where the tight end would normally be positioned), on the punter's kicking-leg side. That position allows the referee to view the snap as well as the action around the kicker before, during and after the kick. The referee must be ready to move in the appropriate direction if an errant snap leads to a loose ball in the offensive backfield.

A verbal alert such as, "Gone!" is an aid to help prevent roughing the kicker after the ball has been kicked. Once the kick is away, the referee takes a quick look to see the flight of the ball. If the kick is short and toward a sideline, the covering sideline official should be prepared to determine the spot the ball went out of bounds. If the kick is long and goes out of bounds, the covering official moves past where he thinks it flew out before walking toward the referee with his hand up — along the sideline — until the referee chops downward, telling him to halt. How each crew defines "short" and "long" kicks should be determined in the pregame meeting.

If the receivers begin a return, the referee should move slowly downfield; if the runner breaks a long return, the referee may assume responsibility for the runner. The referee will get an inside-out look regardless of which sideline is involved since the appropriate wing official has sideline responsibility from endline to endline.

On blocked kicks, the referee should be ready to rule on the recovery and observe the advance of any player who runs with a recovered ball. If the ball is partially blocked, the legal touching signal should be used.

The referee should swing around behind the punter as the kicker steps forward to kick the ball. Federation rules permit a defender to hit the kicker legally if his path has been changed by a blocker. That cannot be determined from the side; it can only be seen from behind the kicker. That position will place the referee in perfect position to line up a kick that veers across a sideline in the air. Lastly, the referee can easily follow the kicker as he drifts downfield, protecting the kicker from an unnecessary hit. The referee should not watch a kick that goes straight down the field. Since you can't tell where a blocked kick will roll, being behind the kicker is just as safe as being off to one side, providing you remain four yards deeper than any player.

Umpire: The umpire sets up four to seven yards deep and favoring the line judge's sideline. Favoring the line judge's side compensates for the line judge moving downfield immediately at the snap.

Remind team R players about rules relating to contact on the snapper. The umpire can see players shooting gaps or lineman chopping rushers at the knees (the ball will be snapped out of the free-blocking/free-clipping zone) as well as contact on the snapper.

The umpire should move toward the line at the snap, which will improve the view of the initial line charge. Once the ball has been kicked and players from both teams have run past, the umpire pivots to the line judge's side. After the pivot, the umpire should move slowly downfield and observe action in front of the runner.

On a return to the middle of the field, the back judge has responsibility for the runner until the umpire takes the coverage (halo coverage); the point at which the transfer occurs depends on how far downfield the umpire has drifted after the kick.

Linesman and line judge: The wing officials' starting position on scrimmage kicks is the same as for other plays from scrimmage. In Federation, the linesman observes the initial line charge and remains on the line until the kick crosses the neutral zone while the line judge releases on the snap and observes action on his side of the field between the neutral zone and the receivers. The linesman waits because whether or not the ball crosses the line is the key element in determining if team K can recover or advance a scrimmage kick. Once the ball crosses the line, the linesman moves slowly downfield to observe the actions of blockers in front of the return. In NCAA, both wings observe the initial line charge but don't move downfield until the ball is beyond the neutral zone.

Both wings must also be cognizant of a fake punt. If a pass is used on the fake, the linesman or line judge must know if the pass was forward or backward. If the kicker initially starts to run before deciding to kick, the covering wing official may have to rule on whether the punter was beyond the line when the ball was kicked.

When it is obvious team R will try to block the kick, *Referee* recommends having the line judge remain on the line. He can see tripping, holding, and other illegal acts by protectors and by rushers. But if the pattern early in the game is for a token rush and a collapse by receivers back to set up a return wall or wedge, a line judge might be better off leaving the line before the snap and setting up about 15 yards downfield. If the line judge breaks at the snap, he won't see one important thing that happens at the line. Hence, there's little point in being there. The reasoning is relatively clear-cut: Why run when you might see something of note if you were better situated? Reliable officiating judgments are usually made when an official is mostly stable. If the line judge starts from a position downfield, all important action (including the punt itself) will be coming toward him and he can pick up the flight of the ball for a moment, then observe the flow of players. He can see the phalanx of receivers jockeying into their protective formation, and he can see the kickers' reacting and attacking. If the kicking team employs wideouts, the line judge can readily see if they're ambushed beyond the line. It is a perfect perspective to adopt, and the line judge can also follow the bouncing ball if it should carry into his side zone or out of bounds.

On the vast majority of punts, however, both wing officials are responsible for their sideline from endline to endline and for covering the runner when the return is to their area. If the run is to the opposite sideline, clean up behind the play.

Back judge: The back judge begins the play seven to 10 yards wider than and in front of the deepest receiver (NCAA: On the sideline slightly ahead of the deepest receiver) on the linesman's side of the field. The back judge must be prepared to move upfield if the kick is short or downfield if the receiver has to retreat.

All deep receivers are the responsibility of the back judge. Good back judges watch the receivers and the players around them rather than the ball as it flies downfield. Remaining far enough away from the receiver to retain a wide-angle view and moving in at a controlled pace, with eyes searching, once the receiver has completed the fair catch helps the back judge look for illegal action around the receiver. In such cases, it is also a good idea not to have the whistle in the mouth; it is possible for a fair catch to be muffed and a whistle blown before the ball dribbles loose from the receiver's grasp.

In addition to the judgment calls listed above, the back judge also has coverage responsibilities for the runner. If the runner breaks into a side zone, coverage transfers to the appropriate wing official. On a return to the middle of the field, the back judge has responsibility for the runner until the umpire takes the coverage; the point at which the transfer occurs depends on how far downfield the umpire has drifted after the kick.

In NCAA, the covering official, regardless of position, must beanbag the spot where the kick ends. That spot may be used for post-scrimmage kick penalty enforcement.

CHALK TALK: FEDERATION SCRIMMAGE KICK POSITIONING AND COVERAGE

Referee: Starting position is three to four yards in front of and five to yards outside the punter, on the punter's kicking-leg side.

Once the kick is away, the referee takes a quick look to see the flight of the ball. If the kick is short and toward a sideline, the covering sideline official should be prepared to determine the spot the ball went out of bounds. If the kick is long and goes out of bounds, the covering official moves past where he thinks it flew out before walking toward the referee with his hand up — along the sideline — until the referee chops downward, telling him to halt. How each crew defines "short" and "long" kicks should be determined in the pregame meeting.

If the receivers begin a return, the referee should move slowly downfield; if the runner breaks a long return, the referee may assume responsibility for the runner.

On blocked kicks, the referee should be ready to rule on the recovery and observe the advance of any player who runs with a recovered ball. If the ball is partially blocked, the legal touching signal should be used.

The referee should swing around behind the punter as the kicker steps forward to kick the ball. That position will place the referee will be in perfect position to line up a kick that veers across a sideline in the air. Lastly, the referee can easily follow the kicker as he drifts downfield, protecting the kicker from an unnecessary hit.

Umpire: Starting position is four to seven yards deep and favoring the line judge's sideline. The umpire should remind team R players about rules relating to contact on the snapper.

The umpire should move toward the line at the snap, which will improve the view of the initial line charge. Once the ball has been kicked and players from both teams have run past, the umpire pivots to the line judge's side. After the pivot, the umpire should move slowly downfield and observe action in front of the runner.

On a return to the middle of the field, the back judge has responsibility for the runner until the umpire takes the coverage; the point at which the transfer occurs depends on how far downfield the umpire has drifted after the kick.

Linesman and line judge: Starting position is straddling the line of scrimmage and more than nine yards outside the widest offensive player. The linesman observes the initial line charge and remains on the line until the kick crosses the neutral zone while the line judge releases on

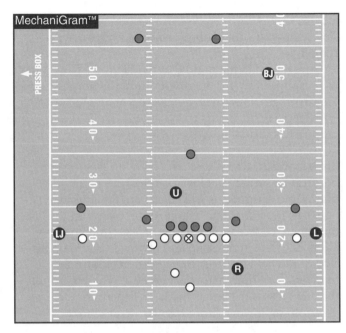

the snap and observes action on his side of the field between the neutral zone and the receivers. Once the ball crosses the line, the linesman moves slowly downfield to observe the actions of blockers in front of the return.

Both wings must also be cognizant of a fake punt. If a pass is used on the fake, the linesman or line judge must know if the pass was forward or backward. If the kicker initially starts to run before deciding to kick, the covering wing official may have to rule on whether the punter was beyond the line when the ball was kicked.

When it is obvious team R will try to block the kick, *Referee* recommends having the line judge remain on the line. He can see tripping, holding, and other illegal acts by protectors and by rushers. But if the pattern early in the game is for a token rush and a collapse by receivers back to set up a return wall or wedge, a line judge might be better off leaving the line before the snap and setting up about 15 yards downfield.

If the run is to the opposite sideline, the off wing should clean up behind the play.

Back judge: Starting position is seven to 10 yards wider than and in front of the deepest receiver on the linesman's side of the field. The back judge must be prepared to move upfield if the kick is short or downfield if the receiver has to retreat.

All deep receivers are the responsibility of the back judge. If the runner breaks into a side zone, coverage transfers to the appropriate wing official. On a return to the middle of the field, the back judge has responsibility for the runner until the umpire takes the coverage; the point at which the transfer occurs depends on how far downfield the umpire has drifted after the kick.

CHALK TALK: NCAA SCRIMMAGE KICK POSITIONING AND COVERAGE

Referee: Starting position is in front of the kicker, wider than where the tight end would normally be positioned, on the punter's kicking-leg side.

Once the kick is away, the referee takes a quick look to see the flight of the ball. If the kick is short and toward a sideline, the covering sideline official should be prepared to determine the spot the ball went out of bounds. If the kick is long and goes out of bounds, the covering official moves past where he thinks it flew out before walking toward the referee with his hand up — along the sideline — until the referee chops downward, telling him to halt. How each crew defines "short" and "long" kicks should be determined in the pregame meeting.

If the receivers begin a return, the referee should move slowly downfield; if the runner breaks a long return, the referee may assume responsibility for the runner.

On blocked kicks, the referee should be ready to rule on the recovery and observe the advance of any player who runs with a recovered ball. If the ball is partially blocked, the legal touching signal should be used.

The referee should swing around behind the punter as the kicker steps forward to kick the ball. That position will place the referee will be in perfect position to line up a kick that veers across a sideline in the air. Lastly, the referee can easily follow the kicker as he drifts downfield, protecting the kicker from an unnecessary hit.

Umpire: The umpire sets up four to seven yards deep and favoring the line judge's sideline. The umpire should remind team R players about rules relating to contact on the snapper.

The umpire can see players shooting gaps or lineman chopping rushers at the knees (the ball will be snapped out of the free-blocking/free-clipping zone) as well as contact on the snapper.

The umpire should move toward the line at the snap, which will improve the view of the initial line charge. Once the ball has been kicked and players from both teams have run past, the umpire pivots to the line judge's side. After the pivot, the umpire should move slowly downfield and observe action in front of the runner.

On a return to the middle of the field, the back judge has responsibility for the runner until the umpire takes the coverage; the point at which the transfer occurs depends on how far downfield the umpire has drifted after the kick.

Linesman and line judge: Starting position is straddling the line of scrimmage, at least seven yards outside the widest offensive player and never inside the top of the numbers. When the snap is from the hashmark, a position on the sideline is required. Both wings observe the initial line charge but don't move downfield until the ball is beyond the neutral zone.

Both wings must also be cognizant of a fake punt. If a pass is used on the fake, the linesman or line judge must know if the pass was forward or backward. If the kicker initially starts

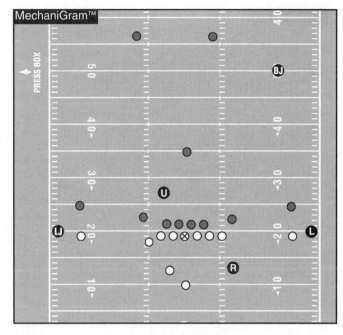

to run before deciding to kick, the covering wing official may have to rule on whether the punter was beyond the line when the ball was kicked.

When it is obvious team R will try to block the kick, *Referee* recommends having the line judge remain on the line. He can see tripping, holding, and other illegal acts by protectors and by rushers. But if the pattern early in the game is for a token rush and a collapse by receivers back to set up a return wall or wedge, a line judge might be better off leaving the line before the snap and setting up about 15 yards downfield.

Both wing officials are responsible for their sideline from endline to endline and for covering the runner when the return is to their area. If the run is to the opposite sideline, they should clean up behind the play.

Back judge: Starting position is on the sideline outside and in front of the deep receivers. When the snap is from the hashmark on the linesman's side of the field, the back judge should favor the wide side of the field. The back judge must be prepared to move upfield if the kick is short or downfield if the receiver has to retreat.

All deep receivers are the responsibility of the back judge. If the runner breaks into a side zone, coverage transfers to the appropriate wing official. On a return to the middle of the field, the back judge has responsibility for the runner until the umpire takes the coverage; the point at which the transfer occurs depends on how far downfield the umpire has drifted after the kick.

All officials: The covering official, regardless of position, must beanbag the spot where the kick ends. That spot may be used for post-scrimmage kick penalty enforcement.

Case Study 13: Federation Scrimmage Kick Out of Bounds to Linesman's Side

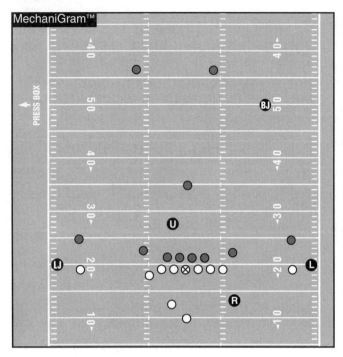

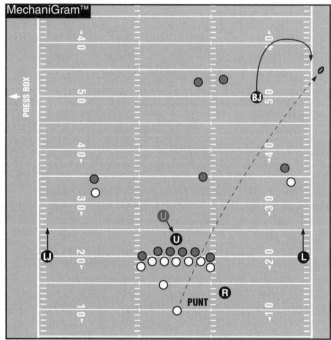

Action on the field: Starting position.

Referee: Three to four yards in front of and five to yards outside the punter, on the punter's kicking-leg side.

Umpire: Four to seven yards deep and favoring the line judge's sideline.

Linesman: Straddling the line of scrimmage and more than nine yards outside the widest offensive player.

Line judge: Straddling the line of scrimmage and more than nine yards outside the widest offensive player.

Back judge: Seven to 10 yards wider than and in front of the deepest receiver on the linesman's side of the field.

Action on the field: Ball kicked toward sideline.

Referee: Observes snap and action around kicker.

Umpire: Moves toward the line at the snap, observing initial charge of linemen and contact on the snapper.

Linesman: Observes initial line charge and remains on the line to rule whether or not the kick crossed the neutral zone. Moves quickly downfield when ball crosses neutral zone.

Line judge: Moves downfield on snap, observing action of players moving downfield.

Back judge: Observes receivers. Retreats to observe result of kick.

KEY

Referee　Umpire　Line Judge　Linesman　Back Judge　Chain Gang　Ballboy　Coach　Offense　Defense　Football　Possession of football

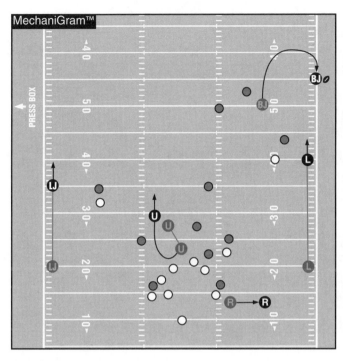

MechaniGram™

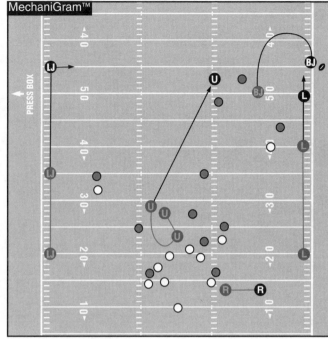

MechaniGram™

Action on the field: Kick is dead out of bounds.

Referee: Moves quickly toward sideline to observe flight of ball.

Umpire: Pivots toward the line judge's side of the field, observing players as they move downfield. Moves downfield on line judge's side of field.

Linesman: Moves down sideline. Observes action of players in front of ball.

Line judge: Moves down sideline. Observes action of players in front of ball.

Back judge: Gives stop-the-clock signal when he sees ball go out of bounds. Moves five to seven yards beyond spot where ball apparently went out of bounds, pivots and makes eye contact with referee.

Action on the field: Ball spotted for new series.

Referee: With arm above head, observes back judge walking toward spot. When back judge reaches spot, drops arm with chopping motion. When certain there are no penalty markers down, signals linesman to move chain crew.

Umpire: Continues to move downfield and observes players. Moves to spot to set ball for new series.

Linesman: Hustles to dead-ball spot to prevent post-play action. Upon signal from referee, instructs chain crew to move to spot.

Line judge: Continues to move downfield and observes players. Squares off and mirrors back judge's spot.

Back judge: Walks slowly toward referee, stopping when referee drops arm with chopping motion. Signals first down for team R.

→ Movement	**U** Previous position	**U**→ Current position (stopped)	**U** Previous position	**U**→ Current position (still moving)

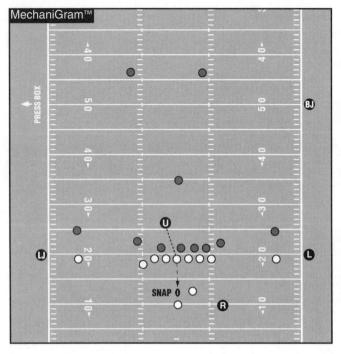

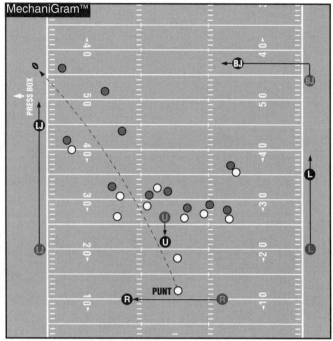

Action on the field: Starting position.

Referee: In front of the kicker, wider than where the tight end would normally be positioned, and on the kicking-leg side. Able to see all the backs and far enough away from the kicker to observe the blockers and kicker at the same time.

Umpire: Four to seven yards deep and favoring the line judge's sideline.

Linesman: Straddling the line of scrimmage, at least seven yards outside the widest offensive player and never inside the top of the numbers. When the snap is from the hashmark, position on the sideline is required.

Line judge: Straddling the line of scrimmage, at least seven yards outside the widest offensive player and never inside the top of the numbers. When the snap is from the hashmark, position on the sideline is required.

Back judge: On the sideline outside and in front of the deep receivers. When the snap is from the hashmark on the linesman's side of the field, favor the wide side of the field.

Action on the field: Ball kicked toward sideline.

Referee: Observes snap and action around kicker. Moves quickly toward sideline when kick flies toward sideline.

Umpire: Moves toward the line at the snap, observing initial charge of linemen and contact on the snapper.

Linesman: Observes initial line charge and remains on the line to rule whether or not the kick crossed the neutral zone. Moves downfield when ball crosses neutral zone.

Line judge: Observes initial line charge. Moves quickly downfield when ball is kicked.

Back judge: Observes receivers. Moves toward ball as it nears sideline.

KEY

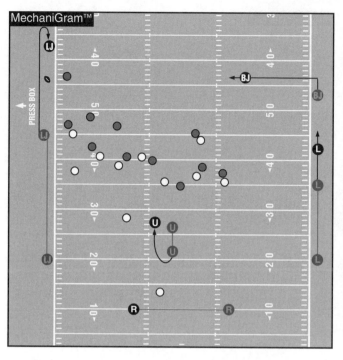

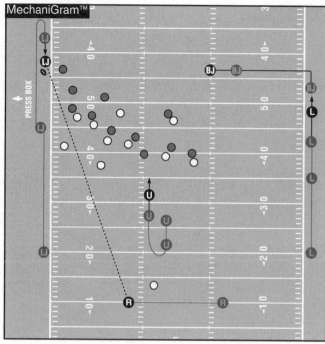

Action on the field: Ball travels out of bounds.

Referee: Moves into position to determine where ball went out of bounds.

Umpire: Pivots toward the direction of kick, observing players as they move downfield. Moves downfield with flow of players.

Linesman: Moves downfield and observes action of players in front of ball.

Line judge: Moves quickly down sideline, stopping clock when he sees ball go out of bounds. Moves five to seven yards beyond spot where ball apparently went out of bounds, pivots and makes eye contact with referee.

Back judge: Observes action of players in front of ball.

Action on the field: Ball spotted for new series.

Referee: With arm above head, observes line judge walking toward spot. When line judge reaches spot, drops arm with chopping motion. When certain there are no penalty markers down, signals linesman to move chain crew.

Umpire: Observes action of players in front of ball. Moves to spot to set ball for new series.

Linesman: Observes action of players in front of ball. Upon signal from referee, instructs chain crew to move to spot.

Line judge: Walks slowly toward referee, stopping when referee drops arm with chopping motion. Signals first down for team R.

Back judge: Observes action of players in front of ball. Mirrors linesman's spot.

Movement →   Previous position Current position (stopped)   Previous position Current position (still moving)

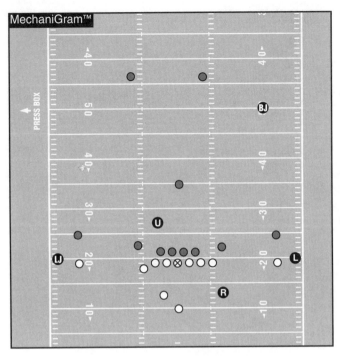

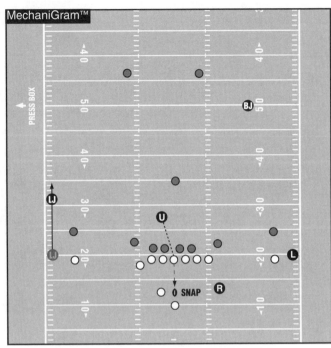

Action on the field: Starting position.

Referee: Three to four yards in front of and five to yards outside the punter, on the punter's kicking-leg side.

Umpire: Four to seven yards deep and favoring the line judge's sideline.

Linesman: Straddling the line of scrimmage and more than nine yards outside the widest offensive player.

Line judge: Straddling the line of scrimmage and more than nine yards outside the widest offensive player.

Back judge: Seven to 10 yards wider than and in front of the deepest receiver on the linesman's side of the field.

Action on the field: Ball snapped to punter.

Referee: Observes snap and action in front of and around kicker.

Umpire: Moves toward the line at the snap, observes initial line charge.

Linesman: Observes initial line charge and remains on the line to rule whether or not the kick crossed the neutral zone.

Line judge: Releases on snap and begins to move downfield, observes action on his side of the field between the neutral zone and the receivers.

Back judge: Observes action of receivers.

KEY

Referee	Umpire	Line Judge	Linesman	Back Judge	Chain Gang	Ballboy	Coach	Offense	Defense	Football	Possession of football

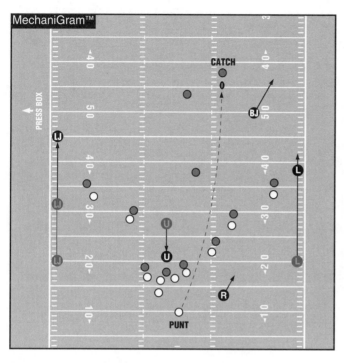

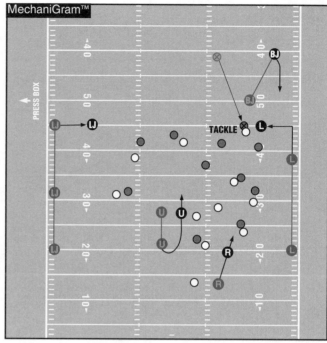

Action on the field: Receiver catches punt.

Referee: Observes line play after ball has cleared neutral zone. Moves slowly downfield.

Umpire: Pivots toward line judge's side of the field. Observes players as they move downfield. Moves downfield with flow of players.

Linesman: Observes action of players in front of ball.

Line judge: Observes action of players in front of ball.

Back judge: Moves with runner.

Action on the field: Runner advances and is downed.

Referee: Observes action of players. When certain there are no penalty markers down, signals linesman to move chain crew.

Umpire: Observes action of players. Moves to spot to set ball for new series.

Linesman: Takes coverage of runner when runner enters coverage area. When runner is downed, squares off to spot and stops the clock. Upon signal from referee, instructs chain crew to move to spot.

Line judge: Observes action of players. Squares off to mirror linesman's spot.

Back judge: Gives up coverage of runner when runner enters linesman's coverage area (halo concept). Observes action of players.

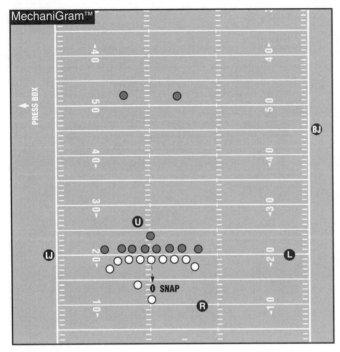

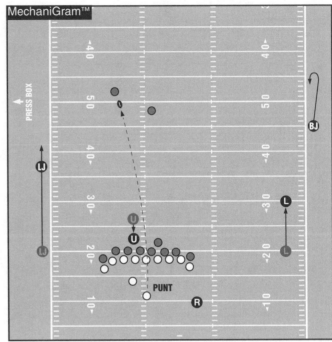

Action on the field: Starting position.

Referee: In front of the kicker, wider than where the tight end would normally be positioned, and on the kicking-leg side. Able to see all the backs and far enough away from the kicker to observe the blockers and kicker at the same time.

Umpire: Four to seven yards deep and favoring the line judge's sideline.

Linesman: Straddling the line of scrimmage, at least seven yards outside the widest offensive player and never inside the top of the numbers.

Line judge: Straddling the line of scrimmage, at least seven yards outside the widest offensive player and never inside the top of the numbers. When the snap is from the hashmark, position on the sideline is required.

Back judge: On the linesman's sideline outside and in front of the deep receivers.

Action on the field: Ball is kicked to line judge's side.

Referee: Observes snap and action around kicker.

Umpire: Moves toward the line at the snap, observing initial charge of linemen and contact on the snapper.

Linesman: Observes initial line charge and remains on the line to rule whether or not the kick crossed the neutral zone. Moves downfield when ball crosses zone.

Line judge: Observes initial line charge, then moves downfield.

Back judge: Observes receivers. Retreats with kick to observe catch.

KEY

| Referee | Umpire | Line Judge | Linesman | Back Judge | Chain Gang | Ballboy | Coach | Offense | Defense | Football | Possession of football |

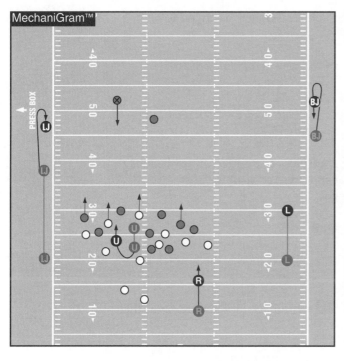

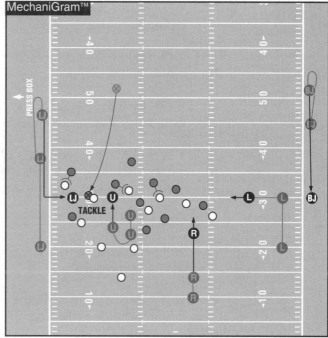

Action on the field: Receiver catches punt and begins advance.

Referee: Moves slowly downfield; observes players in front of ball.

Umpire: Pivots toward the line judge's side of the field; moves downfield and observes players as they move downfield.

Linesman: Moves downfield to end of coverage area and observes action of players in his area.

Line judge: Moves quickly downfield; observes players in front of ball. Pivots and moves upfield to stay ahead of runner (halo coverage).

Back judge: Moves upfield. Observes action around receiver.

Action on the field: Runner advances and is downed.

Referee: Moves slowly downfield; observes players in front of ball. When ball is dead and is certain there are no penalty markers down, signals linesman to move chain crew.

Umpire: Pivots toward the line judge's side of the field; observes players as they move downfield. Moves to spot to set ball for new series.

Linesman: Observes action of players in front of ball. Upon signal from referee, instructs chain crew to move to spot.

Line judge: Observes runner and action in front of runner. When runner is downed, squares off to spot and stops the clock.

Back judge: Continues to move upfield. Observes action around receiver.

• The referee can use a verbal alert such as "Gone!" as an aid to help prevent roughing the kicker.

• The umpire should remind team R players about rules relating to contact on the snapper.

• The line judge should observe the receivers and the players around them rather than the ball as it flies downfield.

• In NCAA, the covering official, regardless of position, must beanbag the spot where the kick ends. That spot may be used for post-scrimmage kick penalty enforcement.

Quiz

Without referring back, you should be able to answer the following true-false questions.

1. The umpire's starting position on a scrimmage kick should favor the line judge's side of the field.

2. If the ball is partially blocked, the legal touching signal should be used.

3. The linesman is responsible for his sideline from the line of scrimmage to team R's endline.

4. The umpire is solely responsible for determining whether or not a kick has crossed the neutral zone.

5. The umpire should pivot and move downfield immediately after observing contact on the snapper.

1. *True* 2. *True* 3. *False* 4. *False* 5. *False*

Chapter 20

Scoring Kicks

Naturally, whether or not a field goal or kick try is good is of prime importance to both teams. Officials need to be especially diligent during any situation that may result in a score.

In addition to ruling on whether the kick passed between the uprights and over the crossbar, officials should watch for an end tripping a rushing linebacker, defenders pulling linemen by the shoulder pads to open gaps for teammates shooting through or a defender leaping on a teammate's back to gain elevation for blocking the kick. All of those techniques have been tried from time to time, and officials must anticipate them and observe them.

Sometimes the officiating manuals offer unreasonable expectations. A scoring kick situation involves putting two officials by the goalposts, effectively forcing three officials to watch the actions of 22 players. But officials have to reconcile those issues, and the best way to do that is to accept the basic dictates, to compromise and to modify where necessary and make plans for contingencies.

The line judge and the back judge rule on the kick. They should confirm their ruling verbally using "good" or "no, no, no." It is too easy to confuse "no good" with "good" and vice versa, thus the recommendation to use two distinctly different phrases.

If the ball flies near one post, that official should call first, which is simply common sense. Both manuals say the back judge should judge the crossbar. If a pair of officials are back there seven yards behind the posts (too close to or directly under the posts makes it difficult to judge), there is probably no sound reason why both can't make the call. Whether they step smartly in front of the posts to signal is a matter of choice, but signals should be held long enough for the referee to see them. The back judge is the designated whistle-blower, sounding the whistle when the ball becomes dead.

If the kick falls short in the end zone, both officials should give the kick failed signal, then the stop-the-clock or touchback signal as appropriate to the situation.

Both deep officials are to head for the sideline, along the endline, if team K fakes the kick or is forced to abort the kick due to a bad snap or other mishap. The line judge has the greater responsibility in such a situation because his sideline is exposed. The recommendation here is that both deep officials fix their eyes on players in the defensive backfield, looking for holding or interference. If a two-point try is going to win the game, players may resort to frantic

behavior to secure an advantage.

If the apparent kick takes place from beyond the 15 yardline and a broken play results instead, the back judge and line judge must assume goalline responsibility, from the sidelines looking inward. No question about it, both goalpost officials have to react with dispatch if a supposed kick turns out to be no kick.

The linesman must focus entirely on the line because the line judge is downfield. He should try to watch action by and against the end and tackle, with a secondary shift of vision to the up back ahead of the holder on the kicking team. When a kick definitely clears the line, the linesman should continue forward to help the umpire police dead-ball post-play unpiling, but he can also serve a critical function as a watchdog, namely, making sure neither the holder nor kicker are hit with a delayed blow while the referee is turning to the pressbox to echo the signal.

If a defender crouches head up on the snapper, the umpire has no alternative but to watch the snapper as the ball is snapped. By the time he sees that the center has not been fouled, the play will be nearly over and the umpire won't be able to see much else.

If there is no defender directly facing the center, the umpire can turn to watch the guard and tackle on the line judge's side. The manuals recommend that the umpire favor that side anyway, but he won't be much help if a runner heads for the open pylon. The umpire can, though, step to the goalline on broken plays and help goalline penetration.

The umpire should stay at the line of scrimmage and supervise the untangling of players after the kick.

The referee should be fairly wide; most referees spread wider than the two to five yards the manuals prescribe. Both manuals also have the referee stand a yard deeper than the kicker, but again that can vary according to preference. The key thing is to have a good perspective on judging the snap, hold and kick, and be ready to react properly to a fake.

Some referees start even with the snapper, about five yards outside the end on the line judge's side of the field, then move back to get an angle on the kicker and holder when the ball is placed. Such an alignment allows the crew to fill the sideline vacancy caused by the line judge's move to the goalposts. However, it gives the referee a lot of ground to cover if the snap gets past the holder and rolls deeper into the offensive backfield. If a fake or broken play results in a passer rolling toward the linesman's side, the linesman will have to make judgments otherwise left to the referee, such as a passer beyond the line or intentional grounding. If the runner is driven out of bounds, the crew's ability to ensure the safety of players who tumble out of bounds will also be compromised.

Alternative coverage: A simple way to have secure and complete coverage is to put only the back judge behind the posts and to leave the line judge at the scrimmage line, where he can move to the goalline at the snap. If a play is run at the pylon on the line judge's side with the line judge behind the post and the referee on the linesman's side, only spectators in the stands may be able to see if a touchdown was scored. Putting the line judge on the line eliminates that possibility.

Regardless of whether the kicker is right- or left-footed, and whether the holder facing him or facing away, the referee can station himself on the line judge's side. An alert and intelligent referee will set up very wide. After all, he doesn't have to get behind the kicker to rule on the kick.

General procedures

Unlike the procedures for four-man crews, the five-man positioning and responsibilities do not change based on the distance of the kick attempt.

The referee faces the holder from a position about one yard behind and two to three yards wide of the kicker (NCAA: Eight yards behind the line and five yards to the side). After the snap, the referee observes the actions of the kicker and holder. If the holder has to leave a kneeling position to catch or recover a poor snap, the referee must rule on the holder's ability to return to a kneeling position.

After the kick, the referee is responsible for ruling on contact on the kicker and holder. A verbal alert such as "Gone!" is an aid to help prevent roughing the kicker and holder. In Federation, if a kick try is blocked, the referee should blow his whistle immediately; a blocked field goal remains live, however. In NCAA, the ball remains live in both instances.

In cases of a fake or a broken play, the referee assists on sideline coverage on the line judge's side of the field.

Once he is confident the kicker and holder are in no danger of being roughed, the referee looks to the deep officials to learn the result of the kick. The signal should then be relayed to the pressbox.

The umpire's position is four to seven yards off the line, favoring the line judge's side of the field (NCAA: Eight to 10 yards deep and on the line judge's side). The umpire is responsible for checking the numbers of the players on the offensive line (team K may use the numbering exception, but the umpire needs to know if a player wearing an eligible receiver's number is in an ineligible position in case a fake kick results in a pass).

Remind team R players about rules relating to contact on the snapper. The umpire can see players shooting gaps or lineman chopping rushers at the knees (the ball will be snapped out of the free-blocking/free-clipping zone) as well as contact on the snapper. Move toward the line at the snap, which will improve the view of the initial line charge.

If a blocked kick or fake results in a play toward the goalline on the line judge's side of the field, the umpire moves toward the goalline to assist on coverage of the runner. The umpire also helps rule whether or not a blocked kick crossed the neutral zone on his side of the field.

The linesman's starting position is on the line of scrimmage and five to seven yards outside the offensive end. On a blocked field goal attempt, the linesman will rule whether or not the kick crossed the neutral zone. That determination is the key element in determining if team K can recover or advance a scrimmage kick. Because the line judge has vacated his position, the linesman also has sole responsibility for encroachment. In NCAA, the linesman also rules on the legality of the snap.

If a pass is used on the fake, the linesman must know if the passer was beyond the line. He can also help rule on ineligibles downfield on fake kicks that lead to passes. When a runner approaches the goalline, the linesman must be at the goalline to rule on the potential score.

The vast majority of scoring kick attempts will be routine — no muffs or fakes. In those instances, the linesman can move toward the offensive and defensive linemen after the kick and use his voice to encourage players to unpile. In NCAA, the linesman should remind the box holder not to move the box after a missed field goal; when the snap is outside team R's 20 yardline, the ball is returned to the previous spot.

The line judge and back judge stand beyond the end zone and behind the upright on their side of the field (NCAA specifies five to seven yards behind the goalposts). The positioning can be adjusted once the ball is kicked to provide the best look possible. The line judge is responsible for ruling whether the ball passed inside or outside the upright on his side; the back judge is responsible for ruling whether the ball passed inside or outside the upright on his side as well as whether the ball cleared the crossbar.

When a successful kick passes the upright or when the ball breaks the goalline plane and it is obvious it will not score, the back judge sounds his whistle and gives the appropriate signals. If the kick is blocked, is obviously short or the play turns out not to be a kick (fake or busted play), the deep officials should move along the endline and toward the nearest sideline. That is especially crucial for the line judge, who is the official in the best position to rule on that sideline. Once the sideline has been reached, the deep official can move toward the goalline to assist on coverage of the runner.

In NCAA, if the kick narrowly misses wide, the official nearest the appropriate upright may signal why the kick failed by giving the appropriate supplementary signal (both arms swept away from the goalposts). *Referee* recommendation: If your association or assigning agency allows, use the signal when appropriate.

CHALK TALK: FEDERATION SCORING KICK POSITIONING AND COVERAGE ZONES

Referee: Starting position is about a yard behind and two to three yards to the side of kicker, facing the holder.

After the snap, the referee observes the actions of the kicker and holder. If the holder has to leave a kneeling position to catch or recover a poor snap, the referee must rule on the holder's ability to return to a kneeling position.

In cases of a fake or a broken play, the referee assists on sideline coverage on the line judge's side of the field.

Once he is confident the kicker and holder are in no danger of being roughed, the referee looks to the deep officials to learn the result of the kick. The signal should then be relayed to the pressbox.

Umpire: Starting position is four to seven yards off line, favoring the line judge's side of field.

The umpire is responsible for checking the numbers of the players on the offensive line and should remind team R players about rules relating to contact on the snapper. The umpire move toward the line at the snap, which will improve the view of the initial line charge.

If a blocked kick or fake results in a play toward the goalline on the line judge's side of the field, the umpire moves toward the goalline to assist on coverage of the runner. The umpire also helps rule whether or not a blocked kick crossed the neutral zone on his side of the field.

Linesman: Starting position is five to seven yards outside widest offensive end.

On a blocked field goal attempt, the linesman will rule whether or not the kick crossed the neutral zone. The linesman also has sole responsibility for encroachment and rules on the legality of the snap.

If a pass is used on the fake, the linesman must know if the passer was beyond the line. He can also help rule on ineligibles downfield on fake kicks that lead to passes. When a runner approaches the goalline, the linesman must be at the goalline to rule on the potential score.

The linesman can move toward the offensive and defensive linemen after the kick and use his voice to encourage players to unpile.

Line judge and back judge: Starting position is beyond the endline and behind the upright.

They should confirm their ruling verbally before signaling, using "good" or "no, no, no."

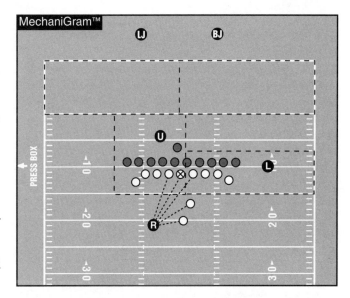

The line judge is responsible for ruling whether the ball passed inside or outside the upright on his side; the back judge is responsible for ruling whether the ball passed inside or outside the upright on his side as well as whether the ball cleared the crossbar.

When a successful kick passes the upright or when the ball breaks the goalline plane and it is obvious it will not score, the back judge sounds his whistle and gives the appropriate signals. If the kick is blocked, is obviously short or the play turns out not to be a kick (fake or busted play), the deep officials should move along the endline and toward the nearest sideline. That is especially crucial for the line judge, who is the official in the best position to rule on that sideline. Once the sideline has been reached, the deep official can move toward the goalline to assist on coverage of the runner.

Referee recommendation: If the kick narrowly misses wide, the official nearest the appropriate upright should signal why the kick failed by giving the appropriate supplementary signal (both arms swept away from the goalposts).

CHALK TALK: NCAA SCORING KICK POSITIONING AND COVERAGE ZONES

Referee: Starting position is eight yards behind the line and five yards to the side of the kicker, facing the holder.

After the snap, the referee observes the actions of the kicker and holder. If the holder has to leave a kneeling position to catch or recover a poor snap, the referee must rule on the holder's ability to return to a kneeling position.

In cases of a fake or a broken play, the referee assists on sideline coverage on the line judge's side of the field.

Once he is confident the kicker and holder are in no danger of being roughed, the referee looks to the deep officials to learn the result of the kick. The signal should then be relayed to the pressbox.

Umpire: Starting position is eight to 10 yards deep, favoring the line judge's side of field.

The umpire is responsible for checking the numbers of the players on the offensive line and should remind team R players about rules relating to contact on the snapper. The umpire move toward the line at the snap, which will improve the view of the initial line charge.

If a blocked kick or fake results in a play toward the goalline on the line judge's side of the field, the umpire moves toward the goalline to assist on coverage of the runner. The umpire also helps rule whether or not a blocked kick crossed the neutral zone on his side of the field.

Linesman: Starting position is five to seven yards outside widest offensive end. Before the snap, the box holder should be reminded not to move the box after a missed field goal; when the snap is outside team R's 20 yardline, the ball is returned to the previous spot.

On a blocked field goal attempt, the linesman will rule whether or not the kick crossed the neutral zone. The linesman also has sole responsibility for encroachment and rules on the legality of the snap.

If a pass is used on the fake, the linesman must know if the passer was beyond the line. He can also help rule on ineligibles downfield on fake kicks that lead to passes. When a runner approaches the goalline, the linesman must be at the goalline to rule on the potential score.

The linesman can move toward the offensive and defensive linemen after the kick and use his voice to encourage players to unpile.

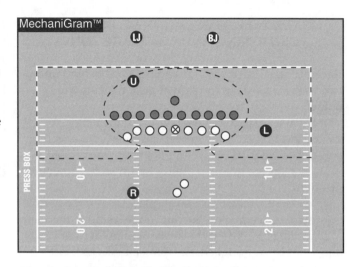

Line judge and back judge: Starting position is five to seven yards beyond endline and behind the upright. The positioning can be adjusted once the ball is kicked to provide the best look possible.

They should confirm their ruling verbally before signaling, using "good" or "no, no, no."

The line judge is responsible for ruling whether the ball passed inside or outside the upright on his side; the back judge is responsible for ruling whether the ball passed inside or outside the upright on his side as well as whether the ball cleared the crossbar.

When a successful kick passes the upright or when the ball breaks the goalline plane and it is obvious it will not score, the back judge sounds his whistle and gives the appropriate signals. If the kick is blocked, is obviously short or the play turns out not to be a kick (fake or busted play), the deep officials should move along the endline and toward the nearest sideline. That is especially crucial for the line judge, who is the official in the best position to rule on that sideline. Once the sideline has been reached, the deep official can move toward the goalline to assist on coverage of the runner.

If the kick narrowly misses wide, the official nearest the appropriate upright may signal why the kick failed by giving the appropriate supplementary signal (both arms swept away from the goalposts).

• The line judge and the back judge should use distinctly different phrases such as "good" or "no, no, no" to prevent confusion when ruling on a scoring kick.

• A verbal alert such as "Gone!" is a preventive officiating tool to help prevent roughing the kicker and holder.

• Another preventive officiating tip: Have the umpire remind team R players not to contact the snapper until allowed by rule.

• The linesman can help the umpire observe dead-ball action by moving toward the offensive and defensive linemen after the kick and using his voice to encourage players to unpile.

Quiz

Without referring back, you should be able to answer the following true-false questions.

1. The line judge is responsible for ruling whether the ball passed inside or outside the upright on his side.

2. The back judge is responsible for ruling whether the ball passed inside or outside the upright on his side as well as whether the ball cleared the crossbar.

3. The CCA-approved signal for indicating a scoring kick was wide is both arms swept away from the goalposts.

4. In Federation mechanics, the referee should blow his whistle immediately if a field goal is blocked.

5. In cases of a fake or a broken play, the referee assists on sideline coverage on the line judge's side of the field.

1. True 2. True 3. True 4. False 5. True

Chapter 21

Timeouts

Either team may request a timeout at any time when the ball is dead. The request must come from a player. The recognizing official should grant the timeout and immediately stop the clock if it is running. That official reports the timeout to the referee. The referee indicates the timeout using a two- or three-step procedure:

• Give the stop the clock signal regardless of whether the clocking is running. Two strokes of the arms are sufficient.

• Indicate the team being charged the timeout by facing the team and extending both arms shoulder high, giving three chucks in that team's direction.

• If it is the final charged timeout, follow with three tugs on an imaginary steam whistle (NCAA only, but recommended for Federation).

In the rare event that both teams request a timeout during the same dead-ball period, the first team requesting the timeout is charged. The other team must then be informed of the other team's timeout and asked if they would like a successive timeout.

All officials must record the number and team of the player requesting the timeout, the quarter and the time remaining on the game clock. Each official then confirms with the referee the number of timeouts each team has remaining. The linesman and line judge inform the coaches on their respective sidelines of the timeouts remaining. The referee informs the head coach when all timeouts have been exhausted. *Referee* recommendation: Inform the coach how many timeouts each team has remaining after each timeout.

The back judge is responsible for timing the timeout. Since the back judge also keeps the game time, it is imperative that the back judge have a watch with multiple modes. Such a watch allows the back judge to switch from a countdown mode to a regular watch mode that allow him to determine the one-minute count.

The one-minute count begins when the referee is informed of the timeout. When 45 seconds have expired, the timing official signals the referee, who signals to the linesman and line judge so they can inform their teams. When the minute has expired, the referee whistles the ball ready for play.

Although the line judge and linesman need to be firm when informing the teams the timeout has ended, there is no need to be gruff. Commands such as, "Coaches out," "Players back on the field," or "Timeout's over," can be replaced with statements such as, "We're ready for you, fellas," or "Time to play ball, guys."

The manuals prescribe that during the timeout, the umpire stands over the ball; the referee stands away from the other officials; the linesman and line judge stay near their respective teams to observe any attempts to use substitutes for deception; and the back judge should maintain a position 15 to 22 yards away from the ball. Those are good guidelines; in practice, the important thing is to avoid clustering and idle chit-chat during timeouts.

Coach-referee conference

If a coach-referee conference is requested, it is held on the field approximately five yards in front of the team area. Only the head coach and the referee participate. The other officials should keep assistant coaches away from the area of the discussion. The referee may be assisted by another official if that official was involved in the decision being questioned.

Injury timeout

The procedure for signaling the timeout is the same as for a charged timeout except that after stopping the clock, the referee taps his chest to indicate it is an official's timeout. Play should resume as quickly as possible after the injured player is safely off the field.

All officials should be alert to ensure neither team does any onfield coaching during the timeout. In Federation, the referee must determine whether an injured player was unconscious.

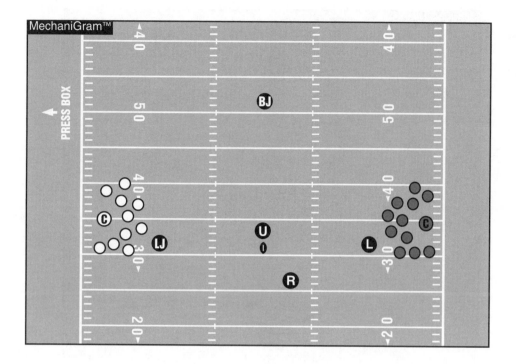

CHALK TALK: FEDERATION TIMEOUT WITH TEAMS AT SIDELINES

Referee: Gives stop the clock signal and indicates team calling timeout by chucking arms three times toward the team's goalline. Records the number and team of the player requesting the timeout, the quarter and the time remaining on the game clock. Confirms with the crew the number of timeouts each team has remaining. Stands away from other officials. On back judge's signal that 45 seconds have expired, points to linesman and line judge so they may tell teams timeout is over. On back judge's signal that 60 seconds have expired, blows whistle and signals ready for play.

Umpire: Records the number and team of the player requesting the timeout, the quarter and the time remaining on the game clock. Confirms with the referee the number of timeouts each team has remaining. Stands over the ball until referee signals ready for play.

Linesman: Records the number and team of the player requesting the timeout, the quarter and the time remaining on the game clock. Confirms with the referee the number of timeouts each team has remaining and relays information to coach or captain. Stands midway between the ball and the team's huddle. On referee's signal, informs team timeout is over.

Line judge: Records the number and team of the player requesting the timeout, the quarter and the time remaining on the game clock. Confirms with the referee the number of timeouts each team has remaining and relays information to coach or captain. Stands midway between the ball and team's huddle. On referee's signal, informs team timeout is over.

Back judge: Records the number and team of the player requesting the timeout, the quarter and the time remaining on the game clock. Confirms with the referee the number of timeouts each team has remaining. Stands away from other officials and times the timeout. Informs the referee when 45 seconds and again when 60 seconds have expired.

Note: Federation rules allow coaches to conduct timeouts on the field or on the sideline.

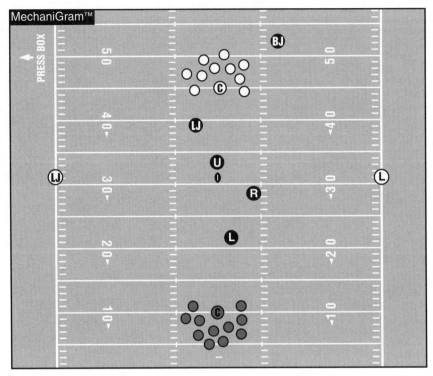

(LJ) (L) = *Referee* recommendation

CHALK TALK: FEDERATION TIMEOUT WITH COACHES ON THE FIELD

Referee: Gives stop the clock signal and indicates team calling timeout by chucking arms three times toward the team's goalline. Records the number and team of the player requesting the timeout, the quarter and the time remaining on the game clock. Confirms with the crew the number of timeouts each team has remaining. Stands away from other officials. On back judge's signal that 45 seconds have expired, points to linesman and line judge. On back judge's signal that 60 seconds have expired, blows whistle and signals ready for play.

Umpire: Echoes timeout signals. Records the number and team of the player requesting the timeout, the quarter and the time remaining on the game clock. Confirms with the referee the number of timeouts each team has remaining. Stands over the ball until referee signals ready for play.

Linesman: Echoes timeout signals. Records the number and team of the player requesting the timeout, the quarter and the time remaining on the game clock. Confirms with the referee the number of timeouts each team has remaining and relays information to coach or captain. Stands midway between ball and team's huddle. On referee's signal, informs team timeout is over. *Referee*

recommendation: Since the referee, umpire and back judge are already in the middle of the field, the linesman can remain on his sideline.

Line judge: Echoes timeout signals. Records the number and team of the player requesting the timeout, the quarter and the time remaining on the game clock. Confirms with the referee the number of timeouts each team has remaining and relays information to coach or captain. Stands midway between ball and visiting team's huddle. On referee's signal, informs team timeout is over. *Referee* recommendation: Since the referee, umpire and back judge are already in the middle of the field, the line judge can remain on his sideline.

Back judge: Echoes timeout signals. Records the number and team of the player requesting the timeout, the quarter and the time remaining on the game clock. Confirms with the referee the number of timeouts each team has remaining. Stands away from other officials and times the timeout. Informs the referee when 45 seconds and again when 60 seconds have expired.

Notes: If one team huddles on the field and the other at the sideline, the respective wing officials should follow the applicable procedure for the team on their sideline. NCAA rules prohibit coaches from conducting timeouts on the field.

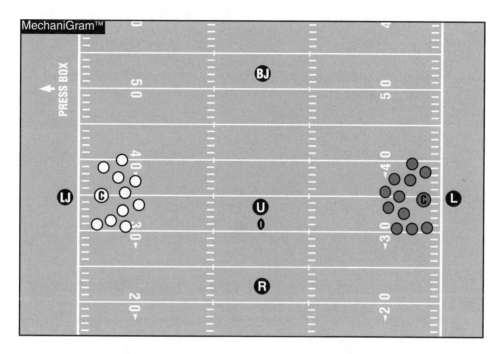

CHALK TALK: NCAA TIMEOUT

Referee: Gives stop the clock signal and indicates team calling timeout by chucking arms three times toward the team's goalline. Records the number and team of the player requesting the timeout, the quarter and the time remaining on the game clock. Confirms with the crew the number of timeouts each team has remaining. Stands away from other officials. On back judge's signal that 45 seconds have expired, points to linesman and line judge. On back judge's signal that 60 seconds have expired, blows whistle and signals ready for play.

Umpire: Records the number and team of the player requesting the timeout, the quarter and the time remaining on the game clock. Confirms with the referee the number of timeouts each team has remaining. Stands over the ball until referee signals ready for play.

Linesman: Records the number and team of the player requesting the timeout, the quarter and the time remaining on the game clock. Confirms with the referee the number of timeouts each team has remaining and relays information to coach or captain. Stands midway between team's huddle and its team area. On referee's signal, informs team timeout is over.

Line judge: Records the number and team of the player requesting the timeout, the quarter and the time remaining on the game clock. Confirms with the referee

the number of timeouts each team has remaining and relays information to coach or captain. Stands midway between team's huddle and its team area. On referee's signal, informs team timeout is over.

Back judge: Records the number and team of the player requesting the timeout, the quarter and the time remaining on the game clock. Confirms with the referee the number of timeouts each team has remaining. Stands away from other officials and times the timeout. Informs the referee when 45 seconds and again when 60 seconds have expired.

Note: NCAA rules do not allow coaches to conduct timeouts on the field.

• The officials observing the teams should ensure neither team uses deceptive substitution practices during timeouts.

• The umpire should remain over the ball until the referee gives the ready signal.

• In CCA mechanics, the referee gives three tugs on an imaginary steam whistle to indicate a team has used its last timeout. Referee recommends the same signal be used in Federation.

• If the timeout is for an injury, the referee should follow the stop-the-clock signal by tapping his chest.

Quiz

Without referring back, you should be able to answer the following true-false questions.

1. A charged timeout lasts 60 seconds.

2. After 45 seconds, the back judge should signal the referee, who instructs the wing officials to tell the teams the timeout is over.

3. When a timeout is called, it is only necessary to give the stop-the-clock signal if the clock is running.

4. Only the referee must record the number and team of the player requesting the timeout, the quarter and the time remaining on the game clock.

5. In Federation, the referee must determine whether an injured player was unconscious.

1. True 2. True 3. False 4. False 5. True

Chapter 22

Measurements

A typical game requires two to three measurements for a first down. On a poorly marked field, you'll have to measure more often. If the line-to-gain stake is right on a five or 10 yardline (e.g. 10 yardline, 25 yardline, et al), it's easier to discern whether the first down has been made and the measurement can possibly be averted. A captain's request for a measurement should be honored unless it is made after the ball is moved from the dead-ball spot or is made after the ready-for-play signal. The defensive captain should be told when a first down is made so he has the opportunity to ask for a measurement.

When the referee signals for a measurement, the line judge should place a beanbag at the intersection of the five yardline where the chain is clipped and a line through the ball parallel to the sideline (some crews have the line judge mark the spot with his foot). That is the spot where the linesman will place the clipped part of the chain; the beanbag enables the linesman to go directly to the spot without fumbling around.

The linesman brings the chain in from the sideline with the chain crew members. Putting one hand on the links on each side of the clip improves the linesman's chances of keeping track of the proper link in case the clip falls off the chain. As the linesman approaches the line judge, the linesman tells his crewmate which part of the line (back, middle or front) the chain crew used to place the clip. The clip must be placed on that part of the line for the measurement. A good double-check is for the linesman to state that the next down will be first if the ball is beyond the stake or the next down of the series if it is short. (Example: "It will either be first or fourth.")

The back judge holds the ball in place from the downfield side (the side of the ball opposite from the sideline the chains are coming from). Holding the ball in that way will preclude the ball from being accidentally displaced. The down marker is moved to the forward point of the ball by the chain crew member.

Once the linesman tells the referee he has the chain on the proper mark, the umpire takes the forward stake from the chain crew member, then pulls the stake to ensure the chain is taut. The referee rules whether or not the ball is beyond the front stake.

Short of a first down

If the measurement is in a side zone and does not result in a first down, the umpire should keep control of the stake. The referee uses his hands (or fingers if the ball is inches short of the front stake) to inform both benches how short the play ended of a first down.

After signaling, the referee grasps the chain at the link in front of the ball and rises. The referee should grasp the chain with two hands with the link that will be used to place the ball between his hands; that will ensure the proper link is maintained. The back judge continues to hold the ball in place. Referee, umpire and linesman walk to the nearest hashmark. The line judge is free to either obtain a new ball from a ballboy or retrieve the ball the back judge is holding. If the latter method is used, the back judge maintains his position until the ball is placed.

When a first down is not made, the linesman must again hold the chain on either side of the clip while he accompanies the chain crew and the chains are moved back to the sideline. Otherwise, the clip could break or simply come off.

The referee must wait for the linesman's signal that the chain crew is back in position before giving the ready-for-play signal.

If the measurement occurred on fourth down and team A is short, the referee signals the change of possession by giving the first down signal toward team A's goalline. The referee then sets the ball in the same position as it was when it became dead so its foremost point becomes the rear point when the direction is changed. The new rear stake is then moved to the new foremost point of the ball.

First down

If the measurement results in the award of a new series, the referee signals the first down. The linesman need not hold the chain as he accompanies the chain crew back to the sideline, but he must go all the way to the sideline and indicate to the chain crew where the new series will begin.

If the measurement occurred in a side zone, the back judge should remain with the ball on the ground as a double-check to ensure the ball is spotted properly for the next play. The line judge may obtain a new ball from a ballboy or the back judge can relay the ball on the ground to the referee who relays it to the umpire at the hashmark. The umpire then spots the ball using either the ball on the ground or the back judge's extended foot as a guide for placement.

Since the down has been completed, moving the down marker forward is routine and having it on the forward point of the ball is necessary in the event the ball is inadvertently moved. The exception is if the measurement is a prelude to a penalty acceptance decision. An example: With about five yards to go, team K punts on fourth down and is happy with the results. Team R is flagged for a five-yard live-ball foul. Team K requests a measurement. They will accept the penalty if it yields a first down and decline it otherwise. In that case the down marker must remain at the previous spot.

The referee must wait for the linesman's signal that the chain crew is back in position before giving the ready-for-play signal.

End of quarter

At the end of the first and third quarters, the referee, umpire and linesman record the following data: the team in possession, the yardline the ball is on, the down, the yards necessary for a first down and the yardline where the chain is clipped.

The linesman should carry a snap clip (in addition to the yardage clip) to place on the chain where the box is. (That can only be done when there are less than 10 yards to go. When there is more than 10 yards to go, the umpire must step off the distance.) The snap clip should be placed on the chain to indicate where the box was located. The box can then be easily placed at the proper spot when the chains are reset. Once the snap clip is in place, the referee signals the linesman to move the chains.

The linesman has the chain crew change direction and trots with them to the opposite end of the field. The linesman must hold the yardage clip at all times and the box holder must hold the snap clip. Do not allow either the yardage clip or secondary clip to drag on the ground; they could easily become dislodged.

The referee and umpire trot to the appropriate yardline on the opposite end of the field. The umpire faces the chain crew, setting the ball on the ground only after the box is in place. By waiting for the box to be placed first, the crew can avoid the possibility of having to move the ball once it is placed. The line judge should note the yardline the yardage clip was on. He can then trot ahead to the same yardline on the other end of the field to ensure the yardage clip is placed on the proper yardline.

When the first or third quarter ends on a play resulting in a first down, set the chains and the clip before you switch sides of the field. Yes, it is seemingly unnecessary and takes a few minutes longer, but if you don't, you lose the double-check on where the umpire places the ball.

Finally, if the period ends with less than a yard to go, the chains should be brought out to the ball to get the exact location of the ball. The crew then proceeds as for a measurement.

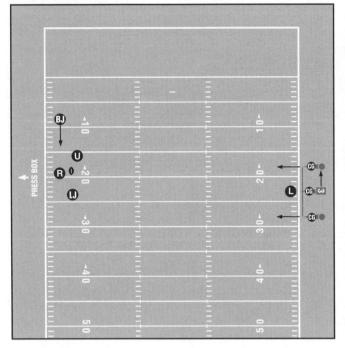

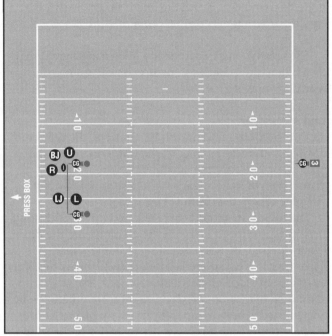

Action on the field: Play ends in side zone close to a first down.

Referee: Stops clock after seeing that measurement is necessary. Waits at spot for arrival of chain gang.

Umpire: Waits at spot for arrival of chain gang.

Linesman: Has box holder move box behind lead stake. Brings chain in from sideline with chain gang members to spot indicated by line judge.

Line judge: Indicates intersection of the five yardline where chain is clipped and line through ball parallel to sideline with beanbag or foot.

Back judge: Moves to spot to hold ball in place on ground.

Action on the field: Team A is short of a first down.

Referee: Rules whether or not ball is beyond front stake. Uses hands or fingers to inform both benches how short the play ended of first down.

Umpire: Holds lead stake.

Linesman: Holds chain in place.

Line judge: Gets spare ball from ballboy.

Back judge: Holds ball in place on ground.

KEY

Referee Umpire Line Judge Linesman Back Judge Chain Gang Ballboy Coach Offense Defense Football Possession of football

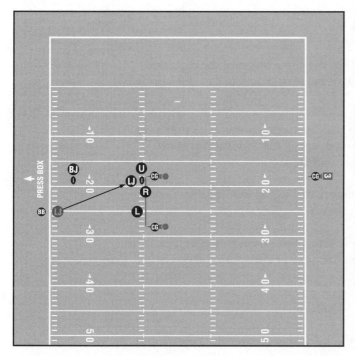

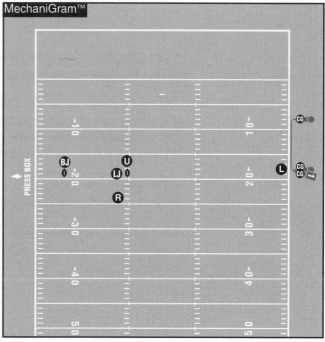

Action on the field: Chains are moved to hashmark for ball placement.

Referee: Grasps chain at link in front of ball and rises. Walks to nearest hashmark. Gets ball from line judge and places it. Waits for linesman's signal that chain gang is back in position and other officials are ready before giving ready-for-play signal.

Umpire: Maintains control of front stake and walks to nearest hashmark.

Linesman: Maintains control of clip and walks to nearest hashmark. Accompanies chain gang back to sideline and sets chains for next down.

Line judge: Delivers ball to referee for placement.

Back judge: Holds ball in place on ground.

Action on the field: Team A is awarded a new series.

Referee: Signals first down. Waits for linesman's signal that chain gang is back in position and other officials are ready before giving ready-for-play signal.

Umpire: Moves to hashmark where ball will next be snapped. Gets ball from line judge and places it.

Linesman: Returns to sideline with chain gang and indicates where new series will begin.

Line judge: Delivers ball to umpire for placement.

Back judge: Holds ball in place on ground.

Movement → | Previous position (U) → Current position (U) (stopped) | Previous position (U) → Current position (U) (still moving)

• Grasping the links on each side of the clip instead of the clip itself allows the linesman to keep track of the proper link in case the clip falls off the chain.

• The linesman should verbalize that the next down will be first if the ball is beyond the stake or the next down of the series if it is short. (Example: "It will either be first or fourth.")

• The referee must wait for the linesman's signal that the chain crew is back in position before giving the ready-for-play signal.

• When changing ends after the first or third quarters, the umpire faces the chain crew, setting the ball on the ground only after the box is in place.

Quiz

Without referring back, you should be able to answer the following true-false questions.

1. The line judge holds the ball in place on the ground to ensure it is not moved off the spot.

2. A captain's request for a measurement should be denied if the request is made after the ready-for-play signal.

3. The referee should signal to both benches when indicating the measurement came up short of a first down.

4. If the first quarter ends with the ball squarely on the 50 yardline, there is no need for the chain crew members to switch ends.

5. The umpire controls the front stake and pulls the chain taut for a measurement.

1. False 2. True 3. True 4. False 5. True

Crew of Four

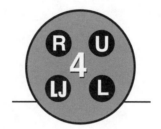

Football Officials Guidebook
Mechanics For Crews of Four and Five Officials

Chapter 23

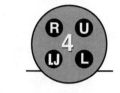

Coin Toss

Coin Toss

In most cases, the players' first contact with the officials will be at the coin toss. Discharging the coin toss duties professionally and efficiently will leave the captains with a positive first impression.

Do not use the coin toss as an opportunity to tell the captains how the game will be officiated. Let the captains know you will do your best to answer any questions they have during the game and that they will serve as the conduit between the officials and the other players.

General procedures

When the referee and umpire meet with the coaches prior to the game, they should obtain the name and number of each captain so they can be greeted by name. At about five minutes prior to game time, the referee and umpire go to their respective sidelines to greet the captains by name (refer to them by title, such as Captain Smith or Mr. Brown), shake their hands and ask them to remove their helmets. Having the captains remove their helmets and carry them to the center of the field allows full face-to-face contact during the toss.

The referee and umpire should ask which captain will make decisions during the toss; that captain (the "talking captain") should be positioned so he is closest to the referee when the group meets in the center of the field. For the sake of uniformity, it is preferable to have the referee face the scoreboard during the toss.

Referee recommendation: Regardless of the location of the pressbox, have the referee escort the home team captains while the umpire takes the visitors.

In Federation, the coin toss is normally conducted in the center of the field five minutes before the game. The state association may prescribe alternative procedures. The toss may be held at an earlier time off the field if both coaches agree. In such a case the results may be simulated in the center of the field three minutes before the game. The umpire goes to the sideline with the line-to-gain equipment and the referee to the opposite sideline. In most situations the visiting team is opposite the pressbox with the line-to-gain equipment on their sideline. The linesman and line judge remain on their respective sidelines. Upon arrival in the center of the field, the umpire and referee will be across from each other.

In NCAA, the toss is normally conducted in the center of the field three minutes before the game. The referee goes to the sideline with the line-to-gain equipment and the umpire to the opposite sideline. In most situations the visiting team is opposite the pressbox with the line-to-gain equipment on their sideline. When they reach the center of the field, the referee and umpire will be next to each other. The line judge, on the sideline opposite the chains, and the linesman, on the opposite sideline, remain on the sideline.

Players who are not involved in the toss should be kept out of the area between the top of the numbers on both sides of the field. The captains stand so their backs are to their own sidelines. The captains are asked to introduce themselves to each other.

The referee should allow all captains to view both sides of the coin, identifying which side is heads and which is tails. A silver dollar or half-dollar is preferred because their size eases identification of heads and tails.

The referee explains the coin flip procedure: The visiting captain is instructed to call heads or tails while the coin is in the air, the coin will be caught by the referee and turned or not turned over. If the coin is dropped, the toss will be repeated. The referee may choose to have the captain declare heads or tails before the coin is flipped; the referee may also choose to have the coin hit the ground.

Once the winner is determined, the winner is offered his choice. *Referee* recommends that the captain of the team winning the toss should be offered choices in the following sequence: defer, receive or defend a goal. The order is that of the most likely selection and omits "kick." Kick is a valid choice, but one that, most likely, will get the captain in trouble. If the captain was told to pick kick, he will pick it whether or not it is offered.

If the choice is to defer, the referee immediately faces the pressbox, taps the shoulder of the deferring captain and signals the declination. The remaining choices are then presented to the other captain and the final selection is made by the deferring captain. If the winner of the coin toss does not defer, no signal is immediately given.

When the final selections are made, the captains are asked to put their backs to their goalline and the referee gives the appropriate signal. If the choice is to kick or receive, only the first selection is signaled. If the choice is to defend a goal, two signals are given: pointing both arms toward the goalline being defended, followed by the appropriate signal for the other captain.

If at any time during the toss the referee errs or gives incorrect information (for instance, giving the wrong team an option), he should speak up immediately.

When the toss is completed, the other officials shall join the referee and umpire in the center of the field and record the results of the toss. All officials simultaneously move to their kickoff positions.

The procedure is repeated before the second half. When the three-minute warmup period ends (NCAA:

When the halftime intermission expires), the referee and umpire go to their respective sidelines and once again escort the captains to the center of the field while the other officials assume the same positions as for the pregame toss. The referee offers the choices to either the deferring captain of the loser of the pregame coin toss, as appropriate.

Overtime procedure

If overtime is necessary, the officials wait for the three-minute intermission to end (NCAA: No intermission is specified; the officials meet to review overtime rules and procedures). The referee and umpire go to their respective sidelines and once again escort the captains to the center of the field while the other officials assume the same positions as for the pregame toss. The coin toss is repeated with the visiting team again calling it. When the winner is determined, the options are explained. The winner may not defer, but may choose offense, defense or the goal to be used.

When the selections are completed, the captains of the team on offense are asked to face the goalline in the direction their team will advance and the opposing captains stand with their backs to that goalline. The referee then taps the shoulder of the captain of the team that won the toss and gives the first down signal in the appropriate direction.

OUTLINE

I. Referee:

1. About five minutes (or as directed by state association) before game time, escort to center of field captains of team whose team box is on side opposite line-to-gain equipment. Speaking captain should be next to referee. Referee faces scoreboard.

2. Have captains face each other with their backs to their respective sidelines.

3. After umpire introduces captains, introduce captains to each other and give them instructions.

4. In presence of umpire:
   a. Instruct visiting captain to call toss while coin is in air.
   b. Inform captains if coin is not caught, you will toss again.
   c. Inform captains if there is question about call, you will toss again.
   d. After making toss and determining winner, place hand on captain's shoulder and have captain choose one of following options: Kick or receive, defend a goal or defer choice to second half.
   e. If winner chooses not to defer and makes a choice, give opposing captain choice of remaining options.
   f. If winner of toss defers, step toward pressbox and give penalty declined signal.
   g. Opposing captain then given choice of options, followed by deferring captain's choice of remaining option.

5. Place captains in position facing each other with backs toward goal they will defend.

6. While facing in same direction as the first choosing captain, signal choice by:
   a. Swing leg simulating kick.
   b. Make catching motion simulating receiving.
   c. If first choosing captain elected to defend a goal, point with both arms extended toward that goalline, then move to other captains and give appropriate signal for choice of other captain.

7. Dismiss captains.

8. Second-half choices:
   a. Prior to beginning of second half, escort to

center of field captains of team whose team box is on side opposite line-to-gain equipment.
   b. Obtain second-half choices and give appropriate signals to pressbox.
   c. Dismiss captains after any further instructions.

NOTES

1. If coin toss is held off field, results may be simulated at center of field three minutes prior to start of game or as directed by state association.

2. If coin toss is needed for overtime, repeat procedures with the following modifications:
   a. Coin toss occurs after three-minute intermission.
   b. Inform captains how many timeouts they have remaining for overtime period.
   c. After making toss and determining winner, place hand on captain's shoulder and have captain choose one of following options (deferment no longer an option): Offense, defense or defend a goal.
   d. Position offensive captain facing goal toward which ball will be advanced and give first down signal.

II. Umpire:

1. About five minutes (or as directed by state association) before game time, escort to center of field the captains of team whose team box is on side where line-to-gain equipment is located. Speaking captain should be next to referee.

2. After introducing captains to referee, remain with referee to listen to instructions and record toss options.

3. Repeat choice of calling captain loudly enough for all captains and referee to hear. If there is a discrepancy in what you heard and what captain says he called, flip should be repeated.

4. Second-half choices:
   a. On signal from referee, escort captains to center of field.
   b. Remain with referee and captains and check on options given teams to ensure accuracy.

III. Linesman

1. Remain at inbounds mark (Federation) or sideline (NCAA) on side where line-to-gain equipment is

located; keep team members who are not involved in toss between you and sideline.

2. Obtain football of kicking team's choice.

3. Second-half choices:

a. Remain on side where line-to-gain equipment is located.

b. Review procedures and correct problems with line-to-gain crew.

c. Indicate end of field line-to-gain crew will be on prior to kickoff.

d. Assume same position at inbounds mark as prior to first half kickoff.

4. Obtain football of kicking team's choice.

IV. Line judge

1. Remain at inbounds mark (Federation) or sideline (NCAA) on side opposite line-to-gain equipment to keep team members who are not involved in toss between you and sideline.

2. Second-half choices:

a. Assume same position at inbounds mark as prior to first-half kickoff.

One of the things that makes a great official is a complete understanding of the game. That goes beyond rules and mechanics. Great referees anticipate plays. They always seem to be in the right place at the right time. It's not an accident or just luck. It's preparation and an understanding of the game. That puts them in the right spot at the right moment.

Studying the game

Part of that preparation is studying the game itself. Just what are the teams trying to do on the field? The novice or unprepared referee doesn't think beyond, "This team is trying to score more points than the other team."

The great referees think about offensive styles, defensive schemes, tempo and tendencies. For example, they'll know or recognize that Central High's motion men always go toward the wide side of the field. They use zone pass defense but double cover the widest receiver on obvious passing downs. They have a history of putting their best offensive lineman at left tackle and usually run the ball behind that tackle on short yardage situations. They isolate a fullback on a blitzing linebacker. They don't save onside kicks for obvious short free kick situations.

The different approaches are obvious: The more you know about the game and a team's tendencies, the better prepared you are.

Recognizing and knowing what coaches and players are trying to do elevates your game. When you have that knowledge, you can adjust your field coverage accordingly. In the section on coverage philosophy (page 20), you read how anticipation is critical to successful officiating. The obvious question is, how do you get better at anticipating plays? You study the game and the specific plays.

As the game of football becomes more complex, officials must be more aware of specific tendencies and strategies. When officials recognize offensive plays and defensive strategies, they make better field coverage adjustments.

Gaining the knowledge

How do you gain the knowledge about specific plays and teams? One way is to talk to other officials. If you know referees who have had a team you're about to officiate, ask them questions about style and tempo. Another way is to carefully watch the players during the pregame warmup.

The most common: Learning and adjusting while the game is in progress. You must develop the ability to see what's happening on the field and adjust accordingly.

Regardless of position, you're not just watching a bunch of players move. Learn to watch specific, orchestrated offensive and defensive plays while on the field. Then, make the necessary adjustments.

For most referees who don't have an extensive playing or coaching background, it takes time to develop those skills. Practice while watching other games (on TV or in person). See what's happening on the field and recognize the offensive plays and defensive schemes. Think about what is likely to happen once you've recognized the play.

Here's an example of how a well-schooled official thinks on the field. Central High, leading by five points with 1:40 remaining in the game, has the ball on its own 17 yardline. It's third down and six yards to go. The clock is running and West High is out of timeouts. The seasoned official realizes Central will likely not pass. Why not? Because an intercepted pass could be returned for the go-ahead touchdown or would at worst put West in prime scoring position. An incomplete pass would stop the clock, something West cannot do since it is out of timeouts.

What is more likely is that Central will use up as much of the 25-second count as possible before running a simple handoff. Central will bring its punt team onto the field and snap the ball after again letting most of the play clock expire. On the punt, West will either forsake a return by putting nine or more men on the line of scrimmage in hopes of blocking the punt, or allow Central to get off the kick and try to set up a long return.

Anticipating all of that action, the officials adjust their field coverage accordingly. An official who doesn't understand the game or recognize specific plays will be caught by surprise; a well-schooled official is prepared.

Reading the case studies

Remember the old "chalk talk" when you were a player? The coach frantically drew circles and lines and pounded the chalk until it became a fine white dust, all the while yelling something like, "If we block this play properly, it's a touchdown!" *Football Officials Guidebook* case studies take the chalk talk a giant step forward.

We've created game-specific plays for officials. We've inserted the officials and diagrammed their movements. The result: *Football Officials Guidebook* teaches officials to recognize specific offensive and defensive plays, help them adjust basic field positioning to properly officiate each play and shows exactly where each official should be looking. It's a referee chalk talk for the new millennium.

Case studies are included in the chapters on free kicks, scrimmage plays, goalline plays, scoring kicks and scrimmage kicks. Each includes actual game plays showing the movements of players and officials. Text accompanies each frame, so officials know where to go and what they're trying to see.

Combined with the chapters on positional and formation keys, you'll understand how to officiate a play from beginning to end.

Use these case studies to learn what plays look like and what you're supposed to do once you recognize them. As you become a student of the game, your officiating will dramatically improve.

One note: The case studies do not depict every conceivable play or variation on the play. For the sake of brevity, a play was depicted only once (e.g. there is a case study for a sweep to the linesman's side of the field but not to the line judge's side of the field).

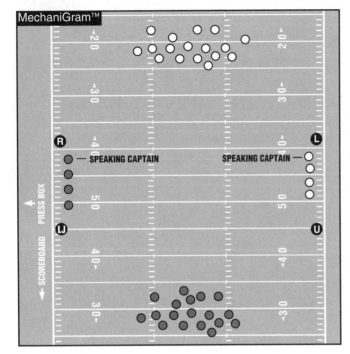

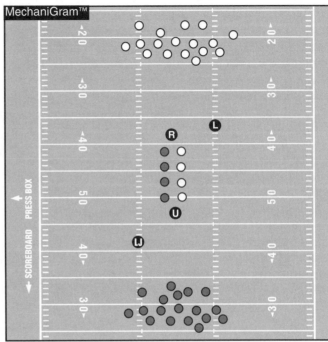

Action on the field: Starting positions.

Referee: At midfield on sideline opposite line-to-gain equipment.

Umpire: At midfield on sideline with line-to-gain equipment.

Linesman: At midfield on sideline with line-to-gain equipment.

Line judge: At midfield on sideline opposite line-to-gain equipment.

Action on the field: Introduction of captains.

Referee: Escorts captains to middle of field. Instructs captains to introduce themselves. Explains coin flip procedure.

Umpire: Monitors referee's discussion with captains; if necessary, corrects referee.

Linesman: Escorts captains as far as hashmark. Prevents players not involved in coin toss from entering area where toss is being conducted.

Line judge: Escorts captains as far as hashmark. Prevents players not involved in coin toss from entering area where toss is being conducted.

KEY

 Referee   Umpire   Line Judge   Linesman   Back Judge   Chain Gang   Ballboy   Coach Offense Defense Football   Possession of football

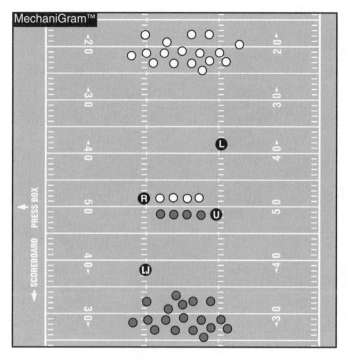

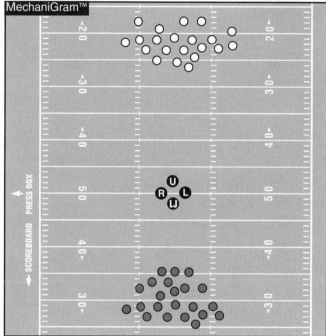

Action on the field: Coin toss winner determined.

Referee: Conducts toss and obtains choices from captains. If toss winner chooses to defer, referee should step away from group and signal that choice to pressbox. Asks captains to turn with backs to goal they will defend and signals toss winner's choice to pressbox. Moves to other set of captains and signals toss loser's choice to pressbox.

Umpire: Monitors referee's discussion with captains; if necessary, corrects referee. Records choices. Moves to other set of captains for referee's signal.

Linesman: Prevents players not involved in coin toss from entering area where toss is being conducted.

Line judge: Prevents players not involved in coin toss from entering area where toss is being conducted.

Action on the field: Final phase.

Referee: Meets with remaining officials in center of field to confirm results of toss. Hustles to position for kickoff.

Umpire: Meets with remaining officials in center of field to confirm results of toss. Hustles to position for kickoff.

Linesman: Meets with remaining officials in center of field to confirm results of toss. Hustles to position for kickoff.

Line judge: Meets with remaining officials in center of field to confirm results of toss. Hustles to position for kickoff.

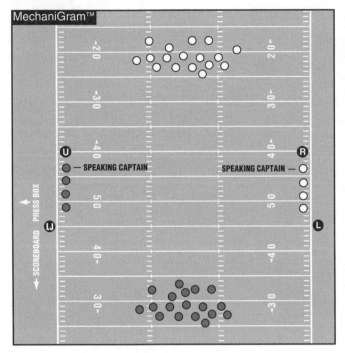

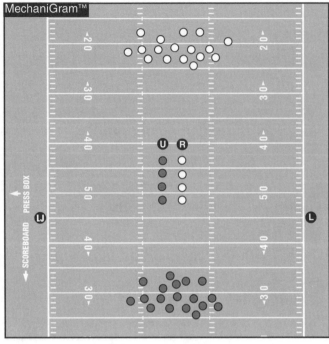

Action on the field: Starting positions.

Referee: At midfield on sideline with line-to-gain equipment.

Umpire: At midfield on sideline opposite line-to-gain equipment.

Linesman: At sideline behind referee.

Line judge: At sideline on umpire's side of field.

Action on the field: Introduction of captains.

Referee: Escorts captains to middle of field. Instructs captains to introduce themselves. Explains coin flip procedure.

Umpire: Monitors referee's discussion with captains; if necessary, corrects referee.

Linesman: Remains at sideline.

Line judge: Remains at sideline.

KEY

 Referee   Umpire   Line Judge   Linesman   Back Judge   Chain Gang   Ballboy   Coach ○ Offense ● Defense ▮ Football ⊗ Possession of football

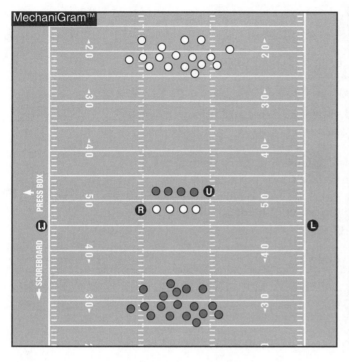 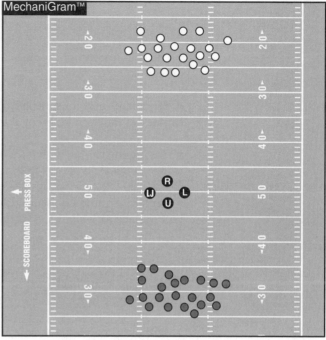

Action on the field: Coin toss winner determined.

Referee: Conducts toss and obtains choices from captains. If toss winner chooses to defer, referee should step away from group and signal that choice to pressbox. Asks captains to turn with backs to goal they will defend and signals toss winner's choice to pressbox. Moves to other set of captains and signals toss loser's choice to pressbox.

Umpire: Monitors referee's discussion with captains; if necessary, corrects referee. Records choices. Moves to other set of captains for referee's signal.

Linesman: Prevents players not involved in coin toss from entering area where toss is being conducted.

Line judge: Prevents players not involved in coin toss from entering area where toss is being conducted.

Action on the field: Final phase.

Referee: Meets with remaining officials in center of field to confirm results of toss. Hustles to position for kickoff.

Umpire: Meets with remaining officials in center of field to confirm results of toss. Hustles to position for kickoff.

Linesman: Meets with remaining officials in center of field to confirm results of toss. Hustles to position for kickoff.

Line judge: Meets with remaining officials in center of field to confirm results of toss. Hustles to position for kickoff.

• The coin toss is not the time to tell the captains how the game will be officiated.

• The referee and umpire should obtain the name and number of each captain so they can be greeted by name.

• Having the captains remove their helmets and carry them to the center of the field allows full face-to-face contact during the toss.

• Captains should be escorted to the center of the field for the second-half options as well as the pregame coin toss.

Quiz

Without referring back, you should be able to answer the following true-false questions.

1. Without exception, the coin toss is conducted in the center of the field five minutes before the game.

2. If the team winning the toss chooses to defer, the referee should wait to signal the declination along with the remaining options.

3. The referee is required to use a silver dollar for the coin toss.

4. If at any time during the toss the referee errs or gives incorrect information (for instance, giving the wrong team an option), the umpire should speak up immediately.

5. Players who are not involved in the toss may stand close to the meeting and observe the toss.

1. False 2. False 3. False 4. True 5. False

Chapter 24

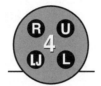

Free Kicks

Officials must realize that teams employ strategies for handling kickoffs, and those strategies should be recognized and officiated.

The kicking team is concerned about containment; that is, not permitting openings in coverage to let a kick returner escape for a long gain. For that purpose, kicking teams adopt two basic strategies. One planned procedure is to have players run straight down the field in imaginary lanes so as to cover the whole area of a runback in a systematic or blanket fashion. The second strategy is retaining one or two players behind the flow of teammates to act as safety valves, final pursuers in case a runner escapes from the first wave of pursuit.

Receiving teams, on the other hand, knowing that kickers stream downfield in lanes, try to open a pre-selected hole where blockers can wedge apart onrushing defenders, much the same as opening a hole in the line on regular scrimmage downs. As a result, receiving team members will often collapse into a makeshift offensive line around their own 25 or 30 yardline, intent on blocking for a runner as they would on a regular play.

Receivers form this makeshift line for two reasons. One, if players strung out across the field (as the ball is kicked) try to block onrushing kickers, it is relatively easy for kicking team players to avoid those blocks by feinting and sidestepping. Two, even if the receivers make contact, it is hard to sustain those open-field blocks, and the kicking team pursuers are likely to free themselves readily on the rebound and continue in their containment lanes. Literally, they'll just bump and charge.

Seeing the receiving team's wedge, kicking team players frequently leave their lanes to converge on the spot where receivers are trying to create an opening. Those convergent spots are where officials should focus their vision, because that is where most of the contact between opponents will take place. In real life, many officials watch the ball and the runner when they could service the game better by observing instead the blocking setup and the kicking team's pursuit.

General procedures

In Federation, the linesman handles the ball and is positioned at team K's free kick line, the line judge is on the sideline at team R's restraining line, the referee is near the top of the numbers near team R's five or 10 yardline on the line judge's side of the field and the umpire is between the numbers and the sideline at team R's 20 yardline on the side of the field with the linesman.

In NCAA, the referee handles the ball and moves

behind the kicker, the umpire is stationed on the sideline at team K's free kick line, the linesman on the sideline at team R's restraining line and the line judge is on the sideline on the umpire's side of the field and in front of the deepest receiver.

The official handling the ball should not give the ball to the kicker until team K has 11 players on the field. The kicker should be reminded not to kick the ball until the referee has sounded the ready for play. In NCAA, the referee is also responsible for ensuring that team K has the correct number of players on either side of the kicker.

All officials can ensure that team personnel are in their team boxes. It's a good idea for the officials on team R's restraining line to identify the free kick line and to remind players that all blocks must be above the waist. Officials signal the referee by lifting an arm overhead when they are ready for the kickoff. After getting ready signals from the rest of the crew and the kicker, the referee blows his whistle and gives the ready for play signal.

The line judge and linesman (NCAA: linesman and umpire) watch for infractions involving their respective free kick lines. When the ball is kicked, the restraining line officials can tell at once whether the kick is going high and deep. Both of them should take a momentary glance at the ball, then move downfield with their eyes on the players. If a team R player apparently stalks the kicker for purposes of blocking him, the linesman (NCAA: referee) should observe contact between the players.

The covering official signals the clock to start if he sees the ball is touched other than first touching by team K (NCAA: if the clock is to start with the kick, the referee gives the signal; otherwise the covering official gives the signal if he sees the ball is touched other than first touching by team K). The covering official is also responsible for signaling the clock to stop if the runner is downed in his area or if the ball goes out of bounds. All officials not responsible for the runner must look for illegal blocks.

If the kick goes out of bounds, the covering official is responsible for either dropping a beanbag (if team R caused the ball to go out of bounds) or a penalty marker (if team K caused the ball to go out of bounds). Officials trailing the runner must clean up after the play.

Coverage responsibilities

In Federation, the referee and umpire are responsible for a rectangular area extending from the goalline to team R's 30 yardline. That rectangle is divided lengthwise so that the referee's coverage area extends from the sideline and slightly more than halfway across. The linesman and line judge share the field from their respective sidelines to the center of the field extending from team R's 30 yardline to team K's goalline.

The umpire should look at the kick only for an instant, to note its trajectory, and should concentrate his vision on the receivers forming a cluster to open a hole for the runner.

The referee should be stationed on the goalline for the simple reason that a kick that breaks the plane of the goalline is a dead ball and an automatic touchback. On kicks inside team R's five yardline, the referee is responsible for determining whether the momentum exception applies and whether the kick is to be ruled a touchback.

If a receiver possesses the ball in the field of play, the referee can follow the runner and observe his progress until the runner moves beyond the 30 yardline or so, after which he should give up coverage to the umpire, line judge or linesman (depending on how far and which direction the runner goes). At that point the referee should watch contact that occurs off to the side and in front of the runner.

In NCAA, the umpire and linesman are responsible for the four players on the kicking team nearest them from the time the ball is kicked until the players reach team R's restraining line. The referee is responsible for the two remaining team K players and for observing contact on the kicker.

The coverage areas for the linesman and umpire are divided lengthwise down the middle of the field and as far as team R's 25 yardline. The line judge is responsible for the area from team R's goalline to team R's 25 yardline. It is crucial for the linesman to remain on the sideline in case team R's return is to his side of the field. Although the line judge is responsible for determining whether the momentum exception applies and whether the kick is to be ruled a touchback, the linesman is the only official who can see a runner step out of bounds on that side of the field. Similarly, the umpire helps the line judge on sideline action on his side of the field.

CHALK TALK: FEDERATION FREE KICK POSITIONING AND COVERAGE ZONES

Referee: Starting position is near the top of the numbers near team R's five or 10 yardline on the line judge's side of the field. After getting ready signals from the rest of the crew and the kicker, the referee blows his whistle and gives the ready for play signal.

On kicks inside team R's five yardline, the referee is responsible for determining whether the momentum exception applies and whether the kick is to be ruled a touchback.

The referee is responsible for a rectangular area on his side of the field extending from the goalline to team R's 30 yardline and slightly more than halfway across the field.

Umpire: Starting position is on the sideline at team R's 20 yardline. The umpire signals the referee by lifting an arm overhead when he is ready for the kickoff.

The umpire is responsible for a rectangular area extending from the goalline to team R's 30 yardline slightly less than halfway across the field.

Linesman: The linesman and line judge move simultaneously toward the center of the field once the players are on the field. The linesman should not give the ball to the kicker until team K has 11 players on the field and should remind the kicker not to kick the ball until the referee has sounded his whistle. After identifying team K's free kick line, the linesman turns toward the line judge. After ensuring that the other is ready, they simultaneously jog off to their sidelines; the linesman is on team K's restraining line. When in position and ready for the kick, the linesman should raise an arm as a ready signal for the referee.

The linesman watches for infractions involving the free kick line. After the ball is kicked, the linesman drifts downfield, maintaining coverage of his sideline. He should not go beyond team R's 30 yardline in case the runner breaks off a long return and enters the linesman's coverage area.

Line judge: The linesman and line judge move simultaneously toward the center of the field once the players are on the field. After identifying team R's free kick line, the line judge turns toward the linesman. After ensuring that the other is ready, they simultaneously jog off to their sidelines; the line judge is on team R's restraining line. When in position and ready for the kick, the line judge should raise an arm as a ready signal for the referee.

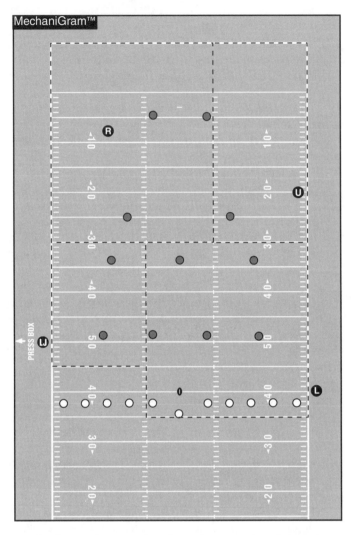

The line judge watches for infractions involving the free kick line. After the ball is kicked, the line judge drifts downfield, maintaining coverage of his respective sideline. He should not go beyond team R's 30 yardline in case the runner breaks off a long return and enters the linesman's coverage area.

All officials: If the kick goes out of bounds, the covering official is responsible for either dropping a beanbag (if team R caused the ball to go out of bounds) or a penalty marker (if team K caused the ball to go out of bounds). Officials trailing the runner must clean up after the play.

The covering official signals the clock to start if he sees the ball is touched other than first touching by team K. The covering official is also responsible for signaling the clock to stop if the runner is downed in his area or if the ball goes out of bounds. All officials not responsible for the runner must look for illegal blocks.

CHALK TALK: NCAA FREE KICK POSITIONING AND COVERAGE ZONES

Referee: The referee handles the ball and should not give the ball to the kicker until team K has 11 players on the field. The kicker should be reminded not to kick the ball until the referee has sounded the ready for play. The referee is also responsible for ensuring that team K has the correct number of players on either side of the kicker. After getting ready signals from the rest of the crew and the kicker, the referee blows his whistle and gives the ready for play signal.

If the clock is to start with the kick, the referee gives the signal. If a team R player blocks the kicker, the referee should observe contact between the players.

After the ball is kicked, the referee shouldn't move beyond the 50 yardline. The referee acts as a safety valve in case the runner breaks off a long return.

Umpire: Starting position is on the sideline at team K's free kick line. The umpire signals the referee by lifting an arm overhead when he is ready for the kickoff. The umpire watches for infractions involving the free kick line and is responsible for the four players on the kicking team nearest him from the time the ball is kicked until the players reach team R's restraining line.

The umpire's coverage area is his side of the field as far as team R's 25 yardline.

Linesman: Starting position is on the sideline at team R's restraining line. The linesman signals the referee by lifting an arm overhead when he is ready for the kickoff. The linesman watches for infractions involving the free kick line and is responsible for the four players on the kicking team nearest him from the time the ball is kicked until the players reach team R's restraining line.

The linesman's coverage area is his side of the field as far as team R's 25 yardline.

Line judge: Starting position is on the sideline on the umpire's side of the field and in front of the deepest receiver. The line judge signals the referee by lifting an arm overhead when he is ready for the kickoff.

The line judge is responsible for determining whether the momentum exception applies and whether the kick is to be ruled a touchback. The line judge is responsible for the runner from the goalline to team R's 25 yardline.

All officials: If the clock is not to start with the kick, the covering official signals the clock to start if he sees the

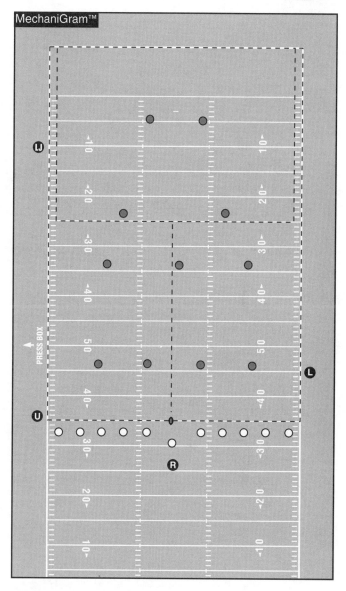

ball is touched (other than first touching by team K).

All officials observe action in front of the runner when the runner is not in their general area.

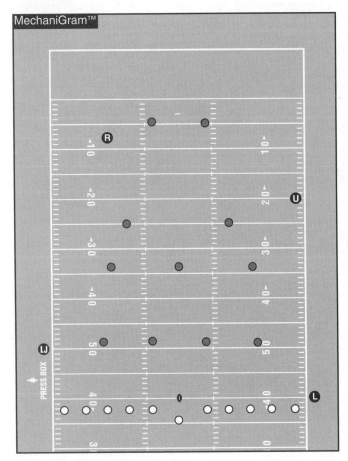

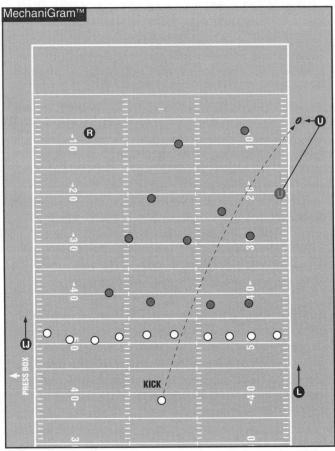

Action on the field: Starting position.

Referee: Near team R's five or 10 yardline inside sideline on line judge's side of the field.

Umpire: At team R's 20 yardline on linesman's side of the field.

Linesman: On sideline at team K's restraining line on sideline with chains.

Line judge: On sideline opposite chains at team R's restraining line.

Action on the field: Kick becomes dead out of bounds.

Referee: Observes action in front of receiver on his side of field.

Umpire: Retreats to observe ball. Signals clock to stop when ball is out of bounds.

Linesman: Watches for infractions involving free kick lines. After kick, moves downfield and observes action in front of receiver on his side of field.

Line judge: Watches for infractions involving free kick lines. After kick, moves downfield and observes action in front of receiver on his side of field.

KEY

Referee	Umpire	Line Judge	Linesman	Back Judge	Chain Gang	Ballboy	Coach	Offense	Defense	Football	Possession of football

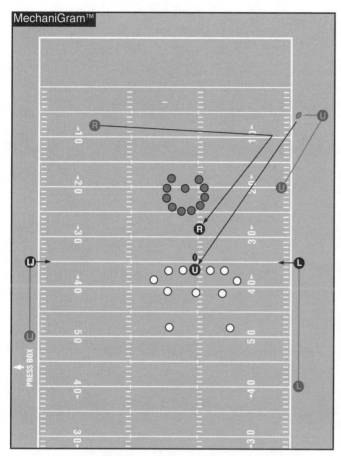

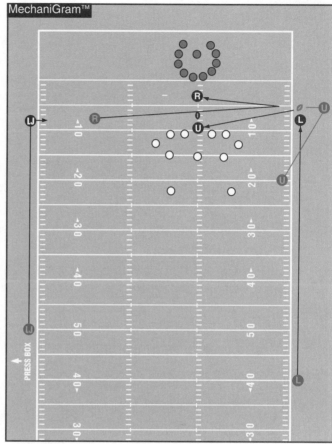

Action on the field: Team R chooses to take ball at its own 35 yardline.

Referee: Observes action in his area. Communicates result of play with umpire. Obtains choice from team R captain. Signals team K's foul and points toward team R's 35 yardline, where ball will next be put in play. (If team R chooses a rekick after enforcement, returns to position for rekick.)

Umpire: Moves downfield and observes action in his area. Gives stop-the-clock signal when ball goes out of bounds. Communicates result of play with referee. Moves to hashmark at team R's 35 yardline, to set ball for new series. (If team R chooses a rekick after enforcement, returns to position for rekick.)

Linesman: Moves downfield and observes action in his area. Moves to team R's 35 yardline, where team R will begin new series, assists chain crew in setting chains. (If team R chooses a rekick after enforcement, signals team K's foul, walks off penalty and returns to position for rekick.)

Line judge: Mirrors spot at team R's 35 yardline, where new series will begin. (If team R chooses a rekick after enforcement, returns to position for rekick.)

Action on the field: Team R caused kick to go out of bounds.

Referee: Observes action in his area. Communicates result of play with umpire. Signals new series will begin at spot where kick went out of bounds.

Umpire: Observes action in his area. Gives stop-the-clock signal when ball goes out of bounds. Communicates result of play with referee. Waits for linesman to arrive and mirror spot; moves to hashmark where new series will begin and sets ball.

Linesman: Moves downfield and observes action in his area. Takes from umpire spot where new series will begin and assists chain crew in setting chains.

Line judge: Moves downfield and observes action in his area. Mirrors linesman's spot where new series will begin.

Movement | Previous position | Current position (stopped) | Previous position | Current position (still moving)

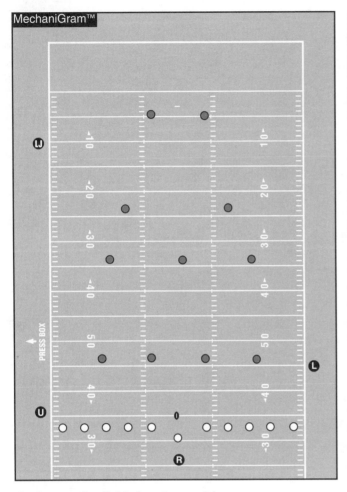

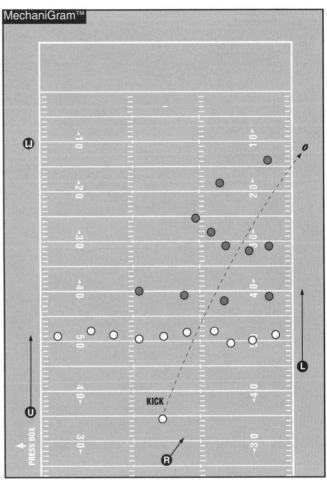

Action on the field: Starting position.

Referee: In middle of the field behind kicker.

Umpire: On sideline at team K's restraining line on side opposite linesman.

Linesman: On sideline at team R's restraining line on sideline with chains.

Line judge: On sideline opposite the chains in front of the deepest receiver.

Action on the field: Ball becomes dead out of bounds.

Referee: Watches for infractions involving free kick lines. When ball is kicked, gives start-the-clock signal if clock is to start with the kick. Observes contact involving two players on either side of kicker and kicker.

Umpire: Watches for infractions involving free kick lines and contact involving four team K players nearest him from the time ball is kicked until players reach team R's restraining line. Moves downfield.

Linesman: Watches for infractions involving free kick lines and contact involving four team K players nearest him from the time ball is kicked until players reach team R's restraining line. Moves downfield.

Line judge: Observes action in his area.

KEY

R	**U**	**LJ**	**L**	**BJ**	**CG**	**BB**	**C**	○	●	◗	⊗
Referee	Umpire	Line Judge	Linesman	Back Judge	Chain Gang	Ballboy	Coach	Offense	Defense	Football	Possession of football

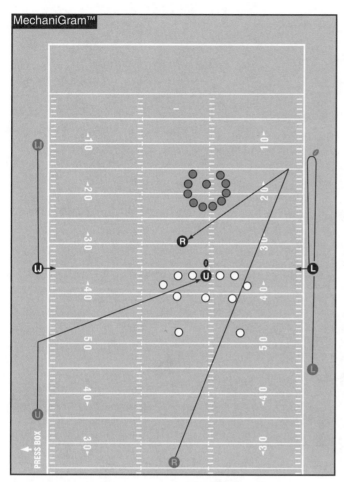

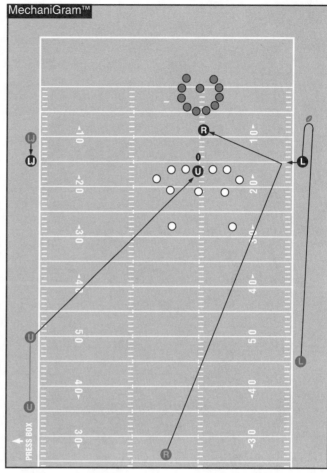

Action on the field: Team R chooses to take ball at its own 35 yardline.

Referee: Observes action in his area. Communicates result of play with linesman. Obtains choice from team R captain. Signals team K's foul and points toward team R's 35 yardline, where ball will next be put in play. (If team R chooses a rekick after enforcement, walks off penalty and returns to position for rekick.)

Umpire: Moves downfield and observes action in his area. Moves to hashmark at team R's 35 yardline, to set ball for new series. (If team R chooses a rekick after enforcement, returns to position for rekick.)

Linesman: Moves downfield and observes action in his area. Gives stop-the-clock signal when ball is out of bounds. Communicates result of play with referee. Moves to team R's 35 yardline, where team R will begin new series, assists chain crew in setting chains. (If team R chooses a rekick after enforcement, returns to position for rekick.)

Line judge: Mirrors linesman's spot at team R's 35 yardline, new series will begin. (If team R chooses a rekick after enforcement, returns to position for rekick.)

Action on the field: Team R caused ball to go out of bounds.

Referee: Moves downfield and observes action in his area. Communicates result of play with linesman. Signals new series will begin at spot where kick went out of bounds.

Umpire: Moves downfield and observes action in his area. Moves to hashmark where new series will begin and sets ball.

Linesman: Moves downfield and observes action in his area. Communicates result of play with referee. Indicates spot where new series will begin and assists chain crew in setting chains.

Line judge: Observes action in his area. Mirrors linesman's spot where new series will begin.

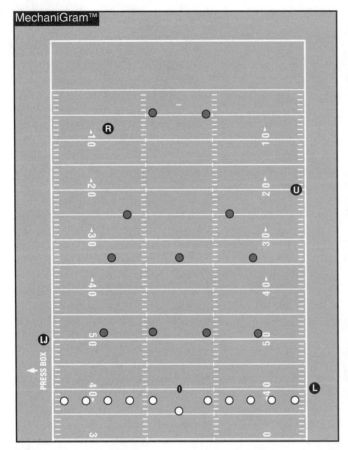

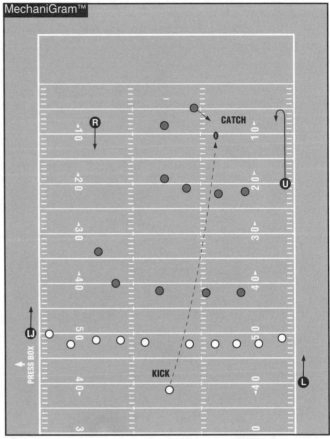

Action on the field: Starting position.

Referee: Near team R's five or 10 yardline inside sideline on line judge's side of the field.

Umpire: At team R's 20 yardline on linesman's side of the field.

Linesman: On sideline at team K's restraining line on sideline with chains.

Line judge: On sideline opposite chains at team R's restraining line.

Action on the field: Receiver catches kick.

Referee: Observes action in front of receiver on his side of field. Moves slowly upfield.

Umpire: Retreats to observe catch. Signals clock to start when ball is caught by receiver. Moves to stay ahead of receiver and observes action of runner during return.

Linesman: Watches for infractions involving free kick lines. After kick, moves downfield and observes action in front of receiver on his side of field.

Line judge: Watches for infractions involving free kick lines. After kick, moves downfield and observes action in front of receiver on his side of field.

KEY

Referee	Umpire	Line Judge	Linesman	Back Judge	Chain Gang	Ballboy	Coach	Offense	Defense	Football	Possession of football

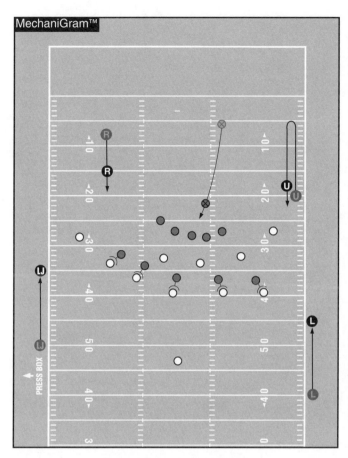

Action on the field: Receiver advances.

Referee: Observes action in front of receiver on his side of field. Moves slowly upfield.

Umpire: Moves to stay ahead of receiver and observes action of runner during return.

Linesman: Stops 15 yards downfield from team R's restraining line. Observes action in front of receiver on his side of field.

Line judge: Stops 15 yards downfield from team K's restraining line. Observes action in front of receiver on his side of field.

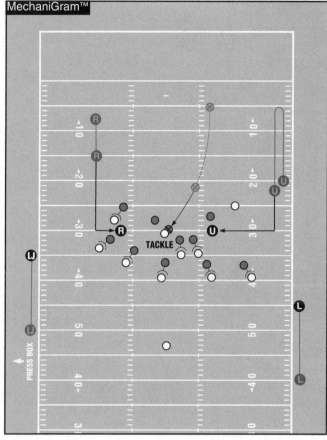

Action on the field: Receiver continues advance and is downed.

Referee: Moves upfield and observes action of players. Takes coverage of runner when runner enters his area (halo coverage). Blows whistle and gives stop-the-clock signal when runner is downed. Squares off and holds spot until umpire can mirror spot.

Umpire: Moves upfield and observes runner until runner leaves coverage area (halo coverage). Squares off to mirror referee's spot.

Linesman: Observes players. When referee signals possession for team R, instructs chain crew to set chains for new series.

Line judge: Observes players.

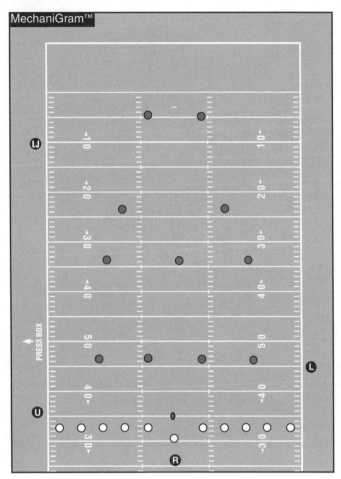

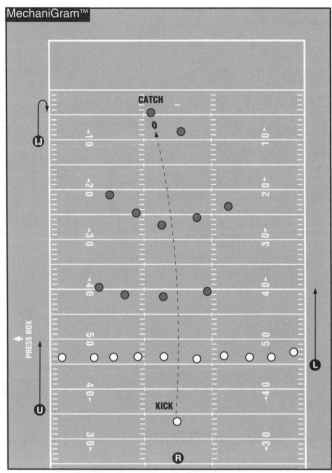

Action on the field: Starting position.

Referee: In middle of the field behind kicker.

Umpire: On sideline at team K's restraining line on side opposite linesman.

Linesman: On sideline at team R's restraining line on sideline with chains.

Line judge: On sideline opposite the chains in front of the deepest receiver.

Action on the field: Receiver catches kick.

Referee: Watches for infractions involving free kick lines. When ball is kicked, gives start-the-clock signal if clock is to start with the kick. Observes contact involving two players on either side of kicker and kicker.

Umpire: Watches for infractions involving free kick lines and contact involving four team K players nearest him from the time ball is kicked until players reach team R's restraining line. Moves downfield and observes players in his area.

Linesman: Watches for infractions involving free kick lines and contact involving four team K players nearest him from the time ball is kicked until players reach team R's restraining line. Moves downfield and observes players in his area.

Line judge: If clock has not started, gives start-the-clock signal when receiver touches kick.

KEY

 Referee Umpire Line Judge Linesman Back Judge Chain Gang Ballboy Coach ○ Offense ● Defense ◗ Football Possession of football

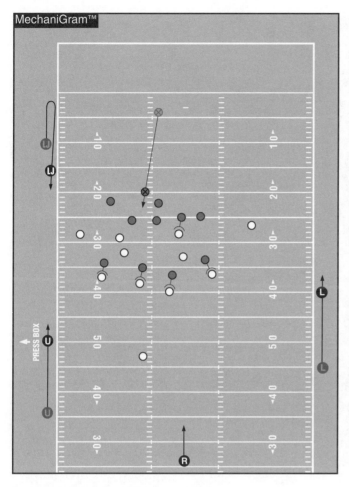

MechaniGram™

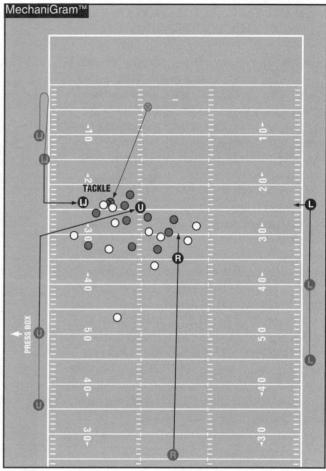

MechaniGram™

Action on the field: Runner advances.

Referee: Moves slowly downfield and observes action in front of ball.

Umpire: Drifts downfield (no farther than team R's 25 yardline) and observes action in front of ball.

Linesman: Drifts downfield (no farther than team R's 25 yardline) and observes action in front of ball.

Line judge: Moves to stay slightly ahead of runner. Observes runner and action around and in front of runner.

Action on the field: Runner continues advance and is downed.

Referee: Moves slowly downfield and observes players. When certain no penalty flags are down, signals new series for team R.

Umpire: Moves downfield and observes players. Hustles to spot to set ball for new series.

Linesman: Moves downfield and observes players. Squares off and mirrors spot. When referee signals possession for team R, instructs chain crew to set chains for new series.

Line judge: Moves with runner. Blows whistle and gives stop-the-clock signal when runner is downed. Squares off and holds spot until umpire arrives and spots ball for next down.

Movement | Previous position | Current position (stopped) | Previous position | Current position (still moving)

CHALK TALK: FEDERATION ONSIDE KICK POSITIONING

Short free kicks are seldom surprise events. Usually they result from clearly anticipated game strategy. Officials should adjust their positions for expected short free kicks. The key elements are determining whether or not either team touched the kick before it traveled 10 yards and who eventually possessed it.

When a kickoff is topped, squibbed or blooped at a time when a short free kick is not customary, such as at the start of either half, the same necessities apply: Who touched it first? Where was it touched? Who eventually recovered it? The kickers have the right to keep the ball if they recover it after it has traveled 10 yards without being touched by a member of the kicking team. Team K also has a right to the ball if the receivers touch the kick before it has gone 10 yards. Receivers may recover the ball anywhere on the field, but the kickers never have the right to advance their own kick. The officials who are guarding their teams' respective restraining lines are ordinarily responsible for making those determinations.

General procedures

In Federation, the linesman and line judge assume their regular positions while the referee moves up to about team R's 10 yardline and the umpire moves up 20 yards (to team R's 40 yardline unless the free kick spot has been moved by penalty). **In NCAA, no adjustments in free kick coverage are made even if it is apparent an onside kick is imminent.**

The umpire, linesman and line judge should have their beanbags in hand to mark the spot if team K first touches the kick and should be prepared to blow the ball dead if a prone player from either team recovers the kick regardless of whether it has traveled 10 yards.

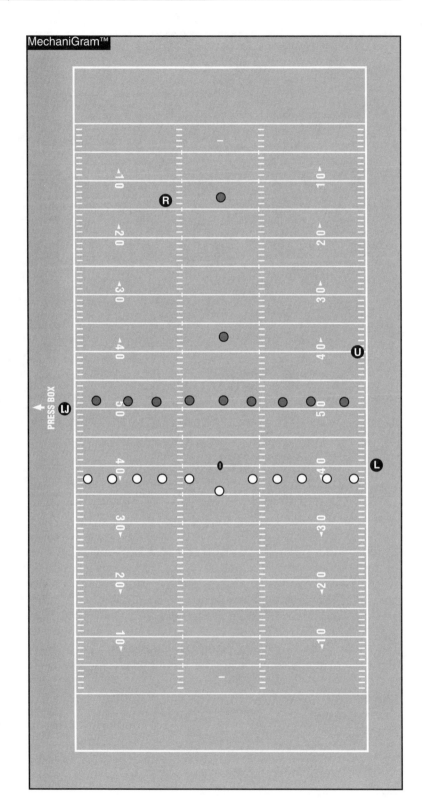

• The official handling the ball should not give the ball to the kicker until team K has 11 players on the field.

• The kicker should be reminded not to kick the ball until the referee has sounded the ready for play.

• If the kick goes out of bounds, the covering official is responsible for either dropping a beanbag (if team R caused the ball to go out of bounds) or a penalty marker (if team K caused the ball to go out of bounds).

• Officials trailing the runner must clean up after the play.

Quiz

Without referring back, you should be able to answer the following true-false questions.

1. In Federation, on kicks inside team R's five yardline, the referee is responsible for determining whether the momentum exception applies and whether the kick is to be ruled a touchback.

2. The covering official is also responsible for signaling the clock to stop if the runner is downed in his area or if the ball goes out of bounds.

3. It's a good idea for the officials on team R's restraining line to remind players that all blocks must be above the waist.

4. In NCAA, no adjustments in free kick coverage are made even if it is apparent an onside kick is imminent.

5. In Federation, the linesman doesn't have to ensure that team K has the correct number of players on either side of the kicker.

1. True 2. True 3. True 4. True 5. True

Notes

Chapter 25

Plays from Scrimmage

Experienced officials know the difference between a four-man crew and a five-man crew goes well beyond the presence of a deep official to help on passes and kicks. While most crews would never turn down the help an extra official provides, a four-man crew can still provide more than adequate coverage and game control.

Keys are much easier to discern in a four-man crew because strength of formation is not an issue; instead officials are responsible for eligible receivers in their area. It takes discipline, hustle and — above all — communication, but four can do the job of five.

Here are the general principles for each position:

Referee: The referee's position varies according to team A's formation, the game situation and player characteristics (i.e. right-handed or left-handed quarterback). The referee must be in a position to see the backs (except flankers or a man in motion toward the referee), as deep as the deepest back and in position to see the snap.

The manuals differ on which tackle should be keyed: the Federation says far-side tackle and the CCA says the tackle on the same side as the referee. *Referee* recommendation: The referee should coordinate with the umpire so that each tackle is keyed on every scrimmage play. By keying on a tackle, the referee can determine if the play is a pass or run. If the tackle fires out or pulls, the play is likely a run; if the tackle retreats, the play is likely a pass or draw.

The referee is responsible for observing the huddle to ensure team A is not violating substitution rules and for identifying eligible receivers in the backfield, as well as observing shifts and watching for false starts and other pre-snap violations by the offense.

On a running play, the referee focuses on the ball, the runner and the blocking around the runner. If the play goes to the opposite side, the referee should move toward or parallel to the line of the scrimmage and maintain a position approximately in line with the runner. Avoid overaggressiveness in case the play is a reverse. If the play is to the referee's side, the referee moves behind the play and is responsible for the runner until he crosses the neutral zone or turns upfield.

On a typical running play, the referee should watch the handoff or the pitchout, see the runner head outside the free clipping/free blocking zone, and watch to see that no one contacts the quarterback before drifting along to follow the play. He will not have much to observe besides the quarterback because little significant action is likely to take place behind the runner, and the runner himself is being watched by the appropriate wing official (halo concept).

The referee's job on such a play is relatively simple and clear-cut: protect the quarterback. At the play's end he can either help relay the ball back inside or go to the hash for a relay and set the ball himself. Only if a runner goes out of bounds (including a scrambling quarterback) behind the scrimmage line will the referee have sideline responsibilities.

On passing plays, the referee observes blocking by the backs as the quarterback drops back. The referee should move to maintain distance between himself and the quarterback (e.g. if the quarterback drops back seven yards, the referee retreats seven yards). By maintaining space between himself and the quarterback, the referee will widen his field of vision. The wider view allows the referee to determine if the pass is forward or backward (use extended arm signal to indicate a backward pass) yet continue to focus attention on the passer.

Once the pass has been released, the referee continues to observe the passer. If the flight of the pass is altered because the passer's arm is hit by a defender, the referee must determine whether the resultant loose ball is a forward pass or a fumble. If the referee rules the play to be an incomplete pass, he must blow his whistle and signal emphatically. If the play results in a fumble, the referee must beanbag the spot where possession was lost.

The referee is also responsible for ruling on intentional grounding and can work with the umpire to determine whether a passer was beyond the line of scrimmage when the pass was thrown. The referee should move to the spot of the pass and observe the location of the passer's feet. If the passer is clearly beyond the line, a penalty marker should be dropped. In cases that are too close for an immediate determination, a beanbag should be dropped. At the end of the play, the referee can compare the spot of the beanbag and the location of the down box in order to make the call.

The referee has to watch the passer (he's supposed to watch the blocking of the opposite tackle too, which is both logical and feasible) and stay with the quarterback if he rolls out or is flushed out of the pocket. And he calls "Gone!" when the pass is released.

On runs that end out of bounds behind the neutral zone, the referee is responsible for marking the spot. He also must beanbag the spot of a muff or fumble and may beanbag a quarterback sack in the offensive backfield.

The referee is responsible for the 25-second count, whether or not a visible 25-second clock is used.

Umpire: Until the referee blows the ready for the play signal, the umpire should stand with his feet straddling the ball. After the signal, the umpire's position is three to eight yards behind team B's line and between the defensive ends (NCAA: a yard behind and to the side of or between the linebackers). The position should be varied so that the umpire does not limit the movement or vision of the linebackers or defensive backs.

The umpire must be able to see the ball from the time the snapper handles the ball until the time it is snapped and is responsible for ensuring that team A has five players numbered 50 to 79 on the offensive line. The umpire should listen for defenders interfering with the offense's snap count. Numerous umpires also help count the defense or offense, according to the crew's preference. Umpires definitely should relay information about the down and distance to fellow crew members; identify the offensive formation; observe the snapper for snap infractions and observe the guards for false starts.

The umpire must read the interior line because the screen of defenders and the offensive line will prevent his getting a good look at backfield players. He shouldn't look at backfield people anyway, because his responsibility at the snap is to judge the legality of play at the line of scrimmage. Stand-up blocking will tell him that a pass or draw is forthcoming. Observing the blocking will help allow the umpire to find the point of attack. For example, if the right tackle blocks down (to his right) and the center joins the right guard on a double-team block taking their man to their left, the point of attack is the gap between the tackle and guard. It is crucial for umpires to determine the point of attack because of the potential for holding, chop blocks and other fouls.

When the hole opens, the umpire should move away from it (to avoid interfering with the defensive pursuit) and laterally (thus turning his head toward the blockers in front of the runner and the tackling efforts of the defense).

The most challenging play for the umpire is one on which the point of attack is aimed at him. An umpire who is lazy or is not paying attention can find himself inadvertently making the tackle, accidentally throwing a block or becoming sandwiched between opposing players. Not only is that poor officiating, it's dangerous. When the point of attack is in the umpire's direction, a quick lateral step followed by a turn toward the play will allow the umpire to get out of harm's way and continue officiating.

When play swings around to one side, the umpire should turn his attention to the blocking ahead of the runner and should prepare to cross outside the hash if the runner is downed in the side zone near the sideline. The umpire can help get the ball back to the hash and set it at the progress spot. He should not automatically halt at the hash and rely on other officials to get him the ball.

The CCA manual advises umpires to blow the whistle when the runner is downed on a short run between the tackles. *Referee* recommends that umpires rarely blow their whistles because it is often difficult for the umpire to see if the runner's knees have touched and that he is still in possession of the ball. If the umpire does blow a whistle, he must be absolutely certain the ball is indeed in possession of a player who is downed before doing so. The collegiate manual also specifies the umpire should take the progress spot from the nearest wing official, a practice *Referee* strongly endorses. Because the umpire is parallel rather than perpendicular to the play, the umpire's position makes it next to impossible to determine the spot. The umpire should get the spot from the covering wing official (or, when the situation dictates, from the referee).

Plays that end in a side zone may require the umpire to move outside the hashmark and toward the sideline in order to clean up behind the play.

On pass plays, the umpire must step up and reach the line of scrimmage. That takes the umpire out of short pass routes and puts him in a position to judge ineligibles downfield and passes thrown from beyond the line of scrimmage. When the pass is thrown, the umpire pivots and follows the flight of the ball. The umpire has catch/trap responsibility if the receiver is facing the umpire.

If a pass is first touched by a team B player, the umpire gives the tipped ball signal; that lets the other officials know that pass interference restrictions are lifted. If a forward pass is caught, touched, batted, muffed or strikes an ineligible team A player, the umpire must know whether the action occurred behind or beyond the neutral zone for purposes of penalty enforcement.

There are virtually no circumstances under which an umpire should spot the ball. Because the umpire is parallel rather than perpendicular to the play, the umpire's position makes it next to impossible to determine the spot. The umpire should get the spot from the covering wing official (or, when the situation dictates, from the referee).

The umpire should have one rubber band-type of device on each hand. One is for keeping track of downs; the other is for keeping of track of the position of the ball relative to the hashmarks. That will help the umpire return to the correct previous spot after an incomplete pass or penalty. If, for instance, the umpire uses his right hand to determine ball position, the thumb indicates the ball was last snapped from the left hash; index finger, between the left upright and the left hash; middle finger, middle of the field; ring finger, between the right upright and the right hash; and pinkie, right hash.

Linesman and line judge: The linesman and line judge straddle the line of scrimmage on their respective side of the field. The Federation manual dictates that, except in goalline or short-yardage situations, neither should be closer than nine yards outside the widest offensive player. The CCA manual places the wingmen at least seven yards outside the widest offensive player and never inside the top of the numbers. *Referee* recommends a compromise between the manuals. Working on the sideline is strongly encouraged because it affords a wide-angle view of the action and prevents the official from interfering in the play. In short-yardage (e.g. fourth down and a half-yard to go) or goalline situations (when the ball is snapped at or inside team B's eight yardline), the wings may choose to "pinch" the ends. However, even when pinching, a wing official should never allow a team A player to get behind him.

Before the snap, the wing officials identify the eligible receivers on their side of the field, count to ensure team A has at least seven players on the line of scrimmage, assist the umpire in checking the legality of uniform numbers of offensive linemen and legality of positions with eligible numbers and assist the referee in monitoring substitutions. If the receiver nearest the official is in the offensive backfield, the wing uses the extended arm signal to alert the opposite wing. Legality of motion is always the responsibility of the official away from whom the player is moving, even if the player reverses his motion.

At the snap, the wing officials observe the two eligible receivers closest to them, including backs. They must be alert for illegal crackback blocks, especially by motion men.

Because they will mark forward progress the vast majority of the time, the line judge and linesman must be especially alert for quick-hitting running plays into the line. On runs to the opposite side of the field, the off wing must clean up after the play but be careful not to venture too far into the middle of the field in case team A runs a reverse or a fumble forces the flow of the play back toward the off wing.

Another major blunder occurs when a wing official reacts too slowly to a run to his side of the field and is unable to stay out of the way of the action (or worse, turns his back to the action). Referee recommendation: back up to the sideline (beyond if necessary) and toward the offensive backfield, then turn and follow the play as it flows downfield.

On pass plays, the wing officials watch initial contact between receivers and defenders. Remember that interference restrictions for team A begin at the snap; for team B, the restrictions begin when the pass is in the air. Be especially alert for pick plays when receivers run short crossing patterns.

On quick passes in the flat, the wings must be ready to rule if the pass is forward or backward. If the pass is backward, the extended arm signal should be directed toward the offensive backfield.

On passes, the wingmen have to follow receivers downfield. When a wing official sees receivers move purposefully off the line of scrimmage, he must trace their paths visually, making sure to see any defenders' contact against the receivers, reading the routes to get to the place where the pass arrives and making sure the receivers do not block downfield. But the wing officials also have to know for sure that the play is really a pass.

Therefore, wing officials should look back at some point to see if a passer is truly setting up to pass. They should do that after traveling no more than five to 10 yards downfield (about two seconds into the play). They should look back only if receivers are running free, i.e., not being bumped by defenders. If contact by defenders is imminent, the wing officials should look at that before checking the offensive backfield to see about the quarterback and his intentions.

If the play is not a screen or a similar short pass, the wings drift cautiously five to seven yards downfield, maintaining a position about halfway between the line of scrimmage (NCAA: five to seven yards downfield) and the deepest receiver on his side. If the pass is to his coverage area, the covering wing official moves quickly to get the best possible angle to observe the attempted catch. If the official is looking at the receiver's back, preventing him from getting a good look, eye contact should be made with the official who has a clearer view. If the other official sees a trap or an incompletion, he must signal immediately. A nod indicates a catch has been made. Referee recommendation: when in doubt, a pass is incomplete.

On pass plays near the sidelines, wing officials have a better chance of determining whether or not a receiver has made a catch if their focus is parallel with the sideline rather than perpendicular to it. By maintaining a look parallel with the sideline, the official can see if the receiver keeps a foot inbounds and whether or not the receiver controlled the pass. The technique is called "looking down the gun barrel." Watch the receiver's feet first; if the player has been unable to get one foot inbounds before going out of bounds (a technique known as "dotting the i"), it doesn't matter if the receiver secured control of the pass because the pass will be ruled incomplete. In order to get that look, the official must avoid being too close to the action. Maintaining proper distance will allow the official to see the feet first, then the ball, with a minimum of head movement.

The Federation does not authorize the official to use supplementary signals such as the pass juggled (hands palm up and alternately moved up and down) or the possession gained out of bounds signal (sweeping motion with both arms) to indicate why the pass was incomplete. *Referee* recommendation: use those signals only if your association or assigning agency allows their use.

Wing officials have responsibility for the passer if he scrambles past the line of scrimmage. Be especially alert if the passer heads for the sideline. If the quarterback is tackled out of bounds the wing official must rule on the legality of the contact.

If the runner is driven out of bounds less than five yards past the scrimmage line, the covering wing official can handle the play and supervise players outside the sideline after marking the spot with his beanbag. When a play is more than a five-yard gain and the runner heads across the sideline, the covering wing official marks the spot while keeping an eye on players.

A play gaining considerably more than 10 yards may find the covering wing official policing activity past the sidelines. Thus, cooperative measures have to be worked out between the referee or covering wing official and the umpire, to be sure the ball is properly spotted and off-the-field activity is monitored.

The CCA manual mandates that the line judge also time the game; the Federation makes that duty mandatory only where there is no field clock. *Referee* recommends having the line judge time the game as a back up in case the stadium clock malfunctions.

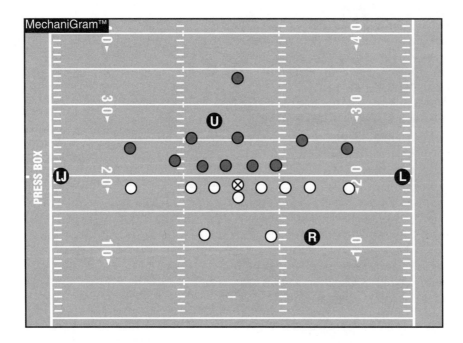

CHALK TALK: SCRIMMAGE PLAY POSITIONING AND COVERAGE

Referee: Starting position is on the passing-arm side of the quarterback, approximately 10 to 12 yards deep and at least as wide as the tight end. The referee is responsible for observing the huddle to ensure team A is not violating substitution rules, identifying eligible receivers in the backfield, observing shifts and watching for false starts and other pre-snap violations by the offense.

On a running play, the referee focuses on the ball, the runner and the blocking around the runner. If the play goes to the opposite side, the referee should move toward or parallel to the line of the scrimmage and maintain a position approximately in line with the runner. If the play is to the referee's side, the referee moves behind the play and is responsible for the runner until he crosses the neutral zone or turns upfield. The referee should watch the handoff or the pitchout, see the runner head outside the free clipping/free blocking zone, and watch to see that no one contacts the quarterback before drifting along to follow the play.

On passing plays, the referee observes blocking by the backs as the quarterback drops back. The referee should move to maintain the 10- to 12-yard distance between himself and the quarterback (e.g. if the quarterback drops back seven yards, the referee retreats seven yards).

The referee is also responsible for ruling on intentional grounding and can work with the umpire to determine whether a passer was beyond the line of scrimmage when the pass was thrown. The referee should move to the spot of the pass and observe the location of the passer's feet. If the passer is clearly beyond the line, a penalty marker should be dropped. In cases that are too close for an immediate determination, a beanbag should be dropped. At the end of the play, the referee can compare the spot of the beanbag and the location of the down box in order to make the call.

On runs that end out of bounds behind the neutral zone, the referee is responsible for marking the spot. He also must beanbag the spot of a muff, fumble or quarterback sack in the offensive backfield.

Umpire: Starting position is three to eight yards behind team B's line and between the defensive ends (NCAA: approximately a yard behind and to the side of or between the linebackers). The umpire must be able to see the ball from the time the snapper handles the ball until the time it is snapped and is responsible for ensuring that team A has five players numbered 50 to 79 on the offensive line. The umpire should listen for defenders interfering with the offense's snap count. observe the snapper for snap infractions and observe the guards for false starts.

The umpire must observe the blocking to find the point of attack. When the hole opens, the umpire should move away from it (to avoid interfering with the defensive pursuit) and laterally (thus turning his head toward the blockers in front of the runner and the tackling efforts of the defense).

Plays that end in a side zone may require the umpire to move outside the hashmark and toward the sideline in order to clean up behind the play. When play swings around to one side, the umpire should turn his attention to the blocking ahead of the runner and should prepare to cross outside the hashmark if the runner is downed in the side zone near the sideline. The umpire can help get the ball back to the hashmark and set it at the progress spot. He should not automatically halt at the hash and rely on other officials to get him the ball.

On pass plays, the umpire must step up and reach the line of scrimmage. If a pass is first touched by a team B player, the umpire gives the tipped ball signal. When the pass is thrown, the umpire pivots to follow the flight of the ball. The umpire has catch/trap responsibility if the receiver is facing the umpire.

Linesman and line judge: Starting position is straddling the line of scrimmage not closer than nine yards (NCAA: at least seven yards) outside the widest offensive player. Working on the sideline is strongly encouraged.

Before the snap, the wing officials identify the eligible receivers on their side of the field, assist the referee in monitoring substitutions, count to ensure team A has at least seven players on the line of scrimmage and assist the umpire in checking the legality of uniform numbers of offensive linemen and receivers. If the receiver nearest the official is in the offensive backfield, the wing uses the extended arm signal to alert the opposite wing.

On runs to the opposite side of the field, the off wing must clean up after the play but be careful not to venture too far into the middle of the field in case team A runs a reverse or a fumble forces the flow of the play back toward the off wing.

On passes, the wing officials watch initial contact between receivers and defenders. The wingmen have to follow receivers downfield; after traveling no more than five to 10 yards downfield (about two seconds into the play), wing officials should look to see if a passer is truly setting up to pass.

On quick passes in the flat, the wings must be ready to rule if the pass is forward or backward. If the play is not a screen or a similar short pass, the wing official should drift cautiously five to seven yards downfield, maintaining a position about halfway between the line of scrimmage and the deepest receiver on his side. If

the pass is to the wing's coverage area, the wing official must move quickly to get the best possible angle to observe the attempted catch.

Wing officials have responsibility for the passer if he scrambles past the line of scrimmage. They must be especially alert if the passer heads for the sideline. If the quarterback is tackled out of bounds the wing official must rule on the legality of the contact. If the runner is driven out of bounds less than five yards past the scrimmage line, the covering wing official can handle the play and supervise players outside the sideline after marking the out of bounds spot with a beanbag. When a play is more than a five-yard gain and the runner heads across the sideline, the covering wing official marks the spot while keeping an eye on players; the referee or umpire must hustle to the spot and escort the players back to the field.

A play gaining considerably more than 10 yards may find the covering wing official policing activity past the sidelines. The covering wing official and the referee or umpire should work together to be sure the ball is properly spotted and off-the-field activity is monitored.

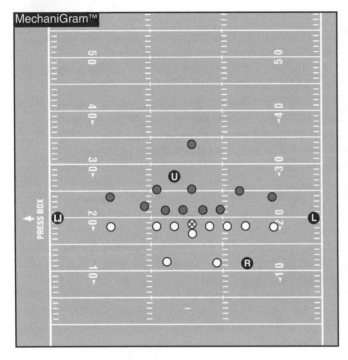

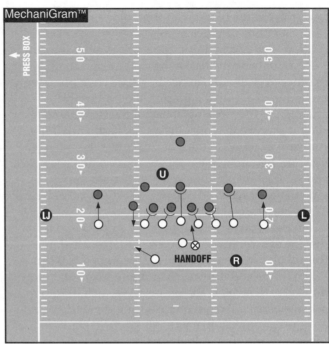

Action on the field: Starting position.

Referee: On the passing-arm side of the quarterback, approximately 10 to 12 yards deep and at least as wide as the tight end.

Umpire: Three to eight yards behind team B's line and between the defensive ends (NCAA: approximately a yard behind and to the side of or between the linebackers).

Linesman: Straddles the line of scrimmage not closer than nine yards (NCAA: at least seven yards) outside the widest offensive player.

Line judge: Straddles the line of scrimmage not closer than nine yards (NCAA: at least seven yards) outside the widest offensive player.

Action on the field: Handoff to back.

Referee: Reads blocking of left tackle and reads run. Observes handoff and action around quarterback after handoff.

Umpire: Reads blocking of center and right guard and reads run. Determines point of attack and observes blocking there.

Linesman: Reads blocking of split end and reads run. Observes initial line charge.

Line judge: Reads blocking of split end and reads run. Observes initial line charge.

KEY

Referee Umpire Line Judge Linesman Back Judge Chain Gang Ballboy Coach Offense Defense Football Possession of football

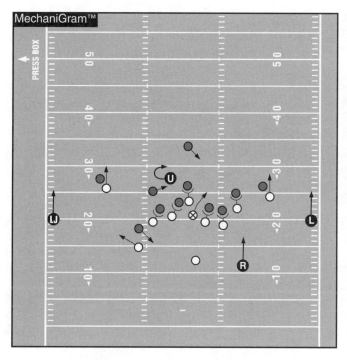

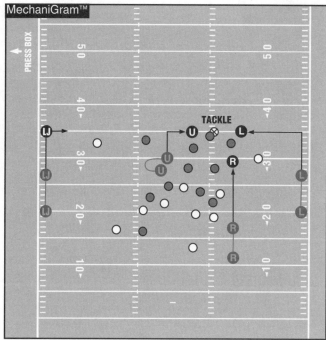

Action on the field: Runner advances.

Referee: Moves slowly downfield and observes action behind runner.

Umpire: Steps back to avoid interfering with play and pivots to observe play. Observes runner and action around runner (halo concept).

Linesman: Moves slowly downfield and observes action in front of runner.

Line judge: Moves slowly downfield and observes action in front of runner.

Action on the field: Runner continues advance and is downed.

Referee: Moves slowly downfield and observes players in his area. If first down has been achieved and no penalty markers are down, signals linesman to have chain crew move the chains.

Umpire: Moves quickly downfield and observes action in front of runner. Squares off to mirror spot. Observes players. Sets ball for next down.

Linesman: Moves quickly downfield and observes action around runner. Blows whistle when runner is downed. (If first down is achieved, also gives stop-the-clock signal.) Observes players. Squares off to mark spot of forward progress. If first down has been achieved, gets signal from referee and instructs chain crew to move to spot. Assists chain crew in setting chains for new series.

Line judge: Observes action in front of runner in his area. Squares off to mirror spot of forward progress. Observes players in his area.

Movement → | Previous position **U** → **U** Current position (stopped) | Previous position **U** → **U** Current position (still moving)

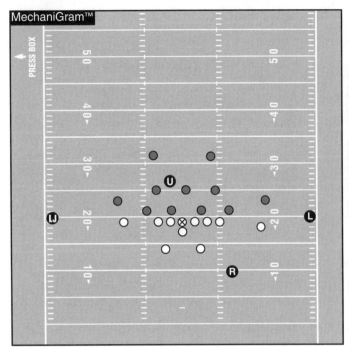

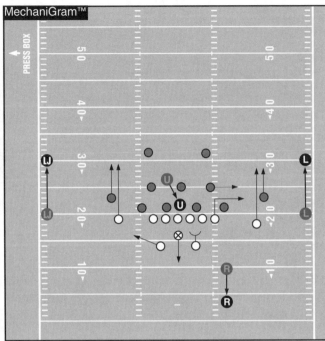

Action on the field: Starting position.

Referee: On the passing-arm side of the quarterback, approximately 10 to 12 yards deep and at least as wide as the tight end.

Umpire: Three to eight yards behind team B's line and between the defensive ends (NCAA: approximately a yard behind and to the side of or between the linebackers).

Linesman: Straddles the line of scrimmage not closer than nine yards (NCAA: at least seven yards) outside the widest offensive player.

Line judge: Straddles the line of scrimmage not closer than nine yards (NCAA: at least seven yards) outside the widest offensive player.

Action on the field: Quarterback drops back.

Referee: Keys on opposite-side tackle; reads pass when tackle retreats. As quarterback drops back, moves back to maintain distance between himself and quarterback. Observes blocking by backs.

Umpire: Observes presnap adjustments and legality of snap. Keys on center and guards; reads pass when linemen retreat. Steps up to the line of scrimmage and observes blocking.

Linesman: Identifies the eligible receivers on his side of the field. Uses extended arm signal to alert line judge that end is in offensive backfield. Keys action of tight end and reads pass. Uses shuffle step to move slowly downfield and watches initial contact between receivers and defenders.

Line judge: Identifies the eligible receivers on his side of the field. Keys split end and reads pass. Uses shuffle step to move slowly downfield and watches initial contact between receivers and defenders.

KEY

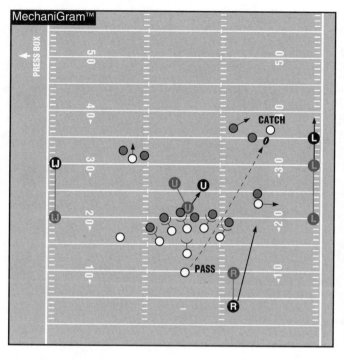

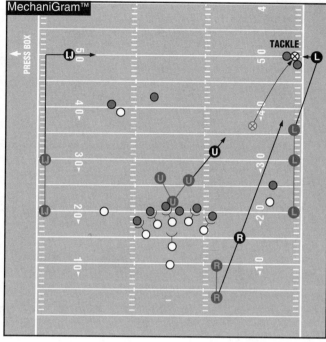

Action on the field: Pass caught by receiver in linesman's side zone.

Referee: Observes passer. Moves downfield with flow of players.

Umpire: Pivots to follow flight of the ball. Moves slowly downfield and observes players in his area.

Linesman: Uses shuffle step to maintain position about halfway between line of scrimmage and deepest receiver on his side. Moves quickly down sideline to get angle to observe attempted catch.

Line judge: Uses shuffle step to maintain position about halfway between line of scrimmage and deepest receiver on his side.

Action on the field: Runner advances and is downed.

Referee: Moves slowly downfield and observes players in front of the ball. If players land in team area, hustles to sideline to observe action.

Umpire: Moves slowly downfield and observes players in front of the ball. Once spot is established, hustles to hashmark to set ball for next down.

Linesman: Blows whistle when receiver is downed. Gives stop-the-clock signal if first down has been acheived. Squares off to mark spot of forward progress. Observes any players who may land in team area.

Line judge: Continues moving downfield and observes players in his area. Squares off to mark spot of forward progress.

Movement | Previous position | Current position (stopped) | Previous position | Current position (still moving)

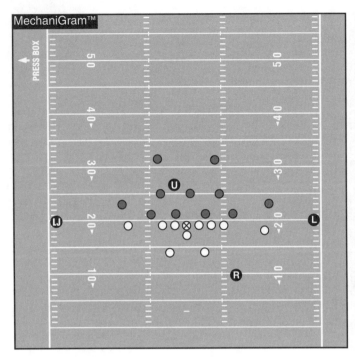

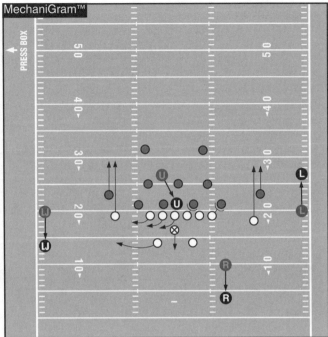

Action on the field: Starting position.

Referee: On the passing-arm side of the quarterback, approximately 10 to 12 yards deep and at least as wide as the tight end.

Umpire: Three to eight yards behind team B's line and between the defensive ends (NCAA: approximately a yard behind and to the side of or between the linebackers).

Linesman: Straddles the line of scrimmage not closer than nine yards (NCAA: at least seven yards) outside the widest offensive player.

Line judge: Straddles the line of scrimmage not closer than nine yards (NCAA: at least seven yards) outside the widest offensive player.

Action on the field: Quarterback drops back.

Referee: Keys on opposite-side tackle; reads screen or draw when tackle pulls. As quarterback drops back, moves back to maintain distance between himself and quarterback. Observes blocking by backs.

Umpire: Observes presnap adjustments and legality of snap. Keys on center and guards; reads screen or draw when linemen pull. Steps up to the line of scrimmage and observes blocking.

Linesman: Identifies the eligible receivers on his side of the field. Uses extended arm signal to alert line judge that end is in offensive backfield. Reads blocking of tight end and reads run. Moves slowly downfield and watches initial contact between receivers and defenders.

Line judge: Identifies the eligible receivers on his side of the field. After snap, observes initial blocking; reads screen or draw when tackle pulls. Moves into offensive backfield to cover receiver out of backfield.

KEY

R	U	LJ	L	BJ	CG	BB	C	O	●	◖	⊗
Referee	Umpire	Line Judge	Linesman	Back Judge	Chain Gang	Ballboy	Coach	Offense	Defense	Football	Possession of football

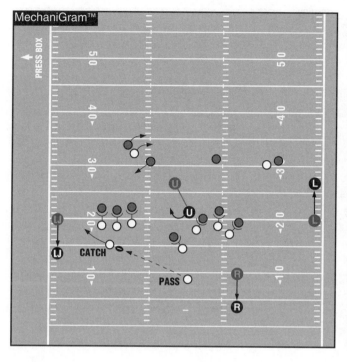

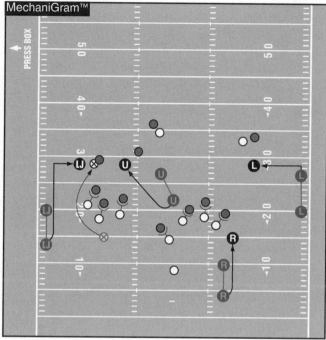

Action on the field: Back catches pass and begins advance.

Referee: Observes passer. Looks to line judge for either backward pass signal, incomplete pass signal or no signal (complete forward pass).

Umpire: Pivots to follow flight of the ball. Observes blockers in front of ball.

Linesman: Moves slowly downfield and observes action of players in his area.

Line judge: Rules on whether pass is backward or forward (punches pass if backward). Observes action in front of runner.

Action on the field: Runner continues advance and is downed.

Referee: Moves slowly downfield and observes players in front of the ball.

Umpire: Moves slowly downfield and observes players in front of the ball. When runner is downed, hustles to hashmark to set ball for next down.

Linesman: Continues to move slowly downfield and observes players in his area. Squares off to mark spot of forward progress.

Line judge: Moves downfield with runner. Observes action of runner and players around runner (halo concept). Blows whistle when receiver is downed. Squares off to mark spot of forward progress. Stops clock if first down has been achieved.

Movement | Previous position | Current position (stopped) | Previous position | Current position (still moving)

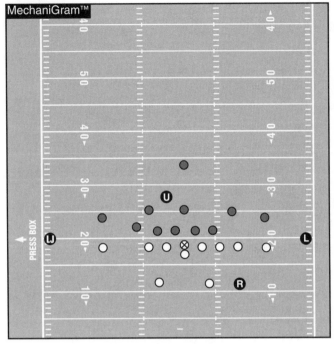

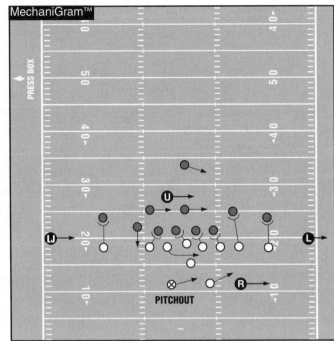

Action on the field: Starting position.

Referee: On the passing-arm side of the quarterback, approximately 10 to 12 yards deep and at least as wide as the tight end.

Umpire: Three to eight yards behind team B's line and between the defensive ends (NCAA: approximately a yard behind and to the side of or between the linebackers).

Linesman: Straddles the line of scrimmage not closer than nine yards (NCAA: at least seven yards) outside the widest offensive player.

Line judge: Straddles the line of scrimmage not closer than nine yards (NCAA: at least seven yards) outside the widest offensive player.

Action on the field: Pitchout to back.

Referee: Reads blocking of left tackle and reads run. Moves with flow of play. Observes runner and action around runner.

Umpire: Reads blocking of pulling left guard and reads sweep. Moves with flow of play. Observes blocking and action in front of runner.

Linesman: Reads blocking of split end and reads run. Steps across sideline to prevent interfering with play. Observes blocking and action in front of runner.

Line judge: Reads blocking of split end and reads run. Moves slowly toward play. Observes blocking and action of players not involved in flow of play.

KEY

Referee   Umpire   Line Judge   Linesman   Back Judge   Chain Gang   Ballboy   Coach   Offense   Defense   Football   Possession of football

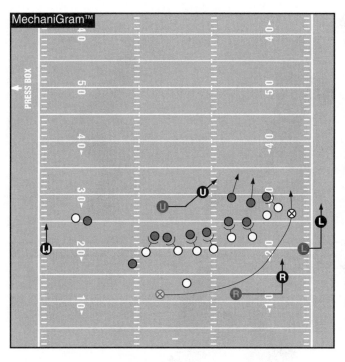

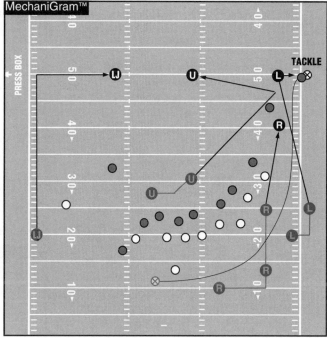

Action on the field: Runner advances.

Referee: Gives up coverage of runner to linesman (halo concept). Moves slowly downfield trailing flow and cleans up after the play.

Umpire: Pivots and moves with flow of play. Observes blocking and action in front of runner.

Linesman: Takes coverage of runner (halo concept) and moves quickly up sideline to stay ahead of runner. Observes runner and action around runner.

Line judge: Moves slowly downfield and cleans up after the play.

Action on the field: Runner continues advance and is downed out of bounds.

Referee: Moves slowly downfield and observes players in front of the ball. If first down has been achieved and no penalty markers are down, signals linesman to have chain crew move the chains.

Umpire: Moves downfield and observes players in front of the ball. Hustles to dead-ball spot to prevent post-play action. Once all players have returned to field, hustles to hashmark to set ball for next down.

Linesman: Continues to move downfield and observes runner and action around runner all the way down sideline. Blows whistle and gives stop-the-clock signal when runner steps out of bounds. Uses inside-out look to observe players and squares off to mark spot of forward progress. If necessary, drops beanbag to indicate spot and moves out of bounds to stop post-play action. Holds spot until umpire arrives to set ball for new series. If first down has been achieved, gets signal from referee and instructs chain crew to move to spot. Assists chain crew in setting chains for new series.

Line judge: Moves downfield with flow of play and cleans up after the play. Squares off to mirror spot of forward progress. Observes players in his area. Holds spot until released by umpire.

MECHANICS ILLUSTRATED: SIDELINE PASS COVERAGE

On pass plays near the sidelines, wing officials have a better chance of determining whether or not a receiver has made a catch if their focus is parallel with the line rather than perpendicular to it.

In PlayPic A, the covering official is behind the receiver as the player tries to catch a pass. From this angle, the official has no way of knowing if the player had control of the ball when he stepped out of bounds.

PlayPic B shows the correct position. The official's gaze is directed parallel with the sideline. From this position the official can see if the receiver keeps a foot inbounds and whether or not the receiver controlled the pass. The technique is called "looking down the gun barrel."

To properly rule on the play, officials must look at the receiver's feet first. If the player has been unable to get a foot inbounds before making the catch (a technique called "dotting the i"), it doesn't matter if the receiver secured control of the pass; the pass will be ruled incomplete. In order to get that look, the official must avoid being too close to the action. Maintaining proper distance will allow the official to see the feet first, then the ball, with a minimum of head movement.

PlayPic C illustrates how two officials working the sideline can communicate before making their ruling. The officials need only make eye contact and nod "yes" to indicate a legal catch or "no" to confirm an incomplete pass. If there is disagreement, both officials should give the stop-the-clock signal but no other signal. They then confer to share information before arriving at a consensus.

MECHANICS ILLUSTRATED: WIDE RUNS THAT END OUT OF BOUNDS

When the ball goes out of bounds, some officials think their work on that play is over. On the contrary, it is just the beginning.

In addition to determining forward progress and stopping the clock, covering officials must keep an eye on the ballcarrier and any other players in the vicinity. An unseen (and unpenalized) personal foul gives players the impression that anything goes outside the boundaries of the field.

Proper coverage on out-of-bounds plays begins when the ball is still inbounds. On sweep plays or quick sideline passes, linesmen and line judges should allow the play to pass them (PlayPic A). Trail the play by a minimum of five yards (PlayPic B). Allow more space if the defensive pursuit is coming from behind the runner.

Trailing in this manner may make you uncomfortable if you feel you are always supposed to be "right on top of the play." But letting the play get by you widens your field of vision, allows you a better view of the action and decreases the chance you will be injured yourself. Keeping your distance also means you'll have a better chance to see a clip or other illegal block, and provide a good look at the runner's feet to see if he steps out of bounds.

When the ballcarrier steps or is taken out of bounds, sound your whistle and get to the spot. Move quickly but cautiously. Be sure to make a one-quarter turn, facing away from the field, and direct your attention to the pile (PlayPic C). You'll need to be doubly alert if the ballcarrier and tacklers have landed in or near the team box; more people in the area means more potential trouble.

Hold your position and wait for the referee to retrieve the ball or obtain a different one from the ballboy. You shouldn't leave this position until the area is cleared of players. Don't mark the spot with a beanbag and retrieve the ball yourself. The beanbag should only be used to mark a spot only if a fight breaks out and you need to intervene.

Once the players have unpiled and are

headed back to their respective huddles, turn around and give the umpire a spot from which he can mark the ball.

While the wing official is facing away from the field and the referee is helping on the sideline, it is important for the umpire and opposite wing official to observe all other players and substitutes. Players not involved in the action must be observed.

• By keying on the opposite-side tackle, the referee can determine if the play is a run or pass.

• *Referee* recommends that the umpire favor the side opposite the tight end because it decreases the number of players who will charge off the line toward the umpire.

• On runs to the opposite side of the field, the off wing must clean up after the play.

• Dead-ball officiating is especially important if the tackle is made in the team area.

Quiz

Without referring back, you should be able to answer the following true-false questions.

1. If the quarterback drops back as if to pass, the referee should move toward the line of scrimmage.

2. The umpire must straddle the ball until the offensive team approaches the line of scrimmage.

3. If the right tackle blocks down (to his right) and the center joins the right guard on a double-team block taking their man to their left, the point of attack most likely is the gap between the center and guard.

4. If a wing official is "pinching" on a short-yardage play, it is OK if a team A player gets behind the official.

5. The umpire should always mirror a touchdown signal.

1. False 2. False 3. False 4. False 5. False

Chapter 26

Goalline Plays

More important than altering positioning near team B's goal is altering behavior. First of all, internalize the tendencies of team A in short-yardage situations. What have they done previously to gain first downs? Have they punched over any touchdowns in the game so far? How? Such thinking will provide clues about likely plays near the goal.

Wing officials must resolve to step to the goalline as prescribed in the manuals. If the run ends up short of the goalline, officiate back toward the progress spot and collapse completely to the ball. A more definitive collapse to the ball and signal are required when the ball barely breaks the plane of the goalline, but if the runner clearly bursts into the end zone, there's no need to make a dramatic show.

But wing officials cannot drift upfield if a run comes at them (sweep or quarterback option). Instead they must retreat and dash outside the sidelines if necessary, determined to be at the goalline to rule on it.

Keep in mind what teams customarily do when down at the goalline. The defensive line usually dives underneath — "submarining" they call it — and linebackers ready themselves to push back the runner. The offensive line surges, even flopping on the defenders, and a back often vaults over the top.

Officials should point the goalline out to each other whenever the ball will be snapped at or inside either team's five yardline. When the line in question is team A's goal the referee should warn deep backs and punters about the endline.

General procedures

The referee's job on a goalline play is much the same as for a standard scrimmage play. He positions himself far enough behind the line to observe the backs and the opposite-side tackle. Federation allows the referee to position himself on either side of the quarterback, depending on the tendencies of team A. For instance, if a team is prone to running behind right tackle on short-yardage plays, a position to the right of the quarterback would be most advantageous because it would give the referee the best view of the point of attack. *Referee* recommendation: The referee can vary his starting position only if he is quick enough to avoid getting too close to the backs; if team A tries to cross up the defense with a pass or wide run, the referee must not interfere with the play.

The umpire sets up in his usual position five to seven yards off the line. Both the referee and the umpire can take positions favoring the strong side of the offense; odds are that a plunge will go that way. Pass plays originating inside team B's 10 yardline are likely to be quick throws. It is crucial for the umpire to recognize a pass quickly and stay out of the pass routes. The tight end is a particularly common target in such situations. The umpire may have the best look to rule on a catch or trap on short passes.

Referee recommendation: Have the wing officials "pinch" the ends in goalline situations. The mechanic should be used only when the ball is snapped at or inside team B's five yardline and when the wings are quick and alert enough to avoid being trapped inside if team A runs wide or throws a screen or a pass in the flat.

When the ball is snapped between team B's 10 and five yardlines, the wing officials release slowly downfield at the snap, staying ahead of the runner all the way to the goalline. The wingman officiates back to the ball when the runner is downed short of the goalline. When the ball is snapped at or inside team B's five yardline, the wings break immediately to the goalline and officiate back to the ball if necessary.

The touchdown signal is given only by an official who actually sees the ball in possession of a runner break the plane of the goalline. Mirroring the signal is dangerous; if the covering official is incorrect, the crew will find it difficult to overcome two officials making a mistake. If the covering official is correct, there is no need for a second signal.

There is virtually no circumstance under which the referee would declare a touchdown. Any touchdown signal from the referee would be one given to the pressbox to verify the signal from a crewmate. The umpire will declare a touchdown in only one specific instance: if the runner crosses the goalline so that the ball is in clear view of the umpire. Under most circumstances, the wing official will be in a much better position to rule if the ball has broken the plane of the goalline. The umpire will rarely determine the spot of forward progress if the run ends short of the goalline. When the runner is stopped short of the goalline, the umpire should ensure that the ball is not pushed forward after it is declared dead.

CHALK TALK: FEDERATION GOALLINE POSITIONING AND COVERAGE

Referee: Starting position is on the passing-arm side of the quarterback, approximately 10 to 12 yards deep and at least as wide as the tight end. The referee must be especially aware of attempts by team A to gain an advantage. Such acts as a rolling start (in which the quarterback walks up behind the snapper and, without stopping, puts his hands under center and immediately receives the snap) and helping the runner must be penalized.

On a running play, the referee focuses on the ball, the runner and the blocking around the runner. If the play goes to the opposite side, the referee should move toward or parallel to the line of the scrimmage and maintain a position approximately in line with the runner. If the play is to the referee's side, the referee moves behind the play and is responsible for the runner until he crosses the neutral zone or turns upfield. The referee should watch the handoff or the pitchout, see the runner head outside the free clipping/free blocking zone, and watch to see that no one contacts the quarterback before drifting along to follow the play.

On passing plays, the referee observes blocking by the backs as the quarterback drops back. The referee should move to maintain the 10- to 12-yard distance between himself and the quarterback (e.g. if the quarterback drops back seven yards, the referee retreats seven yards).

The referee is also responsible for ruling on intentional grounding and can work with the umpire to determine whether a passer was beyond the line of scrimmage when the pass was thrown. The referee should move to the spot of the pass and observe the location of the passer's feet. If the passer is clearly beyond the line, a penalty marker should be dropped. In cases that are too close for an immediate determination, a beanbag should be dropped. At the end of the play, the referee can compare the spot of the beanbag and the location of the down box in order to make the call.

On runs that end out of bounds behind the neutral zone, the referee is responsible for marking the spot. He also must beanbag the spot of a muff, fumble or quarterback sack in the offensive backfield.

Umpire: Starting position is three to eight yards behind team B's line and between the defensive ends.

On runs, the umpire must observe the blocking to find the point of attack. When the hole opens, the umpire should move away from it (to avoid interfering

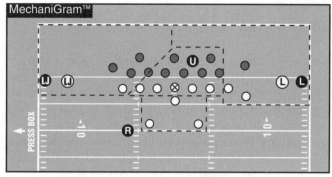

Ⓛ Ⓛ = *Referee* recommendation

with the defensive pursuit) and laterally (thus turning his head toward the blockers in front of the runner and the tackling efforts of the defense).

On pass plays, the umpire must step up and reach the line of scrimmage. If a pass is first touched by a team B player, the umpire gives the tipped ball signal. When the pass is thrown, the umpire pivots to follow the flight of the ball. The umpire has catch/trap responsibility if the receiver is facing the umpire.

Linesman and line judge: Starting position is straddling the line of scrimmage. *Referee* recommendation: Have the wing officials "pinch" the ends in goalline situations. The mechanic should be used only when the ball is snapped at or inside team B's eight yardline and when the wings are quick and alert enough to avoid being trapped inside if team A runs wide or throws a screen or a pass in the flat.

When the snap is at or inside team B's five yardline, the wings move immediately to the goalline and work back toward the ball if the runner is downed short of the goalline. When the snap is between team B's 10 and five yardlines, wingmen should release slowly downfield at the snap and stay ahead of the runner to the goalline.

CHALK TALK: NCAA GOALLINE POSITIONING AND COVERAGE

Referee: Starting position is on the passing-arm side of the quarterback, approximately 10 to 12 yards deep and at least as wide as the tight end. The referee must be especially aware of attempts by team A to gain an advantage. Such acts as a rolling start (in which the quarterback walks up behind the snapper and, without stopping, puts his hands under center and immediately receives the snap) and helping the runner must be penalized.

On a running play, the referee focuses on the ball, the runner and the blocking around the runner. If the play goes to the opposite side, the referee should move toward or parallel to the line of the scrimmage and maintain a position approximately in line with the runner. If the play is to the referee's side, the referee moves behind the play and is responsible for the runner until he crosses the neutral zone or turns upfield. The referee should watch the handoff or the pitchout, see the runner head outside the free clipping/free blocking zone, and watch to see that no one contacts the quarterback before drifting along to follow the play.

On passing plays, the referee observes blocking by the backs as the quarterback drops back. The referee should move to maintain the 10- to 12-yard distance between himself and the quarterback (e.g. if the quarterback drops back seven yards, the referee retreats seven yards).

The referee is also responsible for ruling on intentional grounding and can work with the umpire to determine whether a passer was beyond the line of scrimmage when the pass was thrown. The referee should move to the spot of the pass and observe the location of the passer's feet. If the passer is clearly beyond the line, a penalty marker should be dropped. In cases that are too close for an immediate determination, a beanbag should be dropped. At the end of the play, the referee can compare the spot of the beanbag and the location of the down box in order to make the call.

On runs that end out of bounds behind the neutral zone, the referee is responsible for marking the spot. He also must beanbag the spot of a muff, fumble or quarterback sack in the offensive backfield.

Umpire: Starting position is approximately a yard behind and to the side of or between the linebackers.

On runs, the umpire must observe the blocking to find the point of attack. When the hole opens, the umpire should move away from it (to avoid interfering

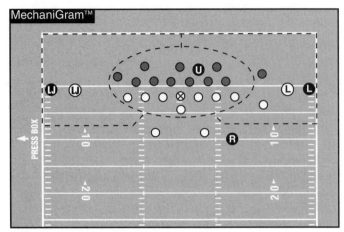

(LJ) (L) = *Referee* recommendation

with the defensive pursuit) and laterally (thus turning his head toward the blockers in front of the runner and the tackling efforts of the defense).

On pass plays, the umpire must step up and reach the line of scrimmage. If a pass is first touched by a team B player, the umpire gives the tipped ball signal. When the pass is thrown, the umpire pivots to follow the flight of the ball. The umpire has catch/trap responsibility if the receiver is facing the umpire.

Linesman and line judge: Starting position is straddling the line of scrimmage. *Referee* recommendation: Have the wing officials "pinch" the ends in goalline situations. The mechanic should be used only when the ball is snapped at or inside team B's eight yardline and when the wings are quick and alert enough to avoid being trapped inside if team A runs wide or throws a screen or a pass in the flat.

When the snap is at or inside team B's five yardline, the wings move immediately to the goalline and work back toward the ball if the runner is downed short of the goalline. When the snap is between team B's 10 and five yardlines, wingmen should release slowly downfield at the snap and stay ahead of the runner to the goalline.

R U
4
LJ L

MECHANICS ILLUSTRATED: GOALLINE COVERAGE

Many scores occur during plays in which the ball is snapped on or inside the 10 yardline. It behooves officials to be at the goalline as soon as possible so they can make decisions based on what they've seen rather than on guesswork.

In PlayPic A, the wing official is straightlined because he is so far behind the play he cannot tell if the ball has broken the plane of the goalline or if the runner's knee has touched down the ground. PlayPic B illustrates the proper position.

Getting to the goalline is paramount, but linesmen and line judges should not get in the way of the play. Get as far as out of bounds as space allows. The position in PlayPic B gives the covering official a wide-angle view of the action, allowing him to see all of the key elements.

The wingmen have the best opportunity to view this specific play, in which the runner's knees, the sideline and the goalline are all involved.

The referee should employ these theories when the offense has the ball deep in its own territory. In PlayPic C, the quarterback is scrambling with a defender in pursuit. If the rusher catches the quarterback, the referee will be able to rule on a fumble that may be caused by the contact, whether or not the quarterback was tackled for a safety or advanced the ball completely out of the end zone and, if the quarterback gets off a pass, whether or not he was roughed.

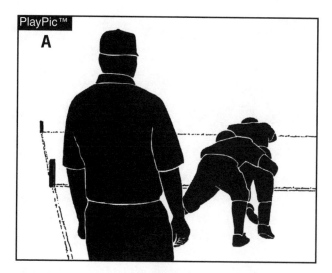

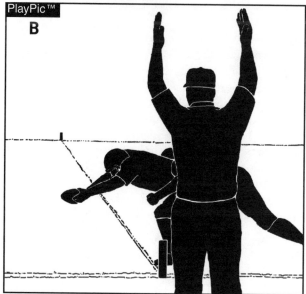

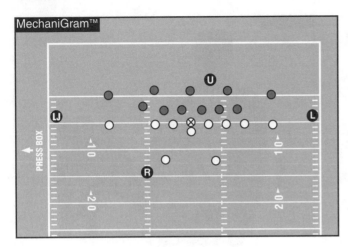

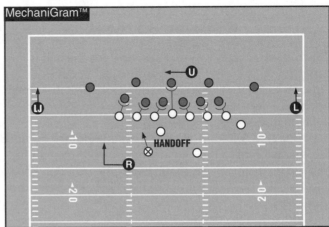

Action on the field: Starting position.

Referee: On the passing-arm side of the quarterback, approximately 10 to 12 yards deep and at least as wide as the tight end.

Umpire: Three to eight yards behind team B's line and between the defensive ends.

Linesman: Straddles the line of scrimmage not closer than nine yards outside the widest offensive player.

Line judge: Straddles the line of scrimmage not closer than nine yards outside the widest offensive player.

Action on the field: Handoff to back.

Referee: Reads blocking of left tackle and reads run. Moves with flow of play. Observes runner and action around runner.

Umpire: Reads blocking of center and right guard and reads run. Determines point of attack and observes blocking there. Moves with flow of play. Observes blocking and action in front of runner.

Linesman: Moves immediately to goalline at snap. Reads blocking of tight end and reads run. Observes initial blocking.

Line judge: Moves immediately to goalline at snap. Reads blocking of split end and reads run. Observes initial blocking.

KEY

 Referee Umpire Line Judge Linesman Back Judge Chain Gang Ballboy Coach ○ Offense ● Defense Football Possession of football

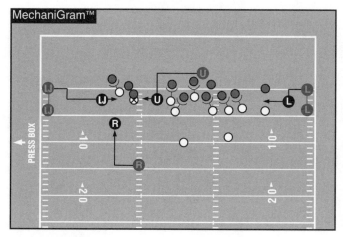

MechaniGram™

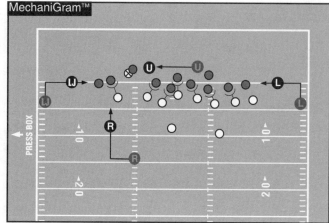

MechaniGram™

Action on the field: Runner stopped short.

Referee: Moves with flow of play and observes players in his area.

Umpire: Moves with flow of play and observes blocking and action in front of runner.

Linesman: Officiates back to the ball and squares off to mirror line judge's spot.

Line judge: Officiates back to the ball to observe contact on runner and squares off to indicate forward progress. Blows whistle when runner is downed.

Action on the field: Runner scores.

Referee: Moves with flow of play and observes action. When line judge signals touchdown (if no flags are down), turns to pressbox and mirrors signal.

Umpire: Moves with flow of play and observes blocking and action in front of runner.

Linesman: Straddles goalline and observes players in his area.

Line judge: Straddles goalline and observes runner and players around runner. When ball in possession of runner breaks plane of goalline, blows whistle and signals touchdown.

Movement →   Previous position → Current position (stopped)   Previous position → Current position (still moving)

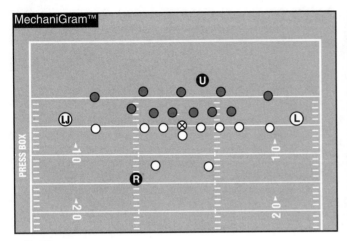

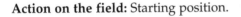

ⓁⒿ Ⓛ = *Referee* recommendation

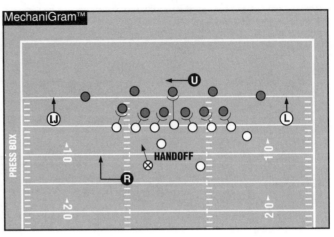

ⓁⒿ Ⓛ = *Referee* recommendation

Action on the field: Starting position.

Referee: On the passing-arm side of the quarterback, approximately 10 to 12 yards deep and at least as wide as the tight end.

Umpire: Three to eight yards behind team B's line and between the defensive ends.

Linesman: Straddles the line of scrimmage pinching the end, but not so far inside as to get trapped.

Line judge: Straddles the line of scrimmage pinching the end, but not so far inside as to get trapped.

Action on the field: Handoff to back.

Referee: Reads blocking of left tackle and reads run. Moves with flow of play. Observes runner and action around runner.

Umpire: Reads blocking of center and right guard and reads run. Determines point of attack and observes blocking there. Moves with flow of play. Observes blocking and action in front of runner.

Linesman: Moves immediately to goalline at snap. Reads blocking of tight end and reads run. Observes initial blocking.

Line judge: Moves immediately to goalline at snap. Reads blocking of split end and reads run. Observes initial blocking.

KEY

| Referee | Umpire | Line Judge | Linesman | Back Judge | Chain Gang | Ballboy | Coach | Offense | Defense | Football | Possession of football |

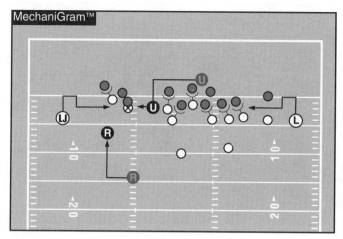

LJ L = *Referee* recommendation

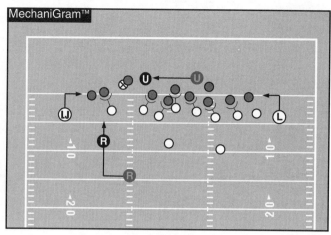

LJ L = *Referee* recommendation

Action on the field: Runner stopped short.

Referee: Moves with flow of play and observes players in his area.

Umpire: Moves with flow of play and observes blocking and action in front of runner.

Linesman: Officiates back to the ball and squares off to mirror line judge's spot.

Line judge: Officiates back to the ball to observe contact on runner and squares off to indicate forward progress. Blows whistle when runner is downed.

Action on the field: Runner scores.

Referee: Moves with flow of play and observes action. When line judge signals touchdown (if no flags are down), turns to pressbox and mirrors signal.

Umpire: Moves with flow of play and observes blocking and action in front of runner.

Linesman: Straddles goalline and observes players in his area.

Line judge: Straddles goalline and observes runner and players around runner. When ball in possession of runner breaks plane of goalline, blows whistle and signals touchdown.

Movement ⟶   U → U Previous position / Current position (stopped)   U → U Previous position / Current position (still moving)

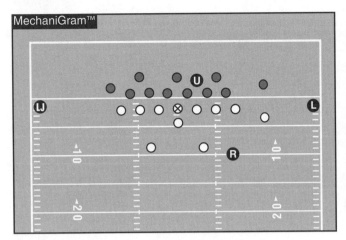

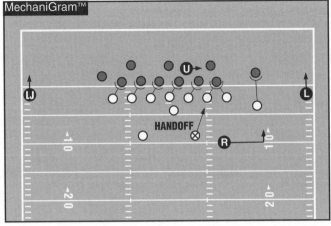

Action on the field: Starting positions.

Referee: On the passing-arm side of the quarterback, approximately 10 to 12 yards deep and at least as wide as the tight end.

Umpire: Approximately a yard behind and to the side of or between the linebackers.

Linesman: Straddles the line of scrimmage at least seven yards outside the widest offensive player.

Line judge: Straddles the line of scrimmage at least seven yards outside the widest offensive player.

Action on the field: Handoff to back.

Referee: Reads blocking of left tackle and reads run. Moves with flow of play. Observes runner and action around runner.

Umpire: Reads blocking of center and right guard and reads run. Determines point of attack and observes blocking there. Moves with flow of play. Observes blocking and action in front of runner.

Linesman: Uses extended arm signal to alert line judge that end is off the line. Moves toward goalline at snap. Reads blocking of tight end and reads run.

Line judge: Moves toward goalline at snap. Reads blocking of tight end and reads run.

KEY

Referee	Umpire	Line Judge	Linesman	Back Judge	Chain Gang	Ballboy	Coach	Offense	Defense	Football	Possession of football

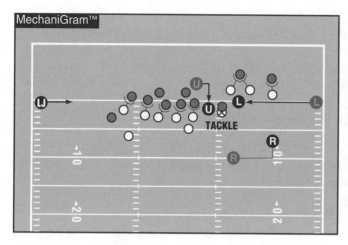

MechaniGram™

TACKLE

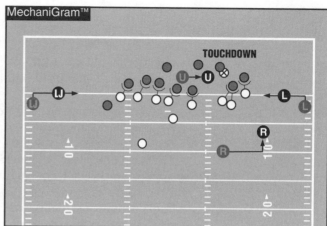

MechaniGram™

TOUCHDOWN

Action on the field: Runner stopped short.

Referee: Moves with flow of play and observes action of players in his area.

Umpire: Moves with flow of play and observes blocking and action in front of runner. When runner is downed, squares off to spot and takes spot from linesman.

Linesman: Officiates back to the ball to observe contact on runner and squares off to indicate forward progress. Blows whistle when runner is downed.

Line judge: Observes action of players in his area.

Action on the field: Runner scores.

Referee: Moves with flow of play and observes action of players in his area. When linesman signals touchdown (if no flags are down), turns to pressbox and mirrors signal.

Umpire: Moves with flow of play and observes blocking and action in front of runner. When ball is dead, moves toward runner and practices dead-ball officiating.

Linesman: Straddles goalline and observes runner and players around runner. When ball in possession of runner breaks plane of goalline, blows whistle and signals touchdown.

Line judge: Straddles goalline and observes players in his area.

Movement | Previous position → Current position (stopped) | Previous position → Current position (still moving)

• Officials should point the goalline out to each other whenever the ball will be snapped at or inside either team's five yardline.

• When team A snaps the ball near its own goalline, the referee should warn deep backs and punters about the endline.

• The wing officials may "pinch" the ends only when the ball is snapped at or inside team B's five yardline.

• The touchdown signal is given only by an official who actually sees the ball in possession of a runner break the plane of the goalline.

Quiz

Without referring back, you should be able to answer the following true-false questions.

1. The referee will rarely declare a touchdown.

2. If a team is prone to running behind right tackle on short-yardage plays, a position to the left of the quarterback would be most advantageous because it would give the referee the best view of the point of attack.

3. The umpire may have the best look to rule on a catch or trap on short passes.

4. When the runner is stopped short of the goalline, the umpire should ensure that the ball is not pushed forward after it is declared dead.

5. Mirroring a touchdown signal lends credibility to the call.

1. True 2. False 3. True 4. True 5. False

Chapter 27

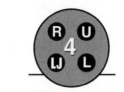

Scrimmage
Kicks

In a four-man scrimmage kick situation, the line judge has to go downfield before the snap to cover the kick, leaving jurisdiction for the entire line of scrimmage to the linesman. That is customary and a linesman ought to be able to handle it. The line judge should remain at the sideline or in the side zone about 30 yards downfield and in front of the receivers.

So far everything is standard, according to both manuals. Where it breaks down is in the execution. Observation has shown that many wing officials watch the ball on punts when they should instead be concentrating on players.

Here's the picture: The referee locks in on the punter and on those approaching the punter. The umpire watches the snap, and the initial contact (usually brush blocks), and the burst of linemen downfield, while the umpire himself is trapped inside the flow of players who are headed downfield. Both wing officials incorrectly gaze upward, the bills of their caps raised like a TV camera, mesmerized by the arc of the ball. As a result, as many as 21 of the 22 players, including the receiver, may be unattended for several seconds until the kick comes down. That is not good.

Instead, the line judge should glance for an instant at the ball and then watch receivers. That quick look and the players themselves will reveal by their reactions where the ball will come down.

The linesman must know what happens to the ball off the kicker's foot. He is supposed to wait until the ball crosses the line before breaking downfield, but if the linesman programs himself not to look upward for the ball, he'll know anyway.

That is, it's not peripheral vision exactly, but it is a "flying-bird-sense" that can tell an individual that a kick has flown by, either straight or shanked, without one's ever having to look at it directly. It's just there, in the sky overhead. Then the linesman breaks, all the while watching players under the punt. He really is the only official who has a good angle on the way receivers are setting up to block for a return and the way team K players are pursuing and converging. Lots of contact, just one official to see it. The umpire can help, but he's sort of in the midst of a storm, with flashes of contact all around, hard to isolate.

The linesman has a secondary obligation, too; namely to see if a player ahead of the probable receiver signals for a fair catch as a way of drawing tacklers to him and away from the player actually in position to make the catch. That is an act with serious consequences (no blocking by the signaler is permitted, and the ball is dead when caught) and must not go undetected.

The referee should pause after the kick, to be sure the punter has not been fouled after his follow-through. Then the referee can trot downfield for backup coverage. Some referees move out to the line judge's side after the kick to be on the outside looking in, in case of an extended runback.

Be advised, because teams frequently change personnel on punts (all kicks, really), both teams should be counted carefully.

Remember also that a kick downfield should be declared dead when it is downed by a member of the kicking team, but when it is still wiggling, a player touching it does not kill it.

Referee: In a five-man crew, the referee can always start on the kicking-leg side of the punter because the sidelines are manned by two wing officials. In a four-man crew, however, the line judge must vacate the sideline in order to observe the deep receivers. The four-man manuals allow the referee to vary his position to an advantageous position. As a result, *Referee* recommends that the referee's position is always on the line judge's side in order to cover the vacated sideline. He should be even with or slightly in front of the punter, in a position to see the snap and the backs.

A verbal alert such as "Gone!" is an aid to help prevent roughing the kicker. Once the kick is away, the referee takes a quick look to see the flight of the ball. If the kick is toward a sideline, he must be prepared to determine the spot the ball went out of bounds. If the kick is short, the referee goes directly to the out-of-bounds spot; if the kick is long and goes out of bounds, the covering official moves past where he thinks it flew out before walking toward the referee with his hand up — along the sideline — until the referee chops downward, telling him to halt (NCAA: the line judge alone determines the spot of any kick to his side that travels out of bounds 25 or more yards beyond the line. On shorter kicks, the line judge works with the referee as described above. The linesman spots a grounded kick out of bounds to his side, but when the kick goes out of bounds in flight, he works with the referee as described above).

If the receivers begin a return, the referee should move slowly downfield; if the runner breaks a long return, the referee may assume responsibility for the runner.

On blocked kicks, the referee should be ready to rule on the recovery and observe the advance of any player who runs with a recovered ball. If the ball is partially blocked, the legal touching signal should be used.

Umpire: The umpire sets up four to seven yards deep and favoring the line judge's sideline. Favoring the line judge's side compensates for the line judge's position farther downfield. Team R players should be reminded about rules relating to contact on the snapper. The umpire should move toward the line at the snap, which will improve the view of the initial line charge and help him see players shooting gaps or lineman chopping rushers at the knees (the ball will be snapped out of the free-blocking/free-clipping zone) as well as contact on the snapper.

Once the ball has been kicked and players from both teams have run past the umpire, the umpire pivots to the line judge's side (NCAA: in the direction of the return) and moves slowly downfield and observe action in front of the runner.

Linesman: The linesman begins the play on the line of scrimmage and no closer than nine yards from the widest offensive player (NCAA: at least seven yards outside the widest offensive player and never inside the top of the numbers). Working on the sideline is necessary when the snap is from the hashmark on the linesman's side of the field.

The linesman observes the initial line charge but doesn't move downfield until the ball is beyond the neutral zone. The linesman is primarily responsible for determining if the ball crossed the line, although the umpire can provide help on that call. The linesman is responsible for his sideline from endline to endline and for covering the runner when the return is to his area. If the run is to the opposite sideline, he should clean up behind the play.

If the kick is short and in the linesman's side zone, he must know who touched a loose ball; if the kicking team is first to touch the kick, a beanbag should be dropped at the spot of the touching.

When kicks go out of bounds to the linesman's side, the linesman should kill the clock at once. If the kick is short and toward a sideline, the referee determines the spot the ball went out of bounds. If the kick is long and goes out of bounds, the linesman moves past where he thinks it flew out before walking toward the referee with his hand up — along the sideline — until the referee chops downward, telling him to halt. How each crew defines "short" and "long" kicks should be determined in the pregame meeting. (NCAA: the linesman spots a grounded kick out of bounds to his side, but when the kick goes out of bounds in flight, the linesman works with the referee as described above.)

On blocked kicks, the linesman should be ready to rule on the recovery and observe the advance of any player who runs with a recovered ball. The linesman must also be cognizant of a fake punt. If a pass to the linesman's flat is used on the fake, the linesman must know if the pass was forward or backward. If the kicker starts to run before deciding to kick, the linesman may have to rule if the punter was beyond the line when the ball was kicked.

Line judge: The line judge's position is seven to 10 yards wider than and the same distance in front of the deepest receiver (NCAA: on his sideline, outside and in front of the deep receivers. If the ball is snapped from a hashmark or on the opposite side of the field, he may adjust to the wide side of the field). The line judge is responsible for covering all kicks down the middle and to his side zone and should be prepared to get to team R's goalline to rule on momentum exception or touchback situations.

All deep receivers are the responsibility of the line judge. He should observe the receivers and the players around them rather than the ball as it flies downfield. Remaining far enough away from the receiver to retain a wide-angle view and moving in at a controlled pace, with eyes searching, once the receiver has completed the fair catch helps the line judge look for illegal action around the receiver. In such cases, it is also a good idea not to have the whistle in the mouth; it is possible for a fair catch to be muffed and a whistle blown before the ball dribbles loose from the receiver's grasp.

The line judge is responsible for his sideline from the line of scrimmage to team R's endline (NCAA: endline to endline) and for covering the runner when the return is to his area. If the runner breaks into the opposite side zone, coverage transfers to the linesman and the line judge cleans up behind the play. On a return to the middle of the field, the line judge has responsibility for the runner until he gives up the runner to the umpire; the point at which the transfer occurs depends on how far downfield the umpire has drifted after the kick. The referee may take over coverage of the runner if the runner breaks off a long return.

When kicks go out of bounds to the line judge's side, the line judge should kill the clock at once. The line judge determines the spot of any kick to his side that travels out of bounds 25 or more yards beyond the line. On shorter kicks, the referee determines the spot the ball went out of bounds. The line judge moves past where he thinks it flew out before walking toward the referee with his hand up — along the sideline — until the referee chops downward, telling him to halt. (NCAA: the line judge alone determines the spot of any kick to his side that travels out of bounds 25 or more yards beyond the line. On shorter kicks, the line judge works with the referee as described above.)

In NCAA, the covering official, regardless of position, must beanbag the spot where the kick ends. That spot may be used for post-scrimmage kick penalty enforcement.

CHALK TALK: FEDERATION SCRIMMAGE KICK POSITIONING AND COVERAGE

Referee: Starting position is three to four yards in front of and five to yards outside the punter, on the punter's kicking-leg side. *Referee* recommendation: The referee should favor the line judge's side and cover that vacated sideline regardless of which leg the punter uses.

Once the kick is away, the referee takes a quick look to see the flight of the ball. If the kick is toward a sideline, he must be prepared to determine the spot the ball went out of bounds. If the kick is short, the referee goes directly to the out-of-bounds spot; if the kick is long and goes out of bounds, the covering official moves past where he thinks it flew out before walking toward the referee with his hand up — along the sideline — until the referee chops downward, telling him to halt.

If the runner breaks a long return, the referee may assume responsibility for the runner.

On blocked kicks, the referee should be ready to rule on the recovery and observe the advance of any player who runs with a recovered ball.

Umpire: Starting position is four to seven yards deep and favoring the line judge's sideline. Team R players should be reminded about rules relating to contact on the snapper.

The umpire should move toward the line at the snap, which will improve the view of the initial line charge. Once the ball has been kicked and players from both teams have run past the umpire, the umpire pivots to the line judge's side and moves slowly downfield.

Linesman: Starting position is straddling the line of scrimmage and more than nine yards outside the widest offensive player.

The linesman observes the initial line charge but doesn't move downfield until

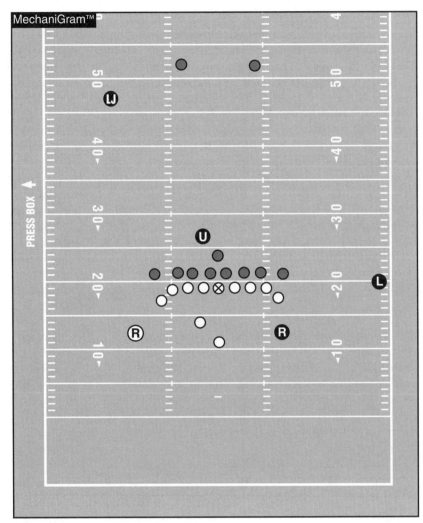

$\textbf{R}$ = *Referee* recommendation

the ball is beyond the neutral zone. The linesman is primarily responsible for determining if the ball crossed the line, although the umpire can provide help on that call. The linesman is responsible for his sideline from endline to endline and for covering the runner when the return is to his area. If the run is to the opposite sideline, he should clean up behind the play.

If the kick is short and in the linesman's side zone, he must who touched a loose ball; if the kicking team is first to touch the kick, a beanbag should be dropped at the spot of the touching.

When kicks go out of bounds to the linesman's side, the linesman should kill the clock at once. If the kick is short and toward a sideline, the referee determines the spot the ball went out of bounds. If the kick is long and goes out of bounds, the linesman moves past where he thinks it flew out before walking toward the referee with his hand up — along the sideline — until the referee chops downward, telling him to halt. How each crew defines "short" and "long" kicks should be determined in the pregame meeting.

On blocked kicks, the linesman should be ready to rule on the recovery and observe the advance of any player who runs with a recovered ball. The linesman must also be cognizant of a fake punt. If a pass to the linesman's flat is used on the fake, the linesman must know if the pass was forward or backward. If the kicker initially starts to run before deciding to kick, the linesman may have to rule whether the punter was beyond the line when the ball was kicked.

Line judge: Starting position is seven to 10 yards wider than and in front of the deepest receiver.

The line judge is responsible for covering all kicks down the middle and to his side zone and should be prepared to get to team R's goalline to rule on momentum exception or touchback situations.

All deep receivers are the responsibility of the line judge. He should observe the receivers and the players around them rather than the ball as it flies downfield. Remaining far enough away from the receiver to retain a wide-angle view and moving in at a controlled pace, with eyes searching, once the receiver has completed the fair catch helps the line judge look for illegal action around the receiver. In such cases, it is also a good idea not to have the whistle in the mouth; it is possible for a fair catch to be muffed and a whistle blown before the ball dribbles loose from the receiver's grasp.

The line judge is responsible for his sideline from the line of scrimmage to team R's endline and for covering the runner when the return is to his area. If the runner breaks into the opposite side zone, coverage transfers to the linesman and the line judge cleans up behind the play. On a return to the middle of the field, the line judge has responsibility for the runner until he gives up the runner to the umpire; the point at which the transfer occurs depends on how far downfield the umpire has drifted after the kick. The referee may take over coverage of the runner if the runner breaks off a long return.

When kicks go out of bounds to the line judge's side, the line judge should kill the clock at once. The line judge determines the spot of any kick to his side that travels out of bounds 25 or more yards beyond the line. On shorter kicks, the referee determines the spot the ball went out of bounds. The line judge moves past where he thinks it flew out before walking toward the referee with his hand up — along the sideline — until the referee chops downward, telling him to halt.

CHALK TALK: NCAA SCRIMMAGE KICK POSITIONING AND COVERAGE

Referee: Starting position is in front of the kicker, wider than where the tight end would normally be positioned, and on the kicking-leg side. *Referee* recommendation: The referee should favor the line judge's side and cover that vacated sideline regardless of which leg the punter uses. He should be able to see all the backs and far enough away from the kicker to observe the blockers and kicker at the same time.

Once the kick is away, the referee takes a quick look to see the flight of the ball. If the kick is toward a sideline, he must be prepared to determine the spot the ball went out of bounds. The line judge alone determines the spot of any kick to his side that travels out of bounds 25 or more yards beyond the line. On shorter kicks, the line judge walks toward the referee with his hand up — along the sideline — until the referee chops downward, telling him to halt. The linesman spots a grounded kick out of bounds to his side, but when the kick goes out of bounds in flight, he uses the walk and chop method described above.

If the receivers begin a return, the referee should move slowly downfield; if the runner breaks a long return, the referee may assume responsibility for the runner.

On blocked kicks, the referee should be ready to rule on the recovery and observe the advance of any player who runs with a recovered ball.

Umpire: Starting position is four to seven yards deep and favoring the line judge's sideline. He should remind team R players about rules relating to contact on the snapper. The umpire should move toward the line at the snap, which will improve the view of the initial line charge.

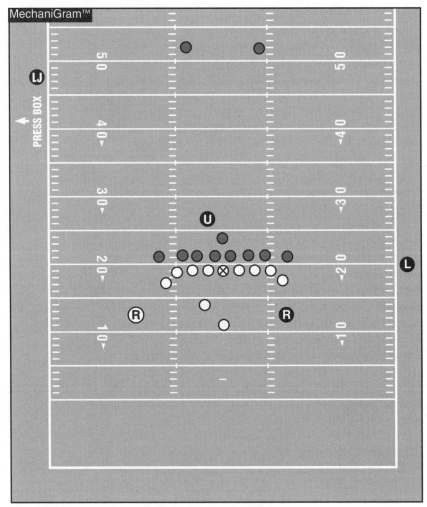

Ⓡ = *Referee* recommendation

Once the ball has been kicked and players from both teams have run past the umpire, the umpire pivots in the direction of the return and moves slowly downfield and observe action in front of the runner.

Linesman: Starting position is straddling the line of scrimmage, at least seven yards outside the widest offensive player and never inside the top of the numbers. When the snap is from the hashmark, position on the sideline is required.

The linesman observes the initial line charge but doesn't move downfield until the ball is beyond the neutral zone. The linesman is primarily responsible for determining if the ball crossed the line, although the umpire can provide help on that call. The linesman is responsible for his sideline from endline to endline and for covering the runner when the return is to his area. If the run is to the opposite sideline, he should clean up behind the play.

If the kick is short and in the linesman's side zone, he must know who touched a loose ball; if the kicking team is first to touch the kick, a beanbag should be dropped at the spot of the touching.

When kicks go out of bounds to the linesman's side, the linesman should kill the clock at once. The linesman spots a grounded kick out of bounds to his side, but when the kick goes out of bounds in flight, he walks toward the referee with his hand up — along the sideline — until the referee chops downward, telling him to halt.

On blocked kicks, the linesman should be ready to rule on the recovery and observe the advance of any player who runs with a recovered ball. The linesman must also be cognizant of a fake punt. If a pass to the linesman's flat is used on the fake, the linesman must know if the pass was forward or backward. If the kicker initially starts to run before deciding to kick, the linesman may have to rule whether the punter was beyond the line when the ball was kicked.

Line judge: Starting position is outside and in front of the deep receivers. The line judge is responsible for covering all kicks down the middle and to his side zone and should be prepared to get to team R's goalline to rule on momentum exception or touchback situations.

All deep receivers are the responsibility of the line judge. He should observe the receivers and the players around them rather than the ball as it flies downfield.

The line judge is responsible for his sideline from endline to endline and for covering the runner when the return is to his area. If the runner breaks into the opposite side zone, coverage transfers to the linesman and the line judge cleans up behind the play. On a return to the middle of the field, the line judge has responsibility for the runner until he gives up the runner to the umpire; the point at which the transfer occurs depends on how far downfield the umpire has drifted after the kick. The referee may take over coverage of the runner if the runner breaks off a long return.

When kicks go out of bounds to the line judge's side, the line judge should kill the clock at once. The line judge alone determines the spot of any kick to his side that travels out of bounds 25 or more yards beyond the line. On shorter kicks, the line judge walks toward the referee with his hand up — along the sideline — until the referee chops downward, telling him to halt.

All officials: The covering official, regardless of position, must beanbag the spot where the kick ends. That spot may be used for post-scrimmage kick penalty enforcement.

Case Study 31: Federation Long Kick Out of Bounds to Linesman's Side

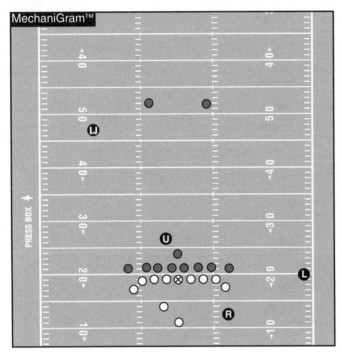

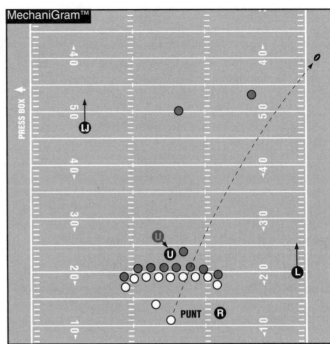

Action on the field: Starting position.

Referee: Three to four yards in front of and five to yards outside the punter, on the punter's kicking-leg side.

Umpire: Four to seven yards deep and favoring the line judge's sideline.

Linesman: Straddling the line of scrimmage and more than nine yards outside the widest offensive player.

Line judge: Seven to 10 yards wider than and in front of the deepest receiver.

Action on the field: Punt to linesman's side.

Referee: Observes snap and action around kicker.

Umpire: Moves toward the line at the snap, observing initial charge of linemen and contact on the snapper.

Linesman: Observes initial line charge and remains on the line to rule whether or not the kick crossed the neutral zone. Moves downfield when kick crosses the neutral zone.

Line judge: Observes receivers. Moves downfield when ball flies deeper than receivers.

KEY

Referee Umpire Line Judge Linesman Back Judge Chain Gang Ballboy Coach Offense Defense Football Possession of football

268 *Football Officials Guidebook*

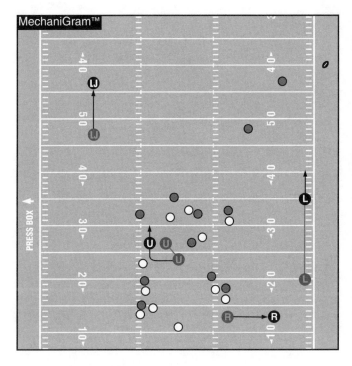

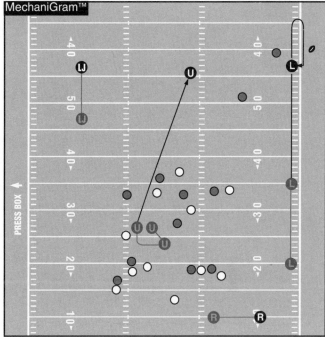

Action on the field: Ball becomes dead out of bounds.

Referee: Moves quickly toward sideline to observe flight of ball.

Umpire: Pivots toward the line judge's side of the field, Moves downfield with flow of players and observes players as they move downfield.

Linesman: Moves quickly down sideline, observing action of players moving downfield. Stops clock when he sees ball go out of bounds.

Line judge: Observes action of players in front of ball.

Action on the field: Ball spotted for next down.

Referee: With arm above head, observes linesman walking toward spot. When linesman reaches spot, drops arm with chopping motion. When certain there are no penalty markers down, signals linesman to move chain crew.

Umpire: Continues to move downfield and observes action of players in his area. Moves to hashmark to set ball for new series.

Linesman: Moves five to seven yards beyond spot where ball apparently went out of bounds, pivots and makes eye contact with referee. Walks slowly toward referee, stopping when referee drops arm with chopping motion. Signals first down for team R. Upon signal from referee, instructs chain crew to move to spot.

Line judge: Observes action of players in front of ball. Squares off and mirrors linesman's spot.

Movement → Previous position ⓤ→ Current position ⓤ (stopped) Previous position ⓤ→ Current position ⓤ (still moving)

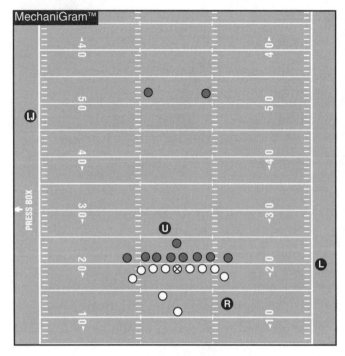

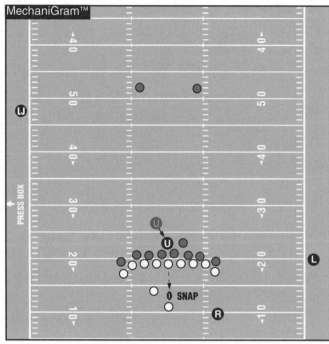

Action on the field: Starting position.

Referee: In front of the kicker, wider than where the tight end would normally be positioned, and on the kicking-leg side. Able to see all the backs and far enough away from the kicker to observe the blockers and kicker at the same time.

Umpire: Four to seven yards deep and favoring the line judge's sideline.

Linesman: Straddling the line of scrimmage, at least seven yards outside the widest offensive player and never inside the top of the numbers. When the snap is from the hashmark, position on the sideline is required.

Line judge: Outside and in front of the deep receivers.

Action on the field: Starting position.

Referee: Observes snap and action around kicker.

Umpire: Moves toward the line at the snap, observing initial charge of linemen and contact on the snapper.

Linesman: Observes initial line charge.

Line judge: Observes receivers.

KEY

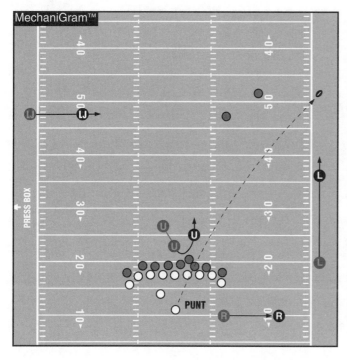

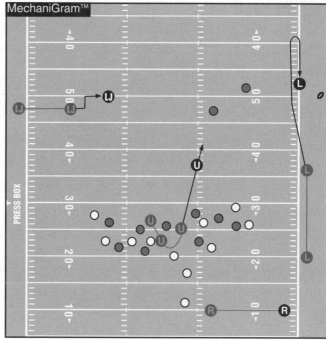

Action on the field: Ball becomes dead out of bounds.

Referee: Moves quickly toward sideline to observe flight of ball.

Umpire: Pivots toward the linesman's side of the field, observing players as they move downfield.

Linesman: Moves downfield after kick has broken the plane of the scrimmage line. Moves quickly down sideline, stopping clock when he sees ball go out of bounds.

Line judge: Moves toward middle of field and observes action of players in front of ball.

Action on the field: Ball spotted for next down.

Referee: With arm above head, observes linesman walking toward spot. When linesman reaches spot, drops arm with chopping motion. When certain there are no penalty markers down, signals linesman to move chain crew.

Umpire: Moves downfield with flow of players and observes action of players in his area. Moves to spot to set ball for new series.

Linesman: Moves five to seven yards beyond spot where ball apparently went out of bounds, pivots and makes eye contact with referee. Walks slowly toward referee, stopping when referee drops arm with chopping motion. Signals first down for team R. Upon signal from referee, instructs chain crew to move to spot.

Line judge: Squares off and mirrors linesman's spot. Continues to practice dead-ball officiating and observes action of players in his area.

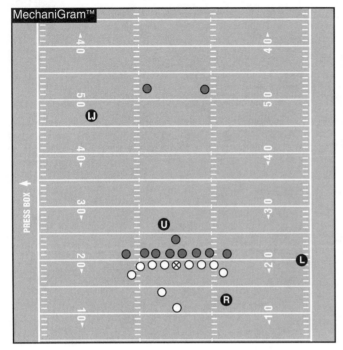

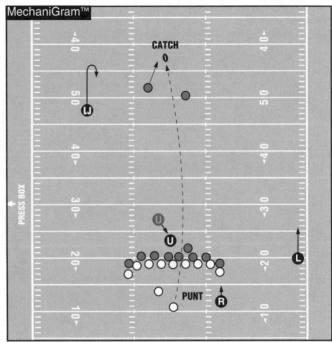

Action on the field: Starting position.

Referee: Three to four yards in front of and five to yards outside the punter, on the punter's kicking-leg side.

Umpire: Four to seven yards deep and favoring the line judge's sideline.

Linesman: Straddling the line of scrimmage and more than nine yards outside the widest offensive player.

Line judge: Seven to 10 yards wider than and in front of the deepest receiver.

Action on the field: Receiver catches kick in line judge's area.

Referee: Observes snap and action around kicker. Moves slowly downfield with flow of players.

Umpire: Moves toward the line at the snap, observing initial charge of linemen and contact on the snapper.

Linesman: Observes initial line charge and remains on the line to rule whether or not the kick crossed the neutral zone. When ball crosses neutral zone, moves downfield and observes players in his area.

Line judge: Retreats to observe catch. Moves upfield slight ahead of runner, observing runner and action in front of runner.

KEY

Referee Umpire Line Judge Linesman Back Judge Chain Gang Ballboy Coach Offense Defense Football Possession of football

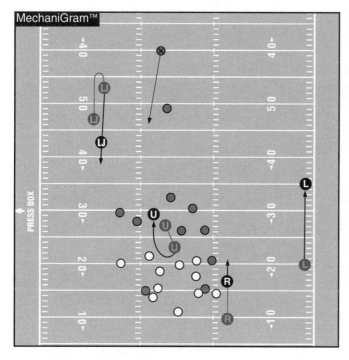

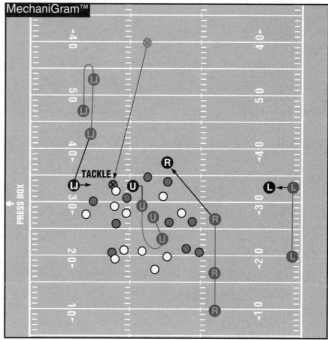

Action on the field: Runner advances.

Referee: Moves slowly downfield and observes action of players in his area.

Umpire: Pivots toward line judge's side. Moves with flow of players downfield and observes action of players in his area.

Linesman: Moves down sideline and observes action of players in front of ball.

Line judge: Moves to stay ahead of and observe runner as runner moves upfield. Observes action in front of runner.

Action on the field: Runner continues advance and is downed.

Referee: Moves slowly downfield and observes action of players in his area. Hustles toward dead-ball spot. If no penalty markers are down, signals linesman to have chain crew move the chains.

Umpire: Continues to move downfield and observes players in his area. Hustles to hashmark to set ball for next down.

Linesman: Observes action of players in front of ball. Squares off to mirror spot of forward progress. When runner is downed, practices dead-ball officiating. Upon signal from referee, instructs chain crew to move to spot. Assists chain crew in setting chains for new series.

Line judge: Blows whistle and gives stop-the-clock signal when runner is downed. Squares off to indicate spot of forward progress and practices dead-ball officiating. Holds spot until released by umpire.

Movement — Previous position / Current position (stopped) — Previous position / Current position (still moving)

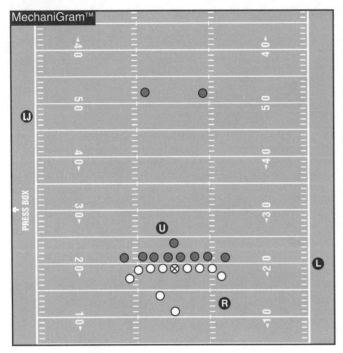

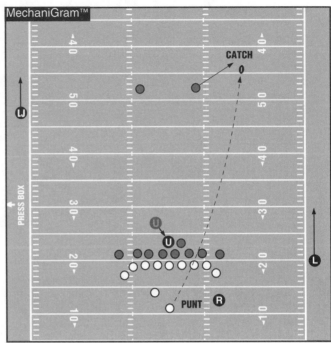

Action on the field: Starting position.

Referee: In front of the kicker, wider than where the tight end would normally be positioned, and on the kicking-leg side. Able to see all the backs and far enough away from the kicker to observe the blockers and kicker at the same time.

Umpire: Four to seven yards deep and favoring the line judge's sideline.

Linesman: Straddling the line of scrimmage, at least seven yards outside the widest offensive player and never inside the top of the numbers. When the snap is from the hashmark, position on the sideline is required.

Line judge: Outside and in front of the deep receivers.

Action on the field: Ball kicked to linesman's side zone.

Referee: Observes snap and action around kicker.

Umpire: Moves toward the line at the snap, observing initial charge of linemen and contact on the snapper.

Linesman: Observes initial line charge. Moves downfield after kick has crossed neutral zone.

Line judge: Retreats when kick flies beyond receivers. Observes receivers.

KEY

Referee Umpire Line Judge Linesman Back Judge Chain Gang Ballboy Coach Offense Defense Football Possession of football

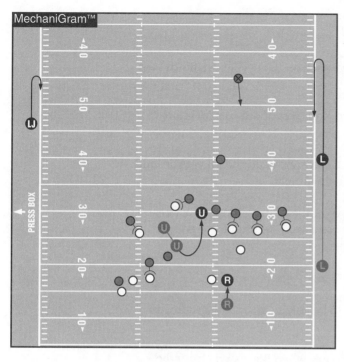

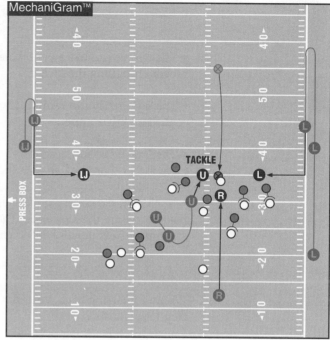

Action on the field: Receiver catches kick and begins advance.

Referee: Moves slowly downfield and observes action of players in his area.

Umpire: Pivots toward linesman's side. Moves with flow of players downfield and observes action of players in his area.

Linesman: Moves to stay ahead of and observe runner as runner moves upfield. Observes action in front of runner.

Line judge: Moves down sideline and observes action of players in front of ball.

Action on the field: Receiver continues advance and is downed.

Referee: Moves slowly downfield and observes players in his area. When certain there are no penalty markers down, signals linesman to move chain crew.

Umpire: Moves slowly downfield and observes players in his area. Once spot is established, hustles to hashmark to set ball for next down.

Linesman: Blows whistle and gives stop-the-clock signal when runner is downed. Squares off to mark spot of forward progress. Practices dead-ball officiating. Holds spot until umpire arrives to set ball for new series. Upon signal from referee, instructs chain crew to move to spot.

Line judge: Continues to move upfield and observes players in his area. Squares off to mark spot of forward progress.

Movement ———→   Previous position ⟶ Current position (stopped)   Previous position ⟶ Current position (still moving)

• The referee can use a verbal alert such as "Gone!" as an aid to help prevent roughing the kicker.

• The umpire should remind team R players about rules relating to contact on the snapper.

• The line judge should observe the receivers and the players around them rather than the ball as it flies downfield.

• In NCAA, the covering official, regardless of position, must beanbag the spot where the kick ends. That spot may be used for post-scrimmage kick penalty enforcement.

Quiz

Without referring back, you should be able to answer the following true-false questions.

1. Working on the sideline is necessary when the snap is from the hashmark on the linesman's side of the field.

2. If the kicking team is first to touch the kick, a beanbag should be dropped at the spot of the touching.

3. In both Federation and NCAA, the line judge alone determines the spot of any kick to his side that travels out of bounds 25 or more yards beyond the line.

4. The line judge should be prepared to get to team R's goalline to rule on momentum exception or touchback situations.

5. It is a good idea not to have the whistle in the mouth to prevent an inadvertent whistle in case a fair catch is muffed.

1. True 2. False 3. False 4. True 5. True

Chapter 28

Scoring Kicks

Positions, duties, and behaviors of officials on attempts to score from placement are difficult to reconcile because customary practices across the nation (and the reasoning behind the practices) vary considerably.

For example, in some places the referee says to the line judge, "You take your post and I'll take mine," which neither the Federation manual nor the CCA manual recommends. In effect, that is a private mechanic. It is basically pointless because it gives two people responsibility for calling the kick, both of whom are widely separated from one another, plus it places 22 players entirely under the jurisdiction of the remaining two officials. Moreover, those remaining two officials are somewhat encumbered because the linesman must judge roughing the kicker and the umpire must judge roughing the snapper, virtually reducing their focus to a pair of players only during the live ball.

Referee recommends one major compromise to a difference in the Federation and CCA manuals: By having the referee rule on all kicks (not just those when the ball is snapped at or inside team R's 15 yardline), no official is placed in an untenable position in terms of coverage. The line judge isn't dashing from the line of scrimmage to the end line when the kick crosses the bar, nor is placed on the endline but expected to cover a sideline in the event of a fake kick (or muffed snap) and run. For most officials those actions are impossible to accomplish, and the reason is that players will initiate their "emergency" or contingency plan before officials (who are screened from view) can react.

By keeping the line judge on the line of scrimmage, the field is covered in a somewhat balanced manner and any broken play can be covered adequately. That balanced coverage is crucial because a score or no-score must be determined with accuracy and such a score may well decide the outcome of a game.

Try that procedure if your association or assigning agency allows experimentation. If not, here are the positioning and mechanics prescribed by the Federation and CCA manuals.

General procedures if the ball is snapped at or inside team R's 15 yardline

The referee faces the holder from a position about one yard behind and two to three yards to the side of the kicker (NCAA: About two yards behind and one yard to the side of the kicker). The referee is responsible for ruling whether the kick is good or no good.

The umpire's position is five to seven yards off the line, favoring the line judge's side of the field.

The linesman straddles the line of scrimmage not closer than nine yards (NCAA: at least seven yards)

outside the widest offensive player and rules on roughing the holder and kicker.

In Federation, the line judge is on the line of scrimmage and five to seven yards outside the offensive end and moves quickly toward the end line after the snap to rule on whether or not the kick passed over the crossbar. In NCAA the line judge is on the endline and under the upright on his side of the field.

If the kick fails because it goes under the crossbar or strikes an upright, the line judge signals the kick no good, then follows with the touchback signal. If the kick clears the crossbar, the line judge blows his whistle and gives a predetermined signal to the referee (a thumb's up is a common signal), but the referee rules on whether the ball went through the uprights. If the kick is good, only the referee signals.

In Federation, if a kick try is blocked or obviously will not score, the referee should blow his whistle to kill the ball and give the appropriate signal (the same mechanic is used if a missed or blocked field goal breaks the plane of the goalline). If a field goal is blocked and does not break the plane of the goalline, the ball remains live and no signal is given.

In NCAA, whether a try or a field goal is blocked or is short and does not break the plane of the goalline, the ball remains live and no signal is given.

General procedures if the ball is snapped outside team R's 15 yardline

The referee faces the holder from a position about one yard behind and two to three yards to the side of the kicker. The referee rules on roughing the holder and kicker and echoes the good or no good signal to the pressbox.

The umpire's position is five to seven yards (NCAA: no more than seven yards) off the line, favoring the line judge's side of the field.

The linesman straddles the line of scrimmage not closer than nine yards (NCAA: at least seven yards) outside the widest offensive player.

The line judge moves five yards behind and directly between the uprights and is the sole judge whether the kick is good or no good.

In Federation, if the kick is no good and breaks the plane of the goalline, the line judge signals the kick no good, followed by the touchback signal. In NCAA, whether a try or a field goal is blocked or is short and does not break the plane of the goalline, the ball remains live and no signal is given.

General procedures regardless of the distance of the kick

If the holder has to leave a kneeling position to catch or recover a poor snap, the referee must rule on the holder's ability to return to a kneeling position. A verbal alert such as "Gone!" is an aid to help prevent roughing the kicker and holder. The referee also must be prepared for a fake kick or a poor snap leading to a broken play.

The umpire is responsible for checking the numbers of the players on the offensive line (team K may use the numbering exception, but the umpire needs to know if a player wearing an eligible receiver's number is in an ineligible position in case a fake kick results in a pass).

Team R players should be reminded about rules relating to contact on the snapper. The umpire can see players shooting gaps or lineman chopping rushers at the knees (the ball will be snapped out of the free-blocking/free-clipping zone) as well as contact on the snapper. Moving toward the line at the snap will improve the view of the initial line charge. If contact on the snapper is legal, the umpire can shift his eyes to watch blocking by the guard and tackle. It is impossible for him to watch the whole line; he must select a pair of players.

If a blocked kick or fake results in a play toward the goalline on the line judge's side of the field, the umpire moves toward the goalline to assist on coverage of the runner. On a blocked field goal attempt, the linesman (with possible help from the umpire) will rule whether or not the kick crossed the neutral zone. That determination is the key element in determining if team K can recover or advance a scrimmage kick.

If a pass is used on the fake, the linesman must know if the passer was beyond the line. Before the snap, he should make a mental note of team K's alignment, noticing whether or not his end has an eligible number, for example, so he can help rule on ineligibles downfield on fake kicks that lead to passes. When the line judge has vacated his position, the linesman has sole responsibility for offside (NCAA only) and encroachment. At the snap he will have only a split-second to watch the clash of the lines. Therefore, he isn't likely to see much of importance unless it's a sudden blatant act, such as a defender leaping on his own teammate or on an opponent to block the kick. When a runner approaches the goalline, the linesman must be at the goalline to rule on the potential score.

If the kick is blocked, is obviously short or the play turns out not to be a kick (fake or busted play), the line judge should officiate back toward the ball. He is responsible for his sideline and may have to rule on a run near the goalline. If a kick does not take place, the best a line judge can do from a place behind the posts in most instances is make it to the corner of the endline and sideline.

The vast majority of scoring kick attempts will be simply that: a kick designed to score. In those instances, the linesman can move toward the offensive and defensive linemen after the kick and use his voice to encourage players to unpile.

In NCAA, the linesman must remind the box holder that the box should not be moved after a missed field goal; when the snap is outside team R's 20 yardline, the ball is returned to the previous spot.

If the kick narrowly passes outside an upright, the CCA authorizes the line judge to indicate that by sweeping his arms to the side. *Referee* recommendation: Use the signal if your association or assigning agency allows.

A word about stances of the offense: Sometimes players come in late, may take up uncertain positions and may be unsure whether to adopt a two-, three-, or four-point stance. The referee also should be certain who's in the backfield and who is on the line. The referee must judge any irregularities in stances (illegal movement or movement at the snap) and positioning. Sometimes a team that is short a player will have a back who has the presence of mind to move forward to create a seven-man line. Also, some up backs may have ineligible numbers. The referee should see those things.

CHALK TALK: FEDERATION SCORING KICK POSITIONING AND COVERAGE ZONES

Referee: If the ball is snapped at or inside team R's 15 yardline, the referee faces the holder from a position about one yard behind and two to three yards to the side of the kicker and is responsible for ruling whether the kick is good or no good. If the ball is snapped outside team R's 15 yardline, the referee faces the holder from a position about one yard behind and two to three yards to the side of the kicker, rules on roughing the holder and kicker and echoes the good or no good signal to the pressbox.

Regardless of the distance of the kick, if the holder has to leave a kneeling position to catch or recover a poor snap, the referee must rule on the holder's ability to return to a kneeling position. The referee also should be certain who's in the backfield and who is on the line. The referee must judge any irregularities in stances (illegal movement or movement at the snap) and positioning.

Umpire: Starting position is five to seven yards off line, favoring the line judge's side of the field. The umpire is responsible for checking the numbers of the players on the offensive line and should remind team R players about rules relating to contact on the snapper. Moving toward the line at the snap will improve the view of the initial line charge.

If a blocked kick or fake results in a play toward the goalline on the line judge's side of the field, the umpire moves toward the goalline to assist on coverage of the runner. On a blocked field goal attempt, the umpire will help rule whether or not the kick crossed the neutral zone.

Linesman: Starting position is straddling the line of scrimmage not closer than nine yards outside the widest offensive player. The linesman rules on roughing the holder and kicker if the ball is snapped on or inside team R's 15 yardline.

On a blocked field goal attempt, the linesman will rule whether or not the kick crossed the neutral zone.

If a pass is used on the fake, the linesman must know if the passer was beyond the line. Before the snap, he should make a mental note of team K's alignment, noticing whether or not his end has an eligible number, for example, so he can help rule on ineligibles downfield on fake kicks that lead to passes. When the line judge has vacated his position, the linesman has sole responsibility for encroachment.

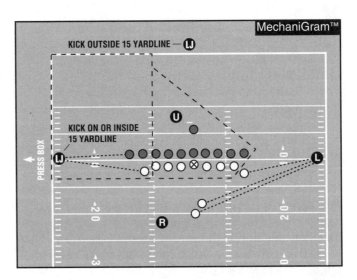

When a runner approaches the goalline, the linesman must be at the goalline to rule on the potential score.

After a kick, the linesman can move toward the offensive and defensive linemen after the kick and use his voice to encourage players to unpile.

Line judge: If the ball is snapped inside team R's 15 yardline, the linesman's starting position is straddling the line, at least five to seven yards outside the widest end. If the ball is snapped on or outside team R's 15 yardline, the line judge moves beyond the endline and between the uprights.

If the kick is blocked, is obviously short or the play turns out not to be a fake or a busted play, the line judge should officiate back toward the ball. He is responsible for his sideline and may have to rule on a run near the goalline.

Referee recommendation: If the kick narrowly misses wide, the linesman should signal why the kick failed by giving the appropriate supplementary signal (both arms swept away from the goalposts).

CHALK TALK: NCAA SCORING KICK POSITIONING AND COVERAGE ZONES

Referee: If the ball is snapped inside team R's 15 yardline, the referee's starting position is two yards behind and one yard to side of kicker, facing the holder. If the kick clears the crossbar, the line judge blows his whistle and gives a predetermined signal to the referee (a thumb's up is a common signal), but the referee rules on whether the ball went through the uprights. If the kick is good, only the referee signals.

If the ball is snapped on or outside team R's 15 yardline, the referee's starting position is one yard behind and two to three yards to the side of the kicker. The referee rules on roughing the holder and kicker and echoes the good or no good signal to the pressbox.

Regardless of the distance of the kick, the referee also should be certain who's in the backfield and who is on the line. The referee must judge any irregularities in stances (illegal movement or movement at the snap) and positioning.

Umpire: Starting position is no more than seven yards off the line, favoring the line judge's side of the field.

The umpire is responsible for checking the numbers of the players on the offensive line and should remind team R players about rules relating to contact on the snapper. Moving toward the line at the snap will improve the view of the initial line charge.

If a blocked kick or fake results in a play toward the goalline on the line judge's side of the field, the umpire moves toward the goalline to assist on coverage of the runner. On a blocked field goal attempt, the umpire will help rule whether or not the kick crossed the neutral zone..

Linesman: Starting position is straddling the line of scrimmage at least seven yards outside the widest offensive player. The linesman must remind the box holder that the box should not be moved after a missed field goal; when the snap is outside team R's 20 yardline, the ball is returned to the previous spot.

On a blocked field goal attempt, the linesman will rule whether or not the kick crossed the neutral zone.

If a pass is used on the fake, the linesman must know if the passer was beyond the line. When the line judge has vacated his position, the linesman has sole responsibility for offside and encroachment.

When a runner approaches the goalline, the linesman must be at the goalline to rule on the potential score. The linesman can move toward the offensive and

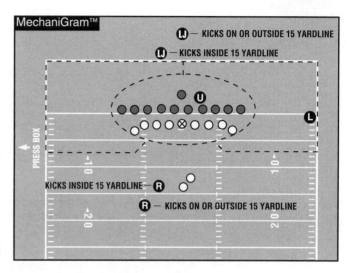

defensive linemen after the kick and use his voice to encourage players to unpile.

Line judge: If the ball is snapped on or outside team R's 15 yardline, the line judge's starting position is on the endline alongside the upright on his side of the field.

If the ball is snapped inside team R's 15 yardline and the kick clears the crossbar, the line judge blows his whistle and gives a predetermined signal to the referee (a thumb's up is a common signal), but the referee rules on whether the ball went through the uprights. If the kick is good, only the referee signals. If the kick fails because it goes under the crossbar or strikes an upright, the line judge signals the kick no good, then follows with the touchback signal.

If the ball is snapped on or outside team R's 15 yardline, the line judge alone rules on the kick.

If the kick narrowly passes outside an upright, the line judge indicates that by sweeping his arms to the side.

• When the snap is at or inside team R's 15 yardline, only the referee signals the result of the kick; when the snap is outside team R's 15 yardline, the line judge signals and the referee echoes the signal to the pressbox.

• The umpire should remind team R players about rules relating to contact on the snapper.

• If a blocked kick or fake results in a play toward the goalline on the line judge's side of the field, the umpire moves toward the goalline to assist on coverage of the runner.

• When the line judge has vacated his position, the linesman has sole responsibility for offside (NCAA only) and encroachment.

Quiz

Without referring back, you should be able to answer the following true-false questions.

1. In NCAA, the linesman must remind the box holder that the box should not be moved after a missed field goal.

2. If the ball is snapped at or inside team R's 15 yardline, the referee rules on roughing the holder and kicker

3. In Federation, whether a try or a field goal is blocked or is short and does not break the plane of the goalline, the ball remains live and no signal is given.

4. The referee faces the holder from a position about one yard behind and two to three yards to the side of the kicker.

5. On a blocked field goal attempt, the umpire alone will rule whether or not the kick crossed the neutral zone.

1. True 2. False 3. False 4. True 5. False

Chapter 29

Timeouts

Either team may request a timeout at any time when the ball is dead. The request must come from a player. The recognizing official should grant the timeout and immediately stop the clock if it is running. That official reports the timeout to the referee. The referee indicates the timeout using a two- or three-step procedure:

• Give the stop-the-clock signal regardless of whether the clocking is running. Two strokes of the arms are sufficient.

• Indicate the team being charged the timeout by facing the team and extending both arms shoulder high, giving three chucks in that team's direction.

• If it is the final charged timeout, follow with three tugs on an imaginary steam whistle (CCA only, but recommended for Federation).

In the rare event that both teams request a timeout during the same dead-ball period, the first team requesting the timeout is charged. The other team must then be informed of the other team's timeout and asked if they would like a successive timeout.

All officials must record the number and team of the player requesting the timeout, the quarter and the time remaining on the game clock. Each official then confirms with the referee the number of timeouts each team has remaining. The linesman and line judge inform the coaches on their respective sidelines of the timeouts remaining. The referee informs the head coach when all timeouts have been exhausted. *Referee recommendation:* Inform the coach how many timeouts each team has remaining after each timeout.

The referee is responsible for timing the timeout. The one-minute count begins when the referee is informed of the timeout. When 45 seconds have expired, the referee informs the linesman and line judge so they can inform their teams. When the minute has expired, the referee whistles the ball ready for play.

Although the line judge and linesman need to be firm when informing the teams the timeout has ended, there is no need to be gruff. Commands such as, "Coaches out," "Players back on the field," or "Timeout's over," can be replaced with statements such as, "We're ready for you, fellas," or "Time to play ball, guys."

During the timeout, the umpire stands over the ball. The referee stands away from the other officials. The linesman and line judge should stay near their respective teams to observe any attempts to use substitutes for deception.

Coach-referee conference

If a coach-referee conference is requested, it is held on the field approximately five yards in front of the team area. Only the head coach and the referee participate. The other officials should keep assistant coaches away from the area of the discussion. The referee may be assisted by another official if that official was involved in the decision being questioned.

Injury timeout

The procedure for signaling the timeout is the same as for a charged timeout except that after stopping the clock, the referee taps his chest to indicate it is an official's timeout. Play should resume as quickly as possible.

All officials should be alert to ensure neither team does any onfield coaching during the timeout. In Federation, the referee must determine whether an injured player was unconscious.

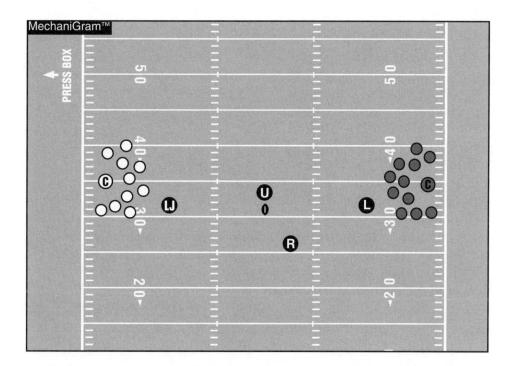

CHALK TALK: FEDERATION OR NCAA TIMEOUT WITH TEAMS AT SIDELINES

Referee: Gives stop the clock signal and indicates team calling timeout by chucking arms three times toward the team's goalline. Records the number and team of the player requesting the timeout, the quarter and the time remaining on the game clock. Confirms with the crew the number of timeouts each team has remaining. Stands away from other officials. Times timeout. When 45 seconds have expired, points to linesman and line judge. When 60 seconds have expired, blows whistle and signals ready for play.

Umpire: Records the number and team of the player requesting the timeout, the quarter and the time remaining on the game clock. Confirms with the referee the number of timeouts each team has remaining. Stands over the ball until referee signals ready for play.

Linesman: Records the number and team of the player requesting the timeout, the quarter and the time remaining on the game clock. Confirms with the referee the number of timeouts each team has remaining and relays information to coach or captain. Stands midway between the ball and the team's huddle. On referee's signal, informs team timeout is over.

Line judge: Records the number and team of the player requesting the timeout, the quarter and the time remaining on the game clock. Confirms with the referee the number of timeouts each team has remaining and relays information to coach or captain. Stands midway between the ball and the team's huddle. On referee's signal, informs team timeout is over.

Note: Federation rules allow coaches to conduct timeouts on the field or on the sideline.

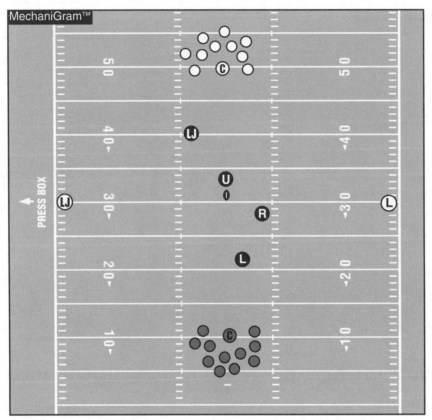

(LJ) (L) = *Referee* recommendation

FEDERATION TIMEOUT WITH COACHES ON FIELD

Referee: Gives stop the clock signal and indicates team calling timeout by chucking arms three times toward the team's goalline. Records the number and team of the player requesting the timeout, the quarter and the time remaining on the game clock. Confirms with the crew the number of timeouts each team has remaining. Stands away from other officials. Times timeout. When 45 seconds have expired, points to linesman and line judge. When 60 seconds have expired, blows whistle and signals ready for play.

Umpire: Echoes timeout signals. Records the number and team of the player requesting the timeout, the quarter and the time remaining on the game clock. Confirms with the referee the number of timeouts each team has remaining. Stands over the ball until referee signals ready for play.

Linesman: Echoes timeout signals. Records the number and team of the player requesting the timeout, the quarter and the time remaining on the game clock.

Confirms with the referee the number of timeouts each team has remaining and relays information to coach or captain. Stands midway between ball and visiting team's huddle. On referee's signal, informs team timeout is over. *Referee* recommendation: Since the referee and umpire are already in the middle of the field, the linesman can remain on his sideline.

Line judge: Echoes timeout signals. Records the number and team of the player requesting the timeout, the quarter and the time remaining on the game clock. Confirms with the referee the number of timeouts each team has remaining and relays information to coach or captain. Stands midway between ball and visiting team's huddle. On referee's signal, informs team timeout is over. *Referee* recommendation: Since the referee and umpire are already in the middle of the field, the line judge can remain on his sideline.

Notes: If one team huddles on the field and the other at the sideline, the respective wing officials should follow the applicable procedure for the team on their sideline. NCAA rules prohibit coaches from conducting timeouts on the field.

• The officials observing the teams should ensure neither team uses deceptive substitution practices during timeouts.

• The umpire should remain over the ball until the referee gives the ready signal.

• In CCA mechanics, the referee gives three tugs on an imaginary steam whistle to indicate a team has used its last timeout. *Referee* recommends the same signal be used in Federation.

• If the timeout is for an injury, the referee should follow the stop-the-clock signal by tapping his chest.

Quiz

Without referring back, you should be able to answer the following true-false questions.

1. A charged timeout lasts 60 seconds.

2. After 30 seconds, the referee should instruct the wing officials to tell the teams the timeout is over.

3. When a timeout is called, it is only necessary to give the stop-the-clock signal if the clock is running.

4. Only the referee must record the number and team of the player requesting the timeout, the quarter and the time remaining on the game clock.

5. In Federation, the referee must determine whether an injured player was unconscious.

1. True 2. False 3. False 4. False 5. True

Notes

Chapter 30

Measurements

A typical game requires two to three measurements for a first down. On a poorly marked field, you'll have to measure more often. If the line-to-gain stake is right on a five or 10 yardline (e.g. 10 yardline, 25 yardline, et al), it's easier to discern whether the first down has been made and the measurement can possibly be averted. A captain's request for a measurement should be honored unless it is made after the ball is moved from the dead-ball spot or is made after the ready-for-play signal. The defensive captain should be told when a first down is made so he has the opportunity to ask for a measurement.

When the referee signals for a measurement, the line judge should place a beanbag at the intersection of the five yardline where the chain is clipped and a line through the ball parallel to the sideline (some crews have the line judge mark the spot with his foot). That is the spot where the linesman will place the clipped part of the chain; the beanbag enables the linesman to go directly to the spot without fumbling around.

The linesman brings the chain in from the sideline with the chain crew members. Putting one hand on the links on each side of the clip improves the linesman's chances of keeping track of the proper link in case the clip falls off the chain. As the linesman approaches the line judge, the linesman tells his crewmate which part of the line (back, middle or front) the chain crew used to place the clip. The clip must be placed on that part of the line for the measurement. A good double-check is for the linesman to state that the next down will be first if the ball is beyond the stake or the next down of the series if it is short. (Example: "It will either be first or fourth.") The down marker is moved by the chain crew member to the forward point of the ball.

Once the linesman tells the referee he has the chain on the proper mark, the umpire takes the forward stake from the chain crew member, then pulls the stake to ensure the chain is taut. The referee rules whether or not the ball is beyond the front stake.

Short of a first down

If the measurement is in a side zone and does not result in a first down, the umpire should keep control of the stake. The referee uses his hands (or fingers if the ball is inches short of the front stake) to inform both benches how short the play ended of a first down.

After signaling, the referee grasps the chain at the link in front of the ball and rises. The referee should grasp the chain with two hands with the link that will be used to place the ball between his hands; that will ensure the proper link is maintained. Referee, umpire and linesman walk to the nearest hashmark. The line judge is free to either obtain a new ball from a ballboy or retrieve the original ball. *Referee* recommendation: In this instance, the line judge should stay with the ball on the ground in the side zone and the ballboy instructed to come onto the field and give the ball to the referee. That ensures the spot will not be lost.

When a first down is not made, the linesman must again hold the chain on either side of the clip while he accompanies the chain crew and the chains are moved back to the sideline. Otherwise, the clip could break or simply come off.

The referee must wait for the linesman's signal that the chain crew is back in position before giving the ready-for-play signal.

If the measurement occurred on fourth down and team A is short, the referee signals the change of possession by giving the first down signal toward team A's goalline. The referee then sets the ball in the same position as it was when it became dead so its foremost point becomes the rear point when the direction is changed. The new rear stake is then moved to the new foremost point of the ball.

First down made

If the measurement results in the award of a new series, the referee signals the first down. The linesman need not hold the chain as he accompanies the chain crew back to the sideline, but he must go all the way to the sideline and indicate to the chain crew where the new series will begin.

Referee recommendation: In this instance, the line judge should stay with the ball on the ground in the side zone and the ballboy instructed to come onto the field and give the ball to the referee. That ensures the spot will not be lost.

Since the down has been completed, moving the down marker forward is routine and having it on the forward point of the ball is necessary in the event the ball is inadvertently moved. The exception is if the measurement is a prelude to a penalty acceptance decision. An example: With about five yards to go, team K punts on fourth down and is happy with the results. Team R is flagged for a five-yard live-ball foul. Team K requests a measurement. They will accept the penalty if it yields a first down and decline it otherwise. In that case the down marker must remain at the previous spot.

End of quarter

At the end of the first and third quarters, the referee, umpire and linesman record the following data: the team in possession, the yardline the ball is on, the down, the yards necessary for a first down and the yardline where the chain is clipped.

The linesman should carry a snap clip (in addition to the yardage clip) to place on the chain where the box is. (That can only be done when there are less than 10 yards to go. When there is more than 10 yards to go, the umpire must step off the distance.) The snap clip should be placed on the chain to indicate where the box was located. The box can then be easily placed at the proper spot when the chains are reset. Once the snap clip is in place, the referee signals the linesman to move the chains.

The linesman has the chain crew change direction and trots with them to the opposite end of the field. The linesman must hold the yardage clip at all times and the box holder must hold the secondary clip. Do not allow either the yardage clip or secondary clip to drag on the ground; they could easily become dislodged.

The referee and umpire trot to the appropriate yardline on the opposite end of the field. The umpire faces the chain crew, setting the ball on the ground only after the box is in place. By waiting for the box to be placed first, the crew can avoid the possibility of having to move the ball once it is placed. The line judge should note the yardline the yardage clip was on. He can then trot ahead to the same yardline on the other end of the field to ensure the yardage clip is placed on the proper yardline.

When the first or third quarter ends on a play resulting in a first down, set the chains and the clip before you switch sides of the field. Yes, it is seemingly unnecessary and takes a few minutes longer, but if you don't, you lose the double-check on where the umpire places the ball.

Finally, if the period ends with less than a yard to go, the chains should be brought out to the ball to get the exact location of the ball. The crew then proceeds as for a measurement.

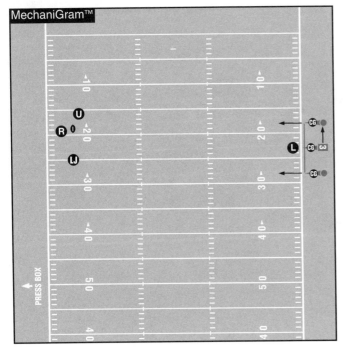

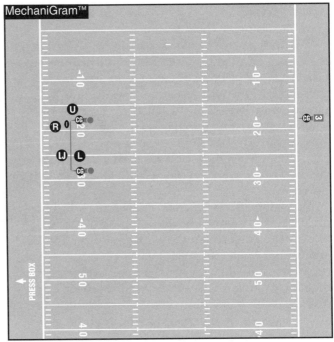

Action on the field: Play ends in side zone close to a first down.

Referee: Stops clock after seeing that measurement is necessary. Waits at spot for arrival of chain gang.

Umpire: Waits at spot for arrival of chain gang.

Linesman: Has box holder move box behind lead stake. Brings chain in from sideline with chain gang members to spot indicated by line judge.

Line judge: Indicates intersection of the five yardline where chain is clipped and line through ball parallel to sideline with beanbag or foot.

Action on the field: Team A is short of a first down.

Referee: Rules whether or not ball is beyond front stake. Uses hands or fingers to inform both benches how short the play ended of first down.

Umpire: Holds lead stake.

Linesman: Holds clip in place.

Line judge: Gets spare ball from ballboy.

KEY

 Referee   Umpire   Line Judge   Linesman   Back Judge   Chain Gang   Ballboy   Coach Offense Defense Football Possession of football

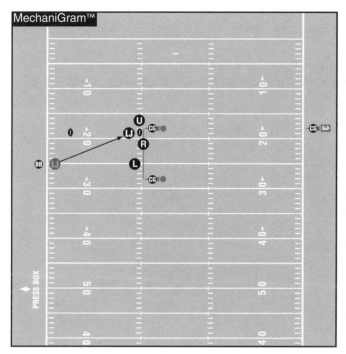

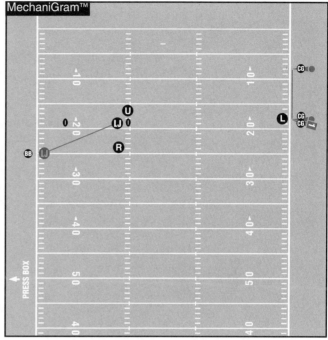

Action on the field: Chains are moved to hashmark for ball placement.

Referee: Grasps chain and rises. Walks to nearest hashmark. Sets chain on ground, maintaining link where ball will be placed. Gets ball from line judge and places it. Waits for linesman's signal that chain gang is back in position and other officials are ready before giving ready-for-play signal.

Umpire: Maintains control of front stake and walks to nearest hashmark.

Linesman: Maintains control of clip and walks to nearest hashmark. Accompanies chain gang back to sideline and sets chains for next down. Signals to referee when chain gang is back in position.

Line judge: Delivers ball to referee for placement.

Action on the field: Team A is awarded a new series.

Referee: Signals first down. Waits for linesman's signal that chain gang is back in position and other officials are ready before giving ready-for-play signal.

Umpire: Moves to hashmark where ball will next be snapped. Gets ball from line judge and places it.

Linesman: Returns to sideline with chain gang and indicates where new series will begin. Signals to referee when chain gang is back in position.

Line judge: Delivers ball to umpire for placement.

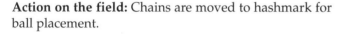

Movement   Previous position   Current position (stopped)   Previous position   Current position (still moving)

• Grasping the links on each side of the clip instead of the clip itself allows the linesman to keep track of the proper link in case the clip falls off the chain.

• The linesman should verbalize that the next down will be first if the ball is beyond the stake or the next down of the series if it is short. (Example: "It will either be first or fourth.")

• The referee must wait for the linesman's signal that the chain crew is back in position before giving the ready-for-play signal.

• When changing ends after the first or third quarters, the umpire faces the chain crew, setting the ball on the ground only after the box is in place.

Quiz

Without referring back, you should be able to answer the following true-false questions.

1. If the measurement occurred on fourth down and team A is short, the referee signals the change of possession by giving the first down signal toward team A's goalline.

2. The line judge holds the ball in place during the measurement.

3. The referee should signal to both benches when indicating the measurement came up short of a first down.

4. It doesn't matter which part of the line (front, middle or back) the clip is placed for the measurement.

5. The umpire controls the front stake and pulls the chain taut for a measurement.

1. True 2. False 3. True 4. False 5. True

Notes

Notes

Notes

IF YOU LIKE THIS BOOK, YOU'LL LOVE THIS MAGAZINE!

The only magazine exclusively for sports officials

Rulings, caseplays, mechanics – in-depth

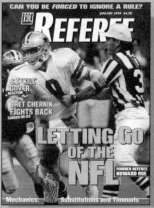

Solid coverage of the sport(s) you work

Important, late-breaking news stories

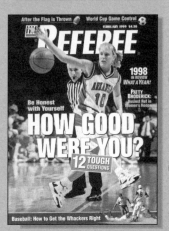

Thought-provoking interviews and features

Opinions/editorials on vital topics

Your source for the best books on football officiating

Better Football Officiating

Practical, hands-on tips and suggestions for football officials at any level! Includes: Gray-area situations and conflicting calls • Working well with others — maximize your effectiveness in dealing with team captains, timers and members of the chain crew • The art of verbal communication • A Challenging Season — one official's journal details a wide array of situations faced by him and his crewmates • On the field during the pregame — a constructive routine will help you mentally prepare for the job ahead • Rules and procedures checklist — this interactive, comprehensive outline encompasses nearly 200 rules, mechanics and procedures questions to be answered by you and your crewmates. (paperback, 68 pages) **BBFO, $12.95, NASO-Member Price: $10.35.** Also available on two audio cassettes: BREBFO, $14.95, NASO-Member Price: $11.95

Take Charge Football Officiating

Author Jerry Grunska shares nearly four decades of football officiating experience at the high school and college levels. Compiled from his best football officiating articles in *Referee*. Includes: Dealing successfully with players and coaches • Working the referee and umpire positions • Working the linesman, line judge and back judge positions • Judging potential infractions • Knowing the nuances of the kicking game • Maximizing crew effectiveness • Making the best of bad situations — all in one source for easy reference! (paperback, 65 pages) **BTCFB, $9.95, NASO-Member Price: $7.95.** Also available on two audio cassettes: BRE102, $14.95, NASO-Member Price: $11.95

The Ball Is Ready

Nine chapters provide football officiating game coverage for crews of four and five officials, including: The keys to working the wings • Sticky situations during pass coverage • Recognizing and reacting to formations and strategies • Determining forward progress • Becoming an informed observer • Improving your concentration • Covering scrimmage kicks • "Tom's Twenty Tips" from former *Referee* editor and co-author Tom Hammill • Plus, "You Make The Call," a selection of play situations and the correct calls. (paperback, 61 pages) **BBIR, $9.95, NASO-Member Price: $7.95.** Also available on two audio cassettes: BRE103, $14.95, NASO-Member Price: $11.95

19 Smart Moves For The Football Official

19 tips for working a better game — tips you will use no matter what level you work! Written by Jeffrey Stern, *Referee* associate editor and veteran high school and college football official. A great handout for association meetings and officiating camps and clinics! (24-page booklet) **BSMFB, $2.95, NASO-Member Price: $2.35**

Qty.	Order Code	Description	Price	NASO Price	Amount
	BBFO	Better Football Officiating	$12.95	$10.35	
	BTCFB	Take Charge Football Officiating	$ 9.95	$ 7.95	
	BBIR	The Ball Is Ready	$ 9.95	$ 7.95	
	BSMFB	19 Smart Moves For The Football Official	$ 2.95	$ 2.35	

Shipping/Handling Chart

Up to $5	$ 2.00
$ 5.01-$ 15	$ 4.00
$ 15.01-$ 30	$ 6.00
$ 30.01-$ 50	$ 8.00
$ 50.01-$ 70	$10.00
$ 70.01-$100	$12.00
$100.01-$250	$15.00
Over $250	CALL FOR RATE

RESIDENTS OUTSIDE 48 CONTIGUOUS STATES:
CALL 800/733-6100 FOR SHIPPING RATES.

Subtotal ___

WI residents add 5% sales tax ___

Shipping & Handling ___

TOTAL ___

VISA/MasterCard holders call 800/733-6100 or 414/632-8855 or Fax: 414/632-5460 or e-mail: orders@referee.com • 24-hour service • 7 days a week. Or send check with order to: REFEREE/NASO Special Services, P.O. Box 12, Franksville, WI 53126

Name_____

Address_____

City/State/Zip_____

Daytime Phone_____

Referee/NASO Account #_____

❑ Check/Money Order   ❑ MasterCard
❑ VISA

Account #_____

Expiration Date_____

Signature_____
(required only if using credit card)

FBG99

The National Association of Sports Officials

All Sports
All Levels
Always
There For You

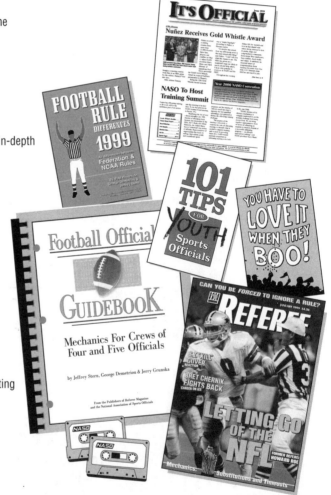

- *Referee* magazine – monthly, colorful, informative.
  For more than 20 years, the voice of officiating and the
  journal of record of all that is vital to officials.

- *It's Official* – monthly 12-page association newsletter

- $3 Million Liability Coverage

- Exclusive Assault Protection Program

- Sport-Specific Educational Updates, Quizzes, Special In-depth
  Reports on issues affecting sports officials

- NASO Legislative Updates

- Educational Seminars and Programs

- Audiocassettes, Books, Manuals
  (member only discounts)

- "Ask Us" Rule Interpretation Service

- Relocation Referral Service

- Rental Car Program

- Affinity MasterCard

- Optional insurance programs that protect your officiating
  income in case of injury.

- And more! All for $72 per year.

For a complete brochure and membership information contact:
NASO • 2017 Lathrop Avenue • Racine, WI 53405 • 414/632-5448 • 414/632-5460 (fax)
naso@naso.org or visit our website at www.naso.org